Spanish AS | para AQA

ánimo 1

Teacher Book

OXFORD

OXFORD
UNIVERSITY PRESS

Great Clarendon Street, Oxford OX2 6DP

Oxford University Press is a department of the University of Oxford.

It furthers the University's objective of excellence in research, scholarship, and education by publishing worldwide in

Oxford   New York   Auckland   Cape Town   Dar es Salaam
Hong Kong   Karachi   Kuala Lumpur   Madrid   Melbourne
Mexico City   Nairobi   New Delhi   Shanghai   Taipei   Toronto

With offices in
Argentina   Austria   Brazil   Chile   Czech Republic   France
Greece   Guatemala   Hungary   Italy   Japan   South Korea
Poland   Portugal   Singapore   Switzerland   Thailand
Turkey   Ukraine   Vietnam

Oxford is a registered trade mark of Oxford University Press
in the UK and in certain other countries

British Library Cataloguing in Publication Data

Data available

ISBN 978 019 912910 2

10 9 8 7 6 5 4

Printed by Bell & Bain Ltd., Glasgow

Paper used in the production of this book is a natural, recyclable
product made from wood grown in sustainable forests.
The manufacturing process conforms to the environmental
regulations of the country of origin.

Contents

Symbols used in this Teacher's Book:

 Listening material available on CD

S   Self-study CD

Summary of unit contents

Unit	Page	Subject content	Grammar	Skills
Puente	6	You and the area you live in Spanish-speaking areas or countries Key people and aspects of the Spanish-speaking world	Key tenses The difference between *ser* and *estar* Making comparisons Agreement, shortening and position of adjectives Cardinal numbers	Research skills
1 La televisión	13	TV viewing habits and preferences The range of channels including satellite and internet The benefits and dangers of watching TV	Negatives *gustar* and *molestar* (third person + noun) *soler* and *poder* (+ infinitive) Irregular preterites (radical changes)	Taking notes when listening Recognising and using synonyms and antonyms Dealing with unfamiliar words
2 Anuncios y publicidad	23	The purposes of advertising Different advertising techniques The benefits and drawbacks of advertising Curbs on advertising	The present subjunctive with verbs of wanting, requesting and advising Suffixes	Recognising and using language of persuasion Recognising and using different registers of language Developing and justifying points of view
3 Los medios de comunicación	33	The popularity of modern technological gadgets The current and potential usage of the Internet The benefits and dangers of the Internet and modern technological gadgets	Using *se* to avoid the passive voice The imperative The subjunctive for value judgements/wanting and not wanting	Using strategies for reading Inferring meaning when listening
4 El cine	43	Types of film The place of cinema in popular culture and changing trends A good film you have seen Different ways of viewing films	The imperfect tense Using a mixture of past tenses *lo* and *lo que* Placing written and spoken accents correctly	Putting forward opinions convincingly (agree and disagree) Inferring meaning when reading
5 La música	53	Different types of music and changing trends The place of music in popular culture Music you like How music defines personal identity	Object pronouns (direct and indirect) The pluperfect tense	Responding to speaking stimulus materials Speaking from notes with the correct intonation Transferring meaning: explaining in Spanish
6 La moda y tendencias	63	How your 'look' defines who you are Different ways we can alter our image Lifestyles and leisure activities The cult of celebrity	The subjunctive mood in past tenses The personal *a* Relative pronouns Time clauses	Writing in paragraphs Transferring meaning: explaining in English

Introduction

The course

Welcome to *ánimo 1 para AQA*!

ánimo 1 para AQA is the first stage of a two-part Spanish course written to match the new AS and A2 specifications for AQA. It has been written by a team of experienced authors, examiners and practising teachers and is suitable for a wide range of learners.

Rationale

The aims of *ánimo 1 para AQA* are:
- to provide thorough coverage of the AS specifications for AQA and prepare students for the AS exams
- to provide material suitable for AS students of all abilities to ease the transition from GCSE to AS level
- to provide comprehensive grammatical coverage and practice of the exam specification grammatical content
- to help students develop specific learning strategies, for example dictionary skills, independent study, vocabulary learning and pronunciation techniques
- to enable students to take control of their own learning by means of learning strategies, reference and revision sections, study skills and opportunities for independent study
- to encourage success by providing clear objectives and by practising language via activities with a clear purpose.

The components of *ánimo 1 para AQA*

Student Book

The Student Book is the complete handbook for advanced level studies, providing a comprehensive and integrated programme of teaching, practice, revision and reference for students. This 176-page book contains the following sections:

Puente

This initial unit bridges the gap between GCSE and AS level by providing revision of key language and grammar and focusing on topics that should be familiar to students from their previous learning.

It also introduces students to the layout of the Student Book and the types of activity they will encounter in *ánimo*.

Unidades 1–12

There are 12 units on different topics. Each unit has been planned to be interesting and motivating, as well as to develop relevant strategies and skills for independent study and preparation for exams. An outline of the content of each unit is given on pages 4–5 of this book.

Exam Practice

At the back of the Student Book there are listening, speaking, reading and writing activities, aimed at providing AQA exam practice of the language of each block of three units. In addition, there are twelve assessments on the OxBox.

Grammar

This detailed reference section at the back of the book complements the grammar explanations given within the body of the Student Book. All explanations are in English so that students are able to use this section independently.

Teacher Book

Detailed teaching notes for each unit are provided. These notes include:

- suggestions for using the material in the Student Book, including the exam practice section
- answers to activities, including possible answers where appropriate
- transcripts for all recorded material
- notes on when to use the worksheets and assessment within each unit.

Resource & Assessment OxBox CD-ROM

There are worksheets and assessments for every unit on the Resource & Assessment OxBox CD-ROM to give further practice on learning skills, grammar, listening, reading, speaking and writing.

Grammar Workbook

This 96-page Workbook contains thorough revision and practice of grammar covered in the Student Book, with an answer booklet for self-marking. The Student Book contains page references to the Workbook where it can most appropriately be used.

Audio CDs

The audio CDs provide the listening material to accompany the Student Book, worksheet and assessment material. The scripted material was recorded by native Spanish speakers. All CDs may be copied within the purchasing institution for use by teachers and students.

CD contents

CD 1:   Puente – Unidad 5
CD 2:   Unidad 6 – Unidad 10
CD 3:   Unidad 11 – Exam Practice 4
CD 4:   Worksheets & Assessment

Features of an *ánimo* unit

Unit objectives

Each unit begins with a list of topics with page references to their place in the unit. There are also objectives in English that provide clear information to students about what they will learn in the unit, including grammar and skills. The first page of each unit contains a visual stimulus and some activities to introduce the theme of the unit.

Core double-page spreads

Each of the three or four core double-page spreads begins with one or two questions to pinpoint what students will learn. Activities in all four skills are included on each double-page spread, leading to a productive spoken and written task at the end of the spread.

Frases clave

These boxes provide key phrases for students to use in their written and spoken outcome tasks.

Gramática

Most double-page spreads feature a *Gramática* box, focusing on a key grammar point. The explanations and instructions in these sections are in English, enabling students to use them independently. Activities are provided to reinforce each grammar point, and examples are included in texts on the double-page spread so that students have an opportunity to see the grammar point in practice.

Técnica

These boxes provide practical skills advice and language-learning tips in English, with activities enabling students to put the advice into practice. They are ideal for self-study and are intended to improve aspects of students' performance and help them develop as independent learners.

Gramática en acción

This page (after the final double-page spread of each unit) provides additional activities to reinforce or extend key grammar points from the unit.

Vocabulario

Each unit has a list of spread-by-spread key vocabulary for students to refer to as they work their way through the course. These vocabulary lists are also accompanied by activities to practise and reinforce the key language.

Extra

At the end of each unit there is an advanced reading or listening text which develops further the theme and grammar of the unit and is particularly aimed at A-A* students. From unit 3 these pages also include a *Técnica* box to help students explore higher level issues of comprehension and language use.

Exam practice

This section at the back of the Student Book provides revision practice with exam-style questions to help students prepare for their AQA AS exam.

ánimo para AQA and the new AS and A2 specifications

ánimo para AQA is a structured two-part course intended for use over two years' study and has been written to follow the revised AS/A2 specifications for AQA. There are 12 units in *ánimo 1 para AQA*, written to match the content of the revised AS specifications (for first teaching from 2008). The style and content of the activities would also be appropriate for use with other exam specifications.

Grammar

ánimo 1 para AQA provides complete coverage of the AS prescribed grammar content. The deductive approach on the Student Book pages and the extensive practice provided in the Grammar Workbook ensure that students are able to master all aspects of language structure required at this level.

Assessment

The assessment material in *ánimo 1 para AQA* has been written to match the style of the AQA exam board. Practice in tackling exam-style questions is provided both in the Exam Practice section at the back of the Student Book and on the Resource & Assessment CD-ROM.

Key skills

The table below provides an overview of key skills coverage in *ánimo 1 para AQA*. It shows where there are opportunities to develop and/or assess some or all of the criteria for each key skill at level 3.

The following notes provide examples of how each key skill may be developed or assessed through the activities in *ánimo 1 para AQA*:

Communication

Teachers should note that, although the study of a modern foreign language helps students to develop their communication skills, *the evidence for this Key Skill must be presented in English, Irish or Welsh.*

		Puente	1	2	3	4	5	6	7	8	9
						ánimo 1 units					
Main key skills	Communication	✓	✓	✓	✓	✓	✓	✓	✓	✓	✓
	Application of number		✓	✓	✓		✓			✓	
	ICT	✓			✓		✓	✓	✓		
Wider key skills	Working with others	✓	✓	✓	✓	✓	✓	✓	✓	✓	✓
	Improving own learning and performance	✓	✓	✓	✓	✓	✓	✓	✓	✓	
	Problem solving	✓	✓	✓	✓	✓	✓	✓	✓	✓	

ánimo 1 offers opportunities for practising and developing communication skills rather than for generating assessed evidence.

For this key skill, students need to:

1a Take part in a group discussion

All *ánimo 1* units provide opportunities for students to discuss topics in pairs, small groups or as whole-class activity.

1b Make a formal presentation of at least eight minutes

Many of the topics covered in the coursebook provide a suitable basis for a presentation. See also the *Técnica* section in Unit 4, which provides specific guidance on putting forward opinions. Students should be encouraged to support their presentations using visuals (e.g. OHP transparencies, photographs, brochures, etc.), PowerPoint, audio clips and other appropriate material.

2 Read and synthesise information from at least two documents about the same subject

ánimo 1 provides reading material on a wide range of topics, with activities designed to help students identify main points and summarize information. Students are also encouraged to undertake wider reading when researching information for productive spoken and written work. Their wider reading might include newspapers, magazines, books, publicity material, and Internet sources.

3 Write two different types of document

Opportunities exist throughout *ánimo 1* for students to attempt extended writing in a variety of styles, e.g. reports, essays and creative material on a wide range of themes, a film review, a biography, publicity material, informal and formal letters, etc.

Application of number

Although it may not be within the scope of a modern foreign language course to generate sufficient evidence to assess this key skill, *ánimo 1* does provide opportunities for students to develop their ability to work with numbers. Numbers feature in most units.

The table indicates only those units where students are involved in interpreting or commenting on statistics.

Information and communication technology

Students need to be able to:

1 search for and select information
2 enter and develop the information, and derive new information
3 present combined information such as text with image, text with number, image with number

Many *ánimo 1* units provide opportunities for students to develop aspects of this key skill. Criteria 1–3 (listed above) can be combined in a single extended piece of work in activities such as the following:

♦ Puente, page 9, activity 4b: Students research a Spanish region using the Internet.
♦ Unit 5, page 58, activity 1b: Students use the Internet to find out about one of the composers listed. They then present the information to the class, for which they could use visual stimuli, produced using desktop publishing.

Working with others

All *ánimo 1* units provide opportunities for students to work together, either in a one-to-one situation or as part of a group. These opportunities may take the form of interviews, discussions, debates and surveys, or they may involve students in a more creative activity such as producing an advertisement or a PowerPoint presentation, or inventing a role-play.

The following example shows how a group task can be developed and expanded in order to become a suitable means of assessing this key skill:

Unit 8, page 37, activity 2b: Students work in groups to conduct a debate on the concept of legalising 'safe' drugs.

1   They begin by dividing into small groups and preparing arguments for and against using the questions listed.
2   Once they have prepared their arguments, they conduct the debate, using the *Frases clave* phrases and the guidance provided in the *Gramática* box on using the subjunctive to express doubt and improbability.
3   After completion of the task, students can review their work, sharing constructive feedback and agreeing on ways to improve collaborative work in future.

Improving own learning and performance

Students are required to:

1   set targets and plan how these will be met
2   take responsibility for own learning and use plans to help meet targets and improve performance
3   review progress and establish evidence of achievements

All *ánimo 1* units provide opportunities to meet these criteria through:

♦   **Clear objectives and means of reviewing progress**
    Each unit begins with a list of objectives, providing clear information to students about what they will learn in the unit, including grammar and skills. Students should also be encouraged to set their own personal targets relating to aspects of their performance that they want to improve, with an action plan showing how they intend to achieve the targets and how they will assess their progress.

♦   **Strategies for improving performance**
    All *ánimo 1* units include *Técnica* sections, which suggest strategies and activities to help students develop as independent learners and improve aspects of their own performance. Strategies range from specific listening, speaking, reading and writing advice to tips on using dictionaries effectively and suggestions on recording and learning new language.

Problem solving

Although a modern foreign language course may not generate sufficient evidence to assess this key skill, it does provide opportunities to practise and develop problem-solving skills. For example, if students are encouraged to 'work out' new language for themselves and take responsibility for their own learning instead of relying on teacher support, they develop problem-solving skills.

All *ánimo 1* units provide opportunities for students to do this. In particular, the *Técnica* sections encourage students to become more independent in their language learning.

Information and communications technology

These notes provide a few examples of ways to use ICT with *ánimo 1*. For more detailed information and practical help and ideas on the use of ICT in the modern foreign languages classroom, you may find the following helpful:

♦   Becta (British Educational Communications and Technology Agency): www.becta.org.uk
♦   CILT (The National Centre for Languages): www.cilt.org.uk
♦   Languages ICT: www.languages-ict.org.uk

Internet

Note on internet safety: before using the internet with students, whether for online communication, the creation of web pages and blogs, or for research purposes, it is vital to be aware of safety issues. Guidance on this can be obtained from Becta (see website above).

Introduction

Online communication

If your school has links with a partner school in a Spanish-speaking country, the internet offers a range of ways in which your students can communicate with their Spanish counterparts, e.g. email, instant messaging, chat rooms, noticeboards and forums, audio- and video-conferencing, web pages and blogs. These enable the exchange of a wide range of information. They are extremely useful for motivating students, encouraging spontaneous communication and generating a source of additional teaching and learning material.

Internet research

The internet can be a valuable research tool, giving both teachers and students easy access to authentic reading materials and cultural information about Spanish-speaking countries. Opportunities for students to research on the internet occur throughout *ánimo*. Themes include:

- Puente, page 6, activity 1h: Students use the internet to prepare a presentation about one of the photographs (a–i).
- Unit 5, page 58, activity 1b: musicians/singers
- Unit 9, page 97, activity 5: holiday destinations.

Word-processing and text manipulation

Word-processing software allows text to be presented in a variety of forms that can be easily edited and manipulated. This makes it easier for students to experiment with language and to draft and redraft their work. Any written task can be completed on the computer, e.g.

- Unit 5, page 58, activity 1b: Students write a biography of a famous musician.
- Unit 6, page 65, activity 4b: Students write about how friends, the media and celebrities influence how they look.
- Unit 8, page 87, activity 4c: Students write about the smoking ban.
- Unit 10, page 109, activity 6: Students write a letter to defend young people.
- Unit 12, page 131, activity 2b: Students write about marriage and cohabitation.

Desktop publishing

Desktop publishing software enables students to design sophisticated documents involving complex layout of text, clip art, digital photos and scanned images, e.g. brochures, posters and articles. Opportunities for students to use desktop publishing in *ánimo 1* include:

- Unit 2, page 27, activity 6: Students produce an advert for a product of their choice.
- Unit 11, page 122, activity 2c: Students write a profile of Erica.

Databases and spreadsheets

Data-processing software allows text- and number-based information gathered by students to be entered into a database then sorted and analyzed in different ways; spreadsheet software is more suitable for dealing with number-based data.

Opportunities to use these in *ánimo 1* include:

- Unit 3, page 37: Students make up a questionnaire on modern communication. They could then compile a database and table of results.

Presentation software

Presentation software (e.g. PowerPoint) allows students to create multimedia 'slides'. These can be displayed to the whole class via a data projector and wall screen or interactive whiteboard. Themes for oral presentations in *ánimo 1* include:

- Unit 4, page 44, activity 2d: actors.
- Unit 7, page 82, activity Extra/Técnica, B: sport and health in Spain.

Unidad 0   Puente

Unit objectives

By the end of this unit students will be able to:
♦ Talk and write about themselves and the area they live in
♦ Talk and write about a Spanish-speaking area or country
♦ Research and write about key people and aspects of the Spanish-speaking world

Grammar

By the end of this unit students will be able to:
♦ Recognise and use key tenses correctly
♦ Make comparisons
♦ Recognise the difference between *ser* and *estar* and use them correctly
♦ Make adjectives agree, shorten them and place them correctly

Skills

♦ Research skills

¡Bienvenidos al mundo hispano de ánimo!

Planner

Skills focus
♦ Research techniques

Resources
♦ Student Book pages 6 and 7
♦ CD 1, track 2

1a Students look at the photos and see how many they recognise. This could be done as a whole class task or as individuals to elicit just how much background knowledge students already possess.

 1b Students listen and match the photos to the commentary to gain a general impression, and identify the photo being talked about.

---

p. 6, actividades 1b y 1c

1   Este raro edificio es un símbolo de la creatividad y el carácter independiente de los catalanes. Si subes más de 400 escalones hasta arriba de una de las ocho torres ya acabadas, tendrás una vista sin igual de la animada ciudad de Barcelona.

---

2   La Ciudad de las Artes y las Ciencias – museo ultramoderno – fue la ingeniosa idea de Santiago Calatrava. Este arquitecto e ingeniero nativo de la ciudad de Valencia decidió reclamar una parte abandonada de la ciudad y diseñar, con otros arquitectos cuatro pabellones que sirven de museo para las artes y las ciencias.

3   Uno de los pintores más famosos del mundo, Pablo Ruiz Picasso, pintó este cuadro en 1937 después del bombardeo atroz del pueblo vasco de Guernica durante la Guerra Civil española.

4   El tango es uno de los bailes más famosos, románticos y sensuales del mundo. Tiene su origen en el barrio del puerto de Buenos Aires, la capital de Argentina. En cualquier momento puedes ver a parejas bailando en la calle acompañados por la música del bandoneón.

5   Desde la muerte del dictador Franco en noviembre de 1975 España es una democracia parlamentaria y monárquica. El rey, Juan Carlos I, vive con su esposa la reina Sofía, en el palacio de la Zarzuela, un edificio modesto comparado con el Palacio Real de Madrid y otros palacios de Europa. Sus tres hijos Elena, Cristina y Felipe están casados y ¡les han dado muchos nietos!

6   Es mundialmente reconocido como uno de los mejores cocineros del mundo. Empezó su vida fregando platos en el hotel Playafels pero a los 19 años tuvo que hacer la mili y fue entonces, mientras formaba parte del ejército español, cuando decidió que quería cocinar.

7   Construido en su mayoría durante el siglo XV, este misterioso lugar fue uno de los palacios del emperador Inca y un santuario religioso. Es considerada una obra maestra de la arquitectura y la ingeniería. Estas ruinas están catalogadas como Patrimonio de la Humanidad desde 1983 y se han convertido en uno de los destinos turísticos más populares del mundo. Son un icono nacional del Perú.

8   En Andalucía, a unos 25 kilómetros de Sevilla, hay un nuevo fenómeno que produce energía para más de 60.000 casas, lo que equivale a un pueblo grande. 624 espejos enormes concentran los rayos del sol produciendo así electricidad.

9   Hoy se puede viajar desde Madrid a Málaga en un tren de alta velocidad que se llama el AVE. El primer trayecto de Madrid a Sevilla se inauguró en 1992 para la Exposición Universal de Sevilla. Si el tren se atrasa más de cinco minutos, te devuelven el valor del billete. Hoy en día, la red se extiende hasta Barcelona de modo que se puede viajar de norte a sur rápida y cómoda.

1c Students listen again for detail and match phrases 1–9 with the appropriate photo A–I.

Answers:
1 = F; 2 = C; 3 = H; 4 = A; 5 = D; 6 = E;
7 = B; 8 = I; 9 = G

1d Students match the titles to six of the photos. Note there are three extra photos for which a title is not given.

Answers:
*una catedral extraordinaria – **A***
*antiguo monumento de los Incas – **B***
*cuadro emblemático de Picasso – **D***
*un baile sensual – **E***
*museo moderno de Valencia – **G***
*un viaje a alta velocidad – **H***

1e Students make up titles for the remaining three photos.

Possible answers could be:
la familia real; la energía solar; Ferrán Adrián, cocinero catalán

1f Students read the text and match it to the appropriate photo.

Answer: F

A useful extra activity would be to ask students to read the text aloud and judge each other's intonation and pronunciation.

1g Students follow the example and write two sentences about the other photos.

1h Students search the Internet for further information about the topics represented in the photos and prepare an oral presentation on one of the photos A–I.

Técnica

Discuss the various research methods, and if necessary, pair up students so that the more confident ones help the weaker ones.

Students present their research to the rest of the class in as much, or as little, detail as appropriate.

Las Españas

Planner

Grammar focus
- The formation and use of the present tense
- The different uses of *ser* and *estar*

Resources
- Student Book pages 8 and 9
- CD 1, tracks 3, 4, 5 and 6
- Grammar Workbook pages 11, 32

Ensure students are familiar with the map of Spain and have a basic knowledge of the regions and their capitals. Explain the term 'las Españas' reflecting the historical and geographical background of Spain. Note that the independent kingdoms, although no longer in existence, still influence the cultural divisions.

1a Students listen and identify who is speaking and where they are from – their region. They can check the list of autonomous regions (CCAA) on page 9.

---

p. 8, actividad 1a

1 Saludos desde el Principado de Asturias – me llamo Victoria.

2 ¡Hola! Me llamo Omar y vivo en Murcia, en el sureste del país.

3 Y yo me llamo Maribel y vivo en Estepona, en Andalucía, en el sur.

4 Bienvenidos a Menorca, una de las islas Baleares – soy Jordi.

5 Y yo soy Raúl, y saludo a todos desde Zaragoza, la capital de Aragón.

6 Y por último voy yo – Silvana. Os saludo desde Lanzarote, en las Islas Canarias.

Answers:
1 *Victoria, Asturias*
2 *Omar, Murcia*
3 *Maribel, Andalucía*
4 *Jordi, Menorca (Baleares)*
5 *Raúl, Aragón*
6 *Silvana, Lanzarote (Canarias)*

1b Students listen and make notes about each speaker. This prepares them for Activity 1c. So it may help to go through the questions of 1c beforehand to help students to focus on the relevant information.

---

p. 8, actividades 1b y 2a

1 – Bueno, Silvana, ¿cómo es la vida en las Islas Canarias?

– Pues, Lanzarote, donde vivo yo, es la cuarta isla más grande de las siete islas Canarias y la más bonita. Arrecife, su capital en la costa este, es bastante comercial y moderna.

– ¿Qué hay de interés en la isla?

– A los turistas les gusta mucho visitar el Parque Nacional de Timanfaya porque les parece muy extraño con su paisaje volcánico.

– ¿A ti, qué te gusta hacer?

– A mí me gusta el arte y suelo visitar a menudo el museo de César Manrique, nuestro pintor más famoso.

2 – Maribel, hay mucho turismo donde vives tú, ¿verdad?

– Sí, porque hace calor y sol casi todo el año, sobre todo en Sevilla, la capital de Andalucía.

– ¿Qué sueles hacer en tu pueblo?

– No hay mucho que hacer para los jóvenes como yo si no te gusta la playa o el deporte y a mí no me gusta ni lo uno ni lo otro.

– Pero ¿qué hay de interés para los turistas entonces?

– Hay varios restaurantes buenos y se pueden visitar los pueblos blancos en las montañas que hay cerca de Ronda.

3 – Raúl, ¿qué nos puedes decir de Zaragoza?

– Es la capital de Aragón en el norte de España. Está situada sobre el río Ebro, en un valle casi en el centro de la región y alrededor todo parece un desierto.

– ¿Te gusta vivir allí?

– Sí, porque es una importante ciudad militar tanto para el Ejército como para las fuerzas aéreas. Está a igual distancia de Madrid, Barcelona, Valencia y Bilbao y ahora el tren de alta velocidad, el AVE, pasa por aquí.

– ¿Hay algo interesante para los turistas allí?

– Sí ... la famosa Basílica Católica de Nuestra Señora del Pilar y las ruinas romanas pero para mí lo más importante es el estadio de fútbol del Real Zaragoza.

4 – ¿Dónde vives exactamente, Victoria, y qué se hace en Asturias?

– Vivo cerca de la capital, Oviedo, en una ciudad que se llama Gijón, que está a orillas del mar y donde hay un puerto industrial. Asturias tiene valles verdes entre montañas grises. Hago bastante deporte y me encanta el surf. Los fines de semana, mis amigos y yo solemos pasarlos en la playa. Lo bueno es que hay mucho de interés para el turista pero lo malo es que estamos un poco aislados.

5 – Omar, ¿cómo es tu pueblo? ¿Y qué te gusta hacer allí?

– Lorca es un pueblo que fue fundado en tiempos de los moros donde hay muchos cultivos de frutas y legumbres. Cuando era joven solía jugar al baloncesto pero hoy prefiero la música y suelo practicar con un grupo llamado Los Tarifeños. Murcia, la capital de la región, tiene muchos monumentos antiguos.

6 – Jordi, háblame de tu región.

– Vivo en Sant Lluís, una bonita aldea no muy lejos de Maó, la capital de Menorca. Tiene unos 3.000 habitantes nada más y normalmente es muy tranquila, pintoresca y encantadora. No me gusta el verano cuando llegan los turistas haciendo ruido y dejando basura por todas partes. Aquí se suele comer muchos mariscos y se vive muy bien.

1c In pairs, students take turns to be interviewee and interviewer. They use the questions provided and base their answers on one of the interviews they have just listened to.

 2a Students study their notes and listen again to the previous transcript in order to elicit phrases and vocabulary that best suit their own situation.

2b Work in pairs. Students then use the questions from 1c to create a dialogue, with a partner, about themselves. They should consult the *frases clave* to help them as well.

3 Dictionary work. Students write a brief description of their own region using all the relevant vocabulary and phrases from the unit so far. Encourage them also to seek further vocabulary in a dictionary or online.
Create text files so that students practise writing using text manipulation. The transcripts could be used as a basis for this activity.

 4a Students listen and make notes on each of the three regions: Andalucía; Galicia, Castilla La Mancha, using the headings provided. This is a more challenging listening task but if students focus on the headings suggested they should be able to make notes under them in English or Spanish. There is an opportunity here to use the transcript for a text manipulation activity as well.

p. 9, actividad 4a

1   Andalucía es la comunidad autónoma más grande de España y cuenta con unos 7.600.000 habitantes. Las ocho provincias que componen la región van desde Cádiz, en la costa atlántica, hasta Almería, en la costa mediterránea. Todos los estereotipos de España son originarios de Andalucía: el flamenco, la guitarra, los pueblos blancos, las fiestas religiosas, los gitanos, los turistas y las tapas. Allí encontrarás una fusión de culturas – la cultura musulmana, la judía y la cristiana. Los cultivos de olivos marcan el paisaje andaluz. Su capital es Sevilla.

2 Galicia, tal vez la región menos descubierta por los turistas y aislada en la punta noroeste, es la zona más verde del país. Allí se encuentra la tumba del Apóstol Santiago. Sus gentes se ganan la vida en las rías de la costa atlántica, abundantes en mariscos y pescado. Pontevedra es el puerto pesquero más importante de España.

3 Castilla la Mancha, meseta abierta salpicada de molinos de viento y castillos, ofrece una imagen clásica de España. Aquí encontrarás los viñedos más extensos del mundo y en otoño los campos se vuelven violetas con el color de la flor del azafrán. En esta parte del centro del país hay también dos parques nacionales, las Tablas de Daimiel y Cabañeros.

4b Students choose one of the autonomous regions listed, but not one mentioned in the recording for Activity 4a, and write a brief description. Basing their descriptions on what they have heard they should include details of where it is, its climate, language, capital city, production, famous monuments, etc. This task extends and develops students' ability to research and elicit relevant information.

The following two websites may be useful for general information:

www.red2000.com/spain

www.SiSpain.org

 5a Students listen to the interview.

---
p. 9, actividad 5a

– A los veintidós años se hizo con la victoria más dulce de su vida ante las narices de su gran ídolo.

– les presento a Fernando Alonso, el ganador más joven de la historia de la Fórmula 1.
¿Qué signo es usted?

– Pues, nací el 29 de julio de 1981, así que soy Leo.

– ¿De qué parte de España es usted?

– Soy de Oviedo, capital del Principado de Asturias, en el norte de España.

– ¿Cuál fue su primer premio?

– Bueno, obtuve mi primera victoria en karting.

– ¿Cuántos años tenía?

– Tenía unos trece años, creo.

– ¿Por qué cambió del karting a la Fórmula 1?

– Porque es un progreso natural si uno es fanático del deporte de automovilismo.

– ¿Cuándo hizo su primera carrera en Fórmula 1?

– Fue en Melbourne, Australia, en 2001.

– ¿Quién es su ídolo?

– Aparte de mi padre, es sin duda Michael Schuhmacher – y también tengo respeto al colombiano Juan Pablo Montoya.

– ¿Cómo se sintió al ganar en Hungría en 2003?

– Muy orgulloso de ser el primer español en subir al podio.

– Así es y enhorabuena – felicitaciones a otro pionero del deporte español.

 5b Students listen a second time and note down the full question form.

5c Students then choose the correct answers from the list A–H.

Answers:

¿Cuál? *H*;   ¿Dónde? *B*;   ¿Cuándo? *A*;
¿Cómo? *G*;   ¿Cuánto? *E*;   ¿Quién? *C*;
¿Qué? *D*;   ¿Por qué? *F*

Gramática

The formation and uses of the present tense

Refer students to the grammar section of the Student Book, pages 164–165.

Radical or stem changing verbs – ensure students understand how they are formed and how they are presented in a dictionary.

A *vuelvo vuelves vuelve volvemos volvéis vuelven*

B *cojo coges coge cogemos cogéis cogen*
    sigo, sigues, sigue etc.

C *digo, voy, estoy, soy, pongo, vengo*

Ser and *estar*

Ask students to provide examples of the different uses to ensure they are fully competent and not just making guesses about which one to use.

D Using the map, students can quiz each other:

A: ¿Dónde está Zaragoza? – B: Está en el norte de España.

A: ¿Cómo es? – B: Es una ciudad grande.

If students are not familiar with the map of Spain, this will help to orientate them as well. students should know the points of the compass (*norte, sur, este, oeste, centro* etc. If not, make sure they revise this basic vocabulary.

Las Américas

Planner

Grammar focus

♦ Comparatives
♦ Agreement of adjectives
♦ Position of adjectives
♦ Cardinal numbers

Resources

♦ Student Book pages 10 and 11
♦ CD 1, tracks 7–8
♦ Grammar Workbook pages 32, 11

 1a Students study the map of Latin America to familiarise themselves with it and gauge how much prior knowledge they already have. They then listen and note the names of the countries mentioned and locate them on the map.

> **p. 10, actividad 1a**
>
> – La parte de América donde se habla español es un subcontinente enorme que empieza en el cono sur, compuesto por Chile, Argentina, Paraguay y Uruguay. Sigue con Bolivia, Perú y Ecuador con sus islas Galápagos en la parte central y Colombia y Venezuela en el norte. Luego se continúa por el istmo de Panamá a través de Costa Rica, Nicaragua, Honduras, El Salvador y Guatemala hasta llegar a México.
> – No hay que olvidar las islas caribeñas de Cuba, Puerto Rico y la República Dominicana y, por supuesto, gran parte de los Estados Unidos donde hay una importante representación latina.

Answers:
Chile, Argentina, Paraguay, Uruguay, Bolivia, Perú, Ecuador, Colombia, Venezuela, Panamá, Costa Rica, Nicaragua, Honduras, El Salvador, Guatemala, México, Cuba, Puerto Rica, República Dominicana, Estados Unidos.

1b In pairs, students look at the map and play the game of "True or False" again to familiarise themselves with basic information about Latin American countries and their capitals. They should try to do this from memory after a few turns each.

Gramática

Comparatives

Refer students to the grammar section of the Student Book, page 159.

Introduce the vocabulary.

A Students compare the countries using the phrases given.

 2 Students listen to the recording of Rosa María talking about Costa Rica. They complete the sentences with the missing numbers.
Depending on how competent students are with numbers, revise the ordinal and cardinal numbers in the *Gramática* box before or after they have completed this task.

> **p. 10, actividad 2**
>
> ¡Hola! les habla Rosa María desde Costa Rica. Mi país es uno de los más bonitos de Latinoamérica y se sitúa entre el océano Atlántico o el Mar Caribe y el océano Pacífico.
> Aquí viven casi 4.000.000 de personas. Es un país bastante pequeño, unos 51km² de tierra, pero no es tan pequeño como El Salvador. Muchas personas son descendientes de españoles pero un 2% de la población es gente indígena.
> Hay muchos parques nacionales que protegen la enorme variedad ecológica que existe aquí. El punto más alto se llama Monte Chiripó a 3819 metros por encima del nivel del mar. Otra cosa importante es que desde 1948 no tenemos ejército – por eso nos llaman la pequeña Suiza.

Answers:
1 = *dos;* **2** = *4,000.000;* **3** = *51km²;*
4 *dos por ciento/2%;* **5** = *3819 metros;* **6** = *1948*

3a Students read this letter and complete the personal details for Roberto.

Answers:
Nombre: *Roberto;* **Edad:** *17;* **Nacionalidad:** *peruano;* **Familia:** *2 hermanos; 3 hermanas;* **Aficiones:** *senderismo, vela, pesca, buceo;* **Profesión:** *estudiante;* **Idiomas:** *Español y Quechua*

3b Students note details from the letter and write a brief description of Roberto.

3c Before completing this task, students could make up personal descriptions of classmates and guess who is being described to help them revise useful vocabulary and phrases. Students compose a letter following the model provided containing their own personal details.

Gramática

Adjectives

Refer students to the grammar sections of the Student Book, page 157 (agreement) and page 158 (position).

Students will be quite familiar by now with the rules for agreement of adjectives, but they will need more practice on the position of adjectives.

A Students find examples of agreement and position of adjectives in the letter and also make up further examples of their own.

B Students reinforce their understanding of how adjectival endings change by making up a sentence for each of the three adjectives listed.

Gramática

Cardinal numbers

Refer students to the grammar section in the Student Book, page 173.

Students should be familiar with numbers by now but will need a reminder about agreements especially of number one.

There is an opportunity here to remind students about percentages, fractions and other number usages.

Gramática en acción

Planner

Grammar focus
♦ Perfect tense
♦ Preterite tense
♦ Genders and articles, pronouns and agreement of adjectives

Resources
♦ Student Book page 12
♦ Grammar Workbook pages 5, and 38–40

Recuerda

Past tenses: preterite versus perfect

Remind students of the different uses of the two forms of the past tense: preterite and perfect.

Refer students to the relevant grammar section of the Student Book for the form of the tenses.

Students will already be quite familiar with the first and third person singular of the preterite, but now they need to be sure they can manage the full paradigm.

♦ The perfect tense is a compound tenses using *haber* (an auxiliary verb) and the past participle. Make sure students understand the terminology of auxiliary verbs and are familiar with the form of the past participle.

A Students write down the infinitive of the verbs used as examples in the *Recuerda* box.

Answers:
sacar; pagar; empezar; averiguar; leer; oír; caer; creer

B Students write down as many past participles as they can from memory.

C Students look at the English sentences and make a note of the tense used in each one.

D Students translate the sentences into Spanish.

Answers for **C** and **D**:
1 perfect: *La Sagrada Familia ha llegado a ser un icono de Barcelona.*
2 perfect: *Costa Rica no ha tenido ejército desde 1948.*
3 perfect: *¿ Has visitado Machu Picchu?*
4 preterite: *Sí, fui el año pasado.*
5 preterite: *Alonso comenzó su carrera en kárting.*
6 perfect: *He tomado muchas fotos.*
7 preterite: *Leyeron mucho sobre Perú antes de su visita.*
8 preterite: *Empecé a estudiar el español hace un año solamente.*

Recuerda

Genders

Refer students to the grammar section of the Student Book, page 154.

E Students write down examples for each of the typical masculine and feminine endings working from memory. They compare their list with that of a partner. Check each list or ask students to share them with the rest of the class. The student who ends up with the longest list, that no other student has, is declared the winner.

F Students compile a list from the texts and then look for exceptions to the rule and learn them.

G Refer to page 155 of the grammar section of the Student Book and ensure that students understand why this happens and can give further examples.

Unidad 1   La televisión

Unit objectives

By the end of this unit students will be able to:
- ♦ Talk and write about TV viewing habits and preferences
- ♦ Comment on the range of channels including satellite and internet
- ♦ Discuss the benefits and dangers of watching TV

Grammar

By the end of this unit students will be able to:
- ♦ Use a range of negatives
- ♦ Use verbs like *gustar* and *molestar* (third person + noun)
- ♦ Use verbs like *soler* and *poder* (+ infinitive)
- ♦ Recognise and use the irregular preterite (radical changes)

Skills

By the end of this unit students will be able to:
- ♦ Take notes when listening
- ♦ Recognise and use synoyms and antonyms
- ♦ Deal with unfamiliar words

Resources

- ♦ Student Book page 13

This page introduces the topic.

1a Students complete the questionnaire.

1b Students discuss their results with a companion.

1c Class discussion. Do the students agree with the description of their TV-viewing habits? Why/why not? How would they describe their viewing? Key phrases are supplied to enable the expression of their opinions.

Los programas más vistos

Planner

Grammar focus
- ♦ Use a range of negatives
- ♦ Use verbs like *gustar* and *molestar* (third person + noun)
- ♦ Use verbs like *soler* and *poder* (+ infinitive)

Gramática

Negatives

Refer students to the relevant grammar section of the Student Book, page 163.
Students study the *Gramática* box on negatives.
For some students this will be a revision process, and for others a new learning one.

 A When they are sufficiently familiar with the negatives, they listen to the recording and identify the negative words used.

Answers:
1 *nunca, no*
2 *nadie, ni siquiera, jamás*
3 *no–nada, ni–ni, no–ningún, ninguna, nada*
4 *tampoco*

 B Students listen again and note down the form of negative used.

Answers:
1 *c* and *a* ; **2** *c, d, c* ; **3** *b, d, b, d* ; **4** *a, d*

Unidad 1 La televisión

p. 14, actividades A y B

1 – ¿Qué estás viendo?

– Deportes.

– Nunca veo programas de deportes, no me gustan.

– Pues, a mí me encantan.

2 – A nadie le gusta el canal 5, ni siquiera a mi abuelo.

– Estoy de acuerdo, jamás lo veo.

3 – No hay nada en la tele esta noche.

– Tienes razón, ni deporte ni música ...

– No hay ningún concurso, ninguna telenovela – en fin, nada.

4 – A mí no me gustan las noticias. ¿A ti te gustan?

– A mí tampoco.

C Work in pairs. Finally students invent similar dialogues and discuss their own viewing preferences.

H 1.4 *Hoja* 1.4 offers additional practice of negatives.

1a and **1b** These activities provide students with key vocabulary and phrases they will need for activities 2 and 3.

Students make sure they know the vocabulary for the different types of TV programmes by studying the programme schedule. They then research on *www. teleprograma.tv* for titles of Spanish programmes for each category and give an equivalent sort of programme in English.

2 Students listen and classify the programmes. This vocabulary is already listed on page 14, but they should be encouraged to complete the task from memory.

p. 14, actividad 2

1 Mira, mira, mira, cómo está adelantando al otro ese fenómeno de chico. Nuestro Fernando Alonso está acelerando y va ganando. Les juro que nuestro campeón mundial va a subir al podio otra vez.

2 Estamos esperando, estamos esperando pero el tiempo pasa y los competidores están pensando, considerando su respuesta – ¿cuál va a ser? Nos preguntamos todos, pendientes de si acertarán o no ... ay no, ¿qué están diciendo ...?

3 Ahora está cantando y moviéndose al compás de la música. ¡Qué voz! ¡Qué letra! Nos entusiasma este joven que está irrumpiendo en la escena musical.

4 Está saliendo, sacando el hocico por el hueco, olfateando, mirando con mucho cuidado antes de sacar a las crías recién nacidas de su hogar.

5 Estamos presenciando un momento clave en el que estos dos líderes cruciales para la paz mundial se están saludando por primera vez tras una época escalofriante llena de tensiones – ahora están sentándose el uno junto al otro y parece que están hablando animadamente – a ver lo que está pasando ...

Answers:

1 *retransmisión deportiva*

2 *concurso*

3 *programa de música*

4 *documental*

5 *telediario*

3 Students discuss the programmes with the highest audience figures in their own country. They then use the internet to find the Spanish TV programmes with the most viewers. Viewing statistics can be found at *www.locosporlatele.net*

4 Students read the letters page of a TV magazine and answer the questions.

Answers should include:

1 *porque tratan a la gente como cifras y dinero; no ponen atención a la calidad ni creatividad de los programas*

2 *Student's own opinion and wording*

3 *Student's own opinion and wording*

4 *Student's own opinion and wording*

5 *Students write their own minisode of a familiar soap.*

6 *Students give their own opinion about reality TV shows.*

7 *Students give their own opinion about 15 minutes of fame.*

Gramática

Verbs in the third person + noun

Refer students to the relevant grammar section of the Student Book, page 172.

Students will think they know all about this already but no doubt they will need reminding about agreement of plural or singular.

A Students make up sentences of their own to illustrate that they know how to use this construction.

Verbs + infinitive

Refer students to the relevant grammar section of the Student Book, page 172.

B Students write sentences about the role of television using the verbs listed.

Tele sin límites

Planner

Skills focus

♦ Listening and taking notes

Key language

el banco digital	digital downloads
el canal de pago	pay per view channel
el canal interactivo	interactive channel
el chisme/cotilleo	tittle-tattle
el liderazgo	leader/way out front
el plató	platform
el portátil	laptop
el prejuicio	prejudice
bajar un programa	to download
dar la gana	to want to do something
encerrarse	to shut oneself away
grabar	to record
quedarse atrás	to get left behind
repasar	to rewind/go over again
seleccionar	to select
transmitir/emitir	to broadcast
cualquier	any (adj)
miope	short sighted
peligroso	dangerous
lo demás	the rest of

Resources

♦ Student Book pages 16 and 17
♦ Vocabulario, Student Book page 21
♦ CD 1, tracks 11 and 12
♦ Hoja 1.5 CD 4, tracks 4, 5, and 6

 1a Students listen to the extracts and classify them.

> **p. 16, actividades 1a y 1b**
>
> 1 Con su apoteósico triunfo en Hungría, donde consiguió doblar a Michael Schumacher, Fernando Alonso ha hecho historia – es el piloto más joven que sube a lo más alto del podio en Fórmula 1 y el primer español que logra tal proeza.
>
> 2 Cóctel de noticias – aunque mi disco se llama *Locura* soy muy tranquilita, nos confesó ayer la joven tras declarar que ya no sigue saliendo con …
>
> 3 Olvide la dieta libre de grasas, nunca conseguirá estar más delgado que nuestro DVD – equipo DVD Home Cinema: el sistema más plano del mundo.
>
> 4 Hoy el primer ministro español viaja a Londres donde se encontrará con su colega, el primer ministro británico, para intercambiar sus opiniones sobre …

> 5 Esta tarde se prevén cielos poco nubosos, con intervalos soleados pero con posibilidad de chubascos tormentosos dispersos, más probables en las zonas de la sierra y en la zona del Estrecho.

Answers:
1 *deportivo*
2 *chisme / cotilleo*
3 *propaganda*
4 *informativo*
5 *pronóstico del tiempo*

 1b Students listen a second time and this time they add two more pieces of information for each extract.

Answers:
1 *piloto más joven; primer español a ganar el Fórmula 1.*
2 *su disco se llama Locura; ya no sale con X.*
3 *Home Cinema – un sistema muy plano*
4 *el primer ministro español viaja a Londres a hablar con el primer ministro británico*
5 *cielos poco nubosos, intervalos soleados*

Técnica

Listening skills

Discuss each point with students to gauge how competent and confident they already feel with listening tasks.

Use the transcript to show students how to focus on key language or vocabulary.

A Discuss with the students how they tackled Activity 1a and 1b.

B Students use the skills discussed to complete Activity 3a.

---

2 Students read the information about newscasts in Spain and then carry out a quick opinion poll by noting the answers to the questions and then comparing their findings with the rest of the class. This could serve as a basis for an essay at a later stage.

 3a Students listen to the seven people describing their viewing habits.

> **p. 16, actividad 3a**
>
> 1 A mí me encanta ver deporte, sobre todo el fútbol, en el portátil porque puedo encerrarme en mi habitación y verlo tumbado en la cama.
>
> 2 ¡No, no y no! Hay que ver los partidos con un grupo de amigos y en una pantalla de plasma grande – ¡así es más divertido!

> **3** Estoy de acuerdo y además así puedes ver con más detalle el juego y repasar los goles cuando quieras en los canales interactivos.
>
> **4** Y si es una película, también prefiero verla en una pantalla de plasma, 3D y, si es posible, con toda la familia porque así parece que estás en el cine. Además puedes seleccionar lo que quieres en los canales de pago.
>
> **5** Bueno pero si me pierdo una película que me gustaría ver entonces la puedo ver en internet Además puedes o en la tele si la he grabado, ¡y todas las veces que me de la gana!
>
> **6** A veces de camino al trabajo en el tren yo veo programas en el móvil aunque sólo se puede ver lo que, están retransmitiendo en ese momento y no se puede volver para atrás ni grabar nada.
>
> **7** ¡Y te vuelves miope con esa pantalla tan minúscula! El móvil y el portátil tienen sus ventajas si estás de viaje y quieres ver las noticias o el tiempo, por ejemplo. Pero para lo demás es mucho mejor sentarte y relajarte delante de la tele normal.

Answers:
1 *el portátil;* **2** *en la pantalla plasma;* **3** *en los canales interactivos;* **4** *los canales de pago;* **5** *en internet o grabado;* **6** *en el móvil;* **7** *la tele convencional*

3b They then write three arguments in favour and three against these ways of viewing.

Answers:
Students' own answers.

4 A group discussion. Students comment on the cartoon which should start a discussion about the pros and cons of TV.

5 This is a group activity. Students carry out a class survey about TV and radio preferences using the questions provided. Remind students that they can check up on numbers on in the grammar section at the back of the Student Book, page 172. Point them to the *frases clave* to see how to express percentages and fractions.

6 Students read the text about the future of television and answer the questions.

Answers:
1 *la programación tradicional*
2 *Podremos elegir de entre un banco digital de programas.*
3 *ver tele en una pantalla plasma enorme, en el móvil o en el ordenador portátil*
4 *Students answer in their own words.*
5 *Students answer in their own words*

7 Students prepare a presentation on the future of television, prompted by the opinion that "the best thing about 'the box' is that it entertains, relaxes and informs us after a day's work". Make sure they understand the subjects listed for inclusion. Students could prepare this as a class discussion first, then as an oral presentation. Finally, this could be done as a piece of written homework, as revsion of the topic or as a follow-up to make sure they have understood the unit so far.

¿Telebasura o programas educativos?

Planner	
Skills focus	
♦ Synonyms and antonyms	

Key language

la basura	rubbish
la broma	joke
la chispa	spark
el equilibrio	balance
el mando	TV control
la pelea	fight
el prejuicio	prejudice
un reflejo	image/reflection
el secuestro	hijack/hostage
días laborables	work days
desarrollar	to develop
matar al mensajero	to kill/shoot the messenger
chocante	shocking
morboso	gruesome
picante	risqué
vago	lazy
a mi modo de ver	in my opinion
no obstante	however
por lo menos	at least

Resources

♦ Student Book pages 18 and 19
♦ Vocabulario, Student Book page 21
♦ CD 1, track 13
♦ Hojas 1.1 CD 4, tracks 2 and 3, 1.2, 1.3

1a Students listen to the opinions about reality TV and make notes. Remind them about the listening skills they discussed on the previous spread especially about anticipating language and vocabulary and also creating their own abbreviations.

p. 18, actividades 1a y 1c

Preguntamos a 20 personas su opinión sobre los programas de tele realidad – he aquí algunas de sus respuestas – a ver lo que opináis vosotros. ¿Son intrusivos o son inofensivos?

1 Ver esta clase de programas, sobre todo los programas rosa, me hace olvidarme de todos mis problemas – que tampoco son demasiado graves.

2 Pues yo creo que la gente joven de mi edad nos reímos bastante y no consideramos nada grave ver accidentes en vídeos domésticos, o a gente aireando sus miserias que acaba pegándose.

3 A mí me emocionan y no me importa que muestren escenas explícitas – me hacen reír y no me las tomo en serio.

4 Yo los considero morbosos y humillantes y no me gustan, pero en fin, sé que la mayoría de la gente disfruta con estos programas y no hay que tomárselos en serio.

5 Lo que pasa es que cuando alguien está describiendo lo que acaba de pasar en un accidente, por ejemplo, me pone la carne de gallina pero si estoy viendo tonterías en casa, me hace reír.

6 No tiene nada de nuevo – desde los romanos, la gente se ha divertido viendo sufrir al prójimo – piensa en los cristianos que se echaban a las fieras o los esclavos que luchaban por su libertad – sólo estamos presenciando las mismas escenas transformadas para el siglo XXI.

7 Digan lo que digan, al público le encanta ventilar sus problemas, sus deseos o ansiedades ya sea a través de la radio, la prensa o la tele. Ahora gracias al holandés John de Mol tenemos cámaras las 24 horas del día enfocadas en los concursantes de Gran hermano.

8 Muchas veces se exagera la realidad porque a la gente le entusiasma tener sus quince minutos de fama – harían lo que fuera para alcanzar la fama y por eso no creo que haya que ser demasiado crítico – déjales que se expresen a su manera. La libertad de expresión es imprescindible en una sociedad democrática y libre.

1b Students read the statements and indicate whether or not they match the notes they have just taken.

Answers:
1 ✗   2 ✓   3 ✓   4 *no se dice*   5 ✗   6 ✓

 1c Students listen a second time and make a list of positive and then negative opinions.

1d Students use the questions and the *frases clave* to help them write 100 words on their opinions about a reality TV programme they know. Remind them they should always try to justify their opinions.

2a Students read the text and answer the questions. Advise them to read the text quickly to get the gist of the piece and then to look at the text with a view to answering the questions.

Answers:
1 *No ha invertido tiempo en educar a sus hijos.*
2 *Es un hombre vago pero acompaña a su hijo cuando ve la tele.*
3 *23% es el porcentaje de los niños españoles que ven entre 2 y 3 horas de tele en días laborables; 55% es el porcentaje de padres españoles que acompañan a sus hijos cuando ven la tele.*
4 *Dice que tendrán más tendencia a la violencia y agresividad cuando cumplen los 20 años.*
5 *Los niños españoles pasan más horas (930) delante de la tele que delante de un profesor (900).*

2b Organise students into groups to discuss among themselves how this compares with their own experience.

2c Get students to use the *frases clave* to give their own reactions to the text.

Cultural note: On 23 Febuary, 1981, a group of Civil Guards took the Congress and all the MPs in it hostage. Only when the king, Juan Carlos, spoke over the radio later that evening did the whole coup fail. It was the fact that he was able to speak directly to the people via the radio and later the television that defused what could have been a disastrous situation.

3 Students read the statements listed and classify them as either "in favour" or "against" TV.

Answers:
a favor = 1, 3, 8   en contra = 2, 4, 5, 6, 7

H 1.4 *Hoja* 1.1 offers additional listening practice for this page.

4a Reading. Students read the two texts and compare the main opinions. These are denser and longer texts than they have probably met so far. This gives an opportunity to illustrate that they do not always have to translate word for word, but rather gain an overall understanding of a text. The two texts could be put side by side on an OHT or whiteboard so that students follow visually with the differences being highlighted in different colours. The *Técnica* box on synonyms and antonyms could be discussed prior to completing this task as it could help students to exploit the vocabulary better.

4b Writing and speaking. Students note down the arguments for and against modern media. Exploit this further with oral questions.

4c Then they answer the questions in full sentences.

Answers should include:
1 *basura en la tele*
2 *hay programas mejor o peor hechos*
3 *que la violencia siempre ha existido*
4 *criticamos a los medios de comunicatión pero exigimos cada vez más inágenes sensacionalistas.*

Técnica

Synonyms and antonyms

This section could be exploited before tackling the texts. The work should be familiar to students from work covered in English lessons so ask for examples in English first. Point out that not just nouns and verbs have synonyms and antonyms but that various other parts of speech do also and that it will help them to write more interesting answers if they can begin to spot these.

A 1 *la violencia;* 2 *el reflejo;* 3 *inánime;*
4 *investigar/registrar/buscar;* 5 *no obstante*

B 1 *gustan;* 2 *la libertad;* 3 *requerimos/damos/ exigimos;* 4 *éxito;* 5 *sencillo*

Continue using the texts as a basis for further exploitation like this.

H 1.2-3 *Hojas* 1.2 and 1.3 offer additional speaking and reading practice for this spread.

Gramática en acción

Planner
Grammar focus
♦ The preterite tense using radical-changing verbs
Resources
♦ Student Book page 20
♦ Hoja 1.4

These sections can be used to revise and reinforce new grammar structures or to test how much students have retained from the unit.

Recuerda

Negatives

Students should revise page 14 and also the relevant grammar section of the Student Book on page 163.

A Ask students to copy the sentences and complete them with an appropriate negative.

Answers:
1 *ninguna; ni ningún*
2 *ningún*
3 *nunca*
4 *tampoco*
5 *nadie*
6 *nada que*

B Students translate the sentences as required.

Answers:
1 *Not even sports interest me./I'm not even interested in sport.*
2 *Has anyone seen the remote control ? No one has.*
3 *They never put anything on that I like.*
4 *No political debate interests me on the news.*
5 *Nada ha cambiado entonces. / No ha cambiado nada entonces.*
6 *Nunca te han gustado las noticias, ¿verdad?*
7 *Ni siquiera las pusiste.*
8 *Ni las noticias ni los documentales.*

Recuerda

The preterite tense continued – radical changes

♦ Ensure students understand the term radical-changing verbs, and then refer them to the relevant grammar section of the Student Book , page 166, and the Grammar Workbook.
♦ Remind them about radical-changing verbs in the present tense as well.
♦ Students then complete tasks A and B.

Answers:
C 1 *sintió* 2 *pidieron* 3 *siguió* 4 *riñeron* 5 *prefirió*

D dar, decir, estar, ser, fuir, hacer, poder, poner, querer, saber, traer, tener, ver

E
1 *Dijo que le gustaba las telenovelas.*
2 *Pusieron el canal de deportes toda la noche.*
3 *Los otros no pudieron ver lo que querían.*
4 *Gran Hermano fue un programa muy popular.*
5 *Dimos un nuevo televisor plasma a nuestros padres como regalo de Navidad.*
6 *¡Estuvieron dichosos!*

H 1.4 *Hoja* 1.4 offers additional practice of preterite tense: radical-changing verbs and negatives.

Unit 1 Assessment offers exam practice for this unit.

Vocabulario

Page 21

Answers:
1 *se repite/repiten*
2 *mejores*
3 *quiere*
4 *suelen*
5 *Gran*

Extra

Planner

Skills focus

♦ Deal with unfamiliar words

Resources

♦ Student Book page 22
♦ CD 1, track 14

This page ia aimed at A-A* students.

1 This text is from the webpage of the Telecinco TV series "Hospital Central", which is Spain's longest running series. Students test and improve their vocabulary by seeking in the text the Spanish equivalents of the words listed.

Answers:
1 *tanto... como...*
2 *ya que*
3 *más de*
4 *convertirse en*
5 *algo*
6 *incluso*
7 *a lo largo de*
8 *volver a +inf*

2 Students read the extract again and test their comprehension by identifying the storylines or characters described in the statements listed.

Suggested answers:
1 *Sandra ha sido amante de Rodolfo y de Fernando.*
2 *Rodolfo*
3 *Esther se ha casado con Maca, pero Raúl es padre de sus hijos.*
4 *Teresa*
5 *Todos!*
6 *Sandra*
7 *Teresa la secretaria, Raúl el joven doctor hedonista, Rodolfo el doctor prepotente*

 3 Students listen to the description of Esther and identify which of the personality traits in Activity 2 are reflected in her personality.

p. 22, actividad 3

Esther ha desarrollado toda su carrera profesional en 'Hospital Central'. Siempre tiene una sonrisa en la boca y está dispuesta a dar un abrazo a quien lo necesite.

Esther ha tenido dos relaciones serias antes de su relación actual, una con un médico residente, Ramón, que tenía problemas con las drogas, y otra con un chico que quedó minusválido cuando estaban juntos y ella le ayudó mucho a asimilar lo sucedido.

La vida de la enfermera dio un giro de 180 grados cuando apareció Maca. Lo que en un principio era una bonita amistad se acabó convirtiendo en una apasionada relación que desembocaría en un matrimonio con tres hijos. Todo empezó cuando, después de un agotador día de trabajo, la pediatra dio un masaje en la espalda a Esther e intentó secucirla; al principio la enfermera se puso a la defensiva, puesto que nunca antes había estado con una mujer.

Desde entonces, el amor y el desamor han sido los protagonistas en la vida de la pediatra y la enfermera. Su relación es como una montaña rusa y sus rupturas nunca parecen definitivas.

Answers:
3, 4, 5

4a Class discussion. Students express their opinion of TV soaps, using examples from the "Hospital Central" text.

Técnica

Dealing with unfamiliar words

Take students through the strategies for working out words that may not immediately be familiar.

A Students read the underlined words in their context and identify which of the four strategies listed is appropriate. Students' first instinct may well be to go straight for the dictionary in all cases. This exercise will generate discusssion about different approaches.

Suggested answers:
1 *SAMUR*
2 *acarreado*
3 *esgrimiendo, cotilla*
4 *muelle, riendas*

4b Students summarise in 150 words the various opinions about TV soaps.

Unit 1 Assessment offers exam practice for this unit.

Unidad 2 Anuncios y publicidad

Unit objectives

By the end of this unit students will be able to:
♦ Comment on the purposes of advertising
♦ Analyse and discuss different advertising techniques
♦ Disuss the benefits and drawbacks of advertising
♦ Give and justify opinions on curbs on advertising

Grammar

By the end of this unit students will be able to:
♦ Understand and use the present subjunctive with verbs of wanting, requesting and advising
♦ Use suffixes

Skills

By the end of this unit students will be able to:
♦ Recognise and use language of persuasion
♦ Recognise and use different registers of language
♦ Develop and justify points of view

Resources

♦ Student Book page 23
♦ This page introduces the topic.

1a Students study the advertisements and answer the questions for each advert.

1b Work in pairs. Students look for more advertisements in Spanish newspapers or magazines or on the Internet and discuss them with a companion. They should use the questions in Activity 1a.

Persuasores y persuadidos

> **Planner**
>
> *Grammar focus*
> ♦ The subjunctive with verbs of wanting, requesting and advising
>
> *Skills focus*
> ♦ The language of persuasion
>
> *Key language*
>
> | | |
> |---|---|
> | *los bienes* | goods |
> | *la cifra* | number |
> | *el freno* | break/restraint |
> | *la inversión* | investment |
> | *una marca* | make |
> | *la meta* | aim/goal |
> | *un mensaje* | message |
> | *el poder* | power |
> | *el propósito* | purpose |
> | *disfrutar* | to enjoy |
> | *entretenerse* | to entertain |
> | *probar (ue)* | to try |
> | *relajar* | to relax |
> | *tratar de* | to be about |
> | *encubierto/a* | hidden/subliminal |
> | *clave* | key (adj.) |
> | *soso/a* | silly/dull |
> | *único/a* | unique |
> | *antiedad* | anti-ageing |
> | *mogollón* | lots/heaps |
>
> *Resources*
> ♦ Student Book pages 24 and 25
> ♦ Vocabulario, Student Book page 31
> ♦ CD 1, track 15
> ♦ Hoja 2.5
> ♦ Grammar Workbook page 53

1a Students listen to the advertisements and answer the questions. Ensure students study the questions before they listen and also anticipate language and vocabulary. They could also make some abbreviations to help them in their note taking. The transcript could be used after they have completed the task to show them where the answers lie.

---

p. 24, actividad 1a

1 El nuevo Audi A1 personalizado – diseñado para que cada uno sea único. Como tu A1 no hay otro. Elige el color que prefieras y combínalo con un color de contraste para el techo. Hay tantos detalles y tantas posibilidades para hacerlo único que no será fácil decidirse. El A1 ya está aquí y pretende reflejar tu estilo.

2 Muy Interesante Junior – la forma más divertida de aprender. Y este mes en tu revista favorita hay Animales ¡Cómo le dan las aves al pico! El Cuerpo Humano – acrobacias increíbles; Economía ¿Qué puedo hacer con1€? Historias en cómic y mucho más. Para más información: www.muyjunior.es

3 Prueba estas fantásticas gafas de masaje. Especialmente diseñadas para relajar tus ojos y tu mente. Estas gafas de masaje te ayudarán a prevenir los dolores de cabeza y la vista cansada. Con diferentes tipos de masajes y temperaturas, que se controlan mediante un mando a distancia, estas gafas mejoran la circulación sanguínea ocular. Además vienen con música relajante para activar las células de tus ojos y de tu cerebro, facilitándote así el sueño.

4 'Una vela, un pupitre'. Desde el 15 de agosto se pondrán a la venta en las papelerías de El Corte Inglés unas velas en forma de lápiz cuyo objetivo es recaudar fondos para ayudar a escolarizar a niñas de todo el mundo. ¡Ayúdanos a que su educación no se apague!

5 El sabor que apaga el verano. Bebe Nestea al limón – la bebida perfecta para 9 de cada 10 consumidores.

6 Lab series presenta MAX. LS crema facial antiedad. Diseñada para el hombre, maximiza el funcionamiento de la piel del hombre. Esta crema hidratante de alto rendimiento reduce visiblemente la aparición de líneas de envejecimiento y arrugas.

7 Este anuncio está dirigido a todos los padres y niños menores de edad de parte de los Ministerios de Salud y de Educación. ¡Vamos a la cama que hay que descansar; para que mañana podamos madrugar – vamos!

1b Work in pairs. Students identify the aim of each advertisement using the terms provided. Remind them to give reasons for their answers.

2a Vocabulary and comprehension. Students read the text about advertising "Diariamente …" and note down the Spanish equivalents of the English words given.

Answers:
1 *los estadounidenses;* **2** *por otro lado;* **3** *se cifra en;* **4** *disparatadas;* **5** *encubierta.*

2b Students translate the sentence in bold in the text.

Answer:
2b *Nowadays it is almost impossible to sell a product without advertising it somehow or other.*

Gramática

The present subjunctive with verbs of wanting, requesting and advising

Allow plenty of time for students to discuss why the subjunctive is used in Spanish and how it affects the whole sentence. This allows a valuable opportunity for students to practise analytical skills on sentence structure and to apply their understanding of language and make comparisons between English and Spanish.

A Students match the halves of the sentences. Remind them that they can check the form of the subjunctive in the Student Book, page 30.

Answers:
There are various possibilities; accept any logical pairings.

B Students translate the sentences into English.

---

3 Students discover what kind of consumer they are by responding to the multiple choice questions.

4a Work in pairs. Students compare their results and discuss their choices. The speech bubbles provide vocalary to aid their discussion.

4b Students discuss whether they are influenced much by publicity or not. Some vocabulary and key phrases are provided.

Técnica

Language of persuasion

Take students through the points one by one, commenting on them and discussing each of them. It would help to show advertisements in Spanish and English to illustrate the kind of language used.

A Students study the advertisement and complete the sentences using the verbs in the subjunctive supplied.

Use the same sentence starters to complete sentences for the other two adverts, but without giving the subjunctive form of the verb.

B Students translate the short passage into English, and explain (in English) how it relates to advertising.

Possible/sample translation:
*No one can force/oblige another person to decide
to buy a certain make of something; they have to be
convinced/you have to convince them. Persuasion
is measured by the level of conviction that the
person receiving it shows; it is quite different from
imposition, submission or lies.*

H 2.5 *Hoja* 2.5 offers additional practice of using language
of persuasion.

Estilos diversos

Planner
Grammar focus
♦ Suffixes
Skills focus
♦ Different registers of language (1)

Key language

el consumidor	consumer
el embalaje	wrapping
el mercadeo	marketing
el truco	trick
una valla de	hoarding/billboard
publicidad aclarar	to make clear
apelar a	to appeal to
caer en la trampa	to fall into the trap
darse el lujo de	to afford
demostrar(ue)	to demonstrate
destacarse	to stand out
estrenar	to show/use for the
	first time
lucir	to shine/show off
fenomenal	great/phenomenal
flipante	ace/crazy
genial	wonderful/genius
imprescindible	essential
ingenioso/a	ingenious/clever
ingenuo/a	naïve/gullible
¡de infarto!	'wicked' (heart attack
	material)

Resources

♦ Student Book pages 26 and 27
♦ Vocabulario, Student Book page 31
♦ CD 1, tracks 16, 17 and 18
♦ Hojas 2.1, CD 4, tracks 7 and 8, 2.2
♦ Grammar Workbook page 6

 1a Students listen to the advertisements and classify
them by types of product they seek to advertise.

p. 26, actividades 1a y 1b

1 ¡Color en los pies! Ha llegado la nueva
increíble colección de zapatos y zapatillas
de Lacoste. Sin renunciar a la elegancia,
destacan por la utilización de fantásticos
colores hasta ahora solo reservados
para el verano.

2 ¡Y ahora precisión a prueba de agua!
Estrenamos la nueva marca de relojes Cat
para hombres y mujeres. Son sumergibles
hasta cien metros de profundidad!

3 ¡Regala un tesoro! Se trata de uno de los
perfumes joya de Lancôme Paris – uno
de los más deseados por lo que sugiere y
provoca. Trésor es como un tesoro escondido
que da brillo y personalidad a quien lo
destapa.¡Regalazo increíble!

4 Este invierno Tomás Burberry se supera y
apuesta por texturas que nunca dejan de
estar de moda, como la pana. Sus abrigos y
cazadoras, diseñados para gente joven, se
presentan en colores beige, caqui o negro.
Imprescindibles para estar a la última.

5 Las últimas ofertas del día en el mostrador
de lácteos y refrigerados – vengan todos y
aprovechen las gangas. Jamón curado en
lonchas; comprando dos la segunda unidad
sale a 1,75€. Huevos natura un envase de
seis unidades sale a 1,10€ pero comprando
dos, la segunda unidad sale a 0,55€. ¡Ultima
hora – mogollón de gangas!

6 Sólo Samsung podía hacerlo. La obra
maestra de Samsung con su televisor de perfil
extraplano – lo mejor del mundo.

7 ¡Resultados visibles geniales! Dentiblanc
es un blanqueador súper intensivo. Con
Dentiblanc tendrás los dientes más blancos,
reirás más y verás los resultados en tu estado
de ánimo. ¡Es flipante!

Answers:
1 *pasatiempo/deporte;* **2** *pasatiempo/deporte;*
3 *cosméticos;* **4** *ropa;* **5** *comida;* **6** *hogar;*
7 *cosméticos*

 1b Students listen again. Then they give their views
on the impact of the adverts, noting the language
used. Ask students to go online or leaf through
Spanish magazines to find more up-to-date examples
of jingles and spots so that they analyse the latest
language for selling a product.

2 Students describe a favourite product, including
how it is branded and advertised, following the
guidance given.

3 Students listen to the young people analysing some advertisements and note down the product or advertisement under discussion and what is said about it. They could describe what is said in either English or Spanish.

> **p. 26, actividad 3**
>
> **1** A mí me gustaría tener el reloj porque me encanta hacer buceo, ¡pero ya me imagino cuánto debe de costar! Un precio desorbitado para alguien como yo. Este tipo de anuncios siempre suenan engañosos. Te seducen y te hacen creer que puedes darte el lujo de comprar uno cuando en realidad no puedes.
>
> **2** Según mi padre pasa lo mismo con los televisores. Uno siempre quiere el último modelo pero salen tantos y con tanta frecuencia que cuando te acabas de comprar uno cuando ya sale otro. ¡Son elegantes pero a fin de cuentas el partido de fútbol va a terminar igual sea en alta definición o en blanco y negro!
>
> **3** A mí me llama la atención cuando la publicidad utiliza música, historias de familias o amores románticos como en los anuncios de nescafé o del Internet. Me fascinan porque tienen que ver con nuestra actualidad cotidiana y por eso parece que son reales y no de fantasía.
>
> **4** Lo que pasa con los anuncios de los supermercados es que los hacen sonar tan urgentes que parece que el producto se va a agotar. Entonces caes en la trampa, y acabas comprando algo que en realidad no necesitas.
>
> **5** Bueno, bueno, vosotros sois unos ingenuos; hay que abrir más los ojos y los oídos y no dejarse seducir por la voz melosa ni por la urgencia ni por la exclusividad; hay que pensar que necesitas unas zapatillas pero para hacer deporte, no para lucir delante de los amigos, entonces acabarás comprando unas zapatillas prácticas por un precio asequible ¡y no te gastarás un dineral!

Possible answers:

1 *Watch, advert sounds false but seduces you to buy beyond your means.*
2 *Television: looks so elegant, turn out so many, game is the same whether watched on high definition or black and white.*
3 *Likes ads with music or storyline – more believable.*
4 *Supermarket ads – urgency makes you fall into trap of buying what you don't need.*
5 *Don't be gullible. Remember you only need trainers for sport not to show off.*

Técnica

Different registers of language (1)

Take students through the points raised and ask for their reactions and comments. They should provide examples of their own to make sure they have a clear idea about the term 'registers of language'.

A Students make a list of some recent adverts they have watched, heard, read or seen.

Work in pairs. Students discuss their answers for **B** and **C** with a partner. But first they prepare their thoughts.

B Students consider differences of register in adverts in various media. Some phrases are given to help the discussion.

C Students describe in Spanish an advert that appeals to them They use questions from page 24 Activity 1 and page 26 Activity 1b to guide them.

4 What makes for a good advert. Students look at the table of techniques used to make advertisements effective. They match the techniques to the reasons.

Answers:
1 *f;* **2** *l;* **3** *a;* **4** *d;* **5** *e;* **6** *j;* **7** *b;* **8** *k;* **9** *i;* **10** *c;* **11** *h;* **12** *g*

5 Students analyse the advertisement using the criteria 1–12 in Activity 4.

Gramática

Suffixes

Ensure students understand the terms diminutive, augmentative and pejorative. Ask for examples in English and then see how many words they already know that have suffixes in Spanish. This could be done as a whole class exercise to make a comprehensive list. They could also discuss how suffixes are used in advertising to add to the shade of meaning desired.

A Students translate the examples into English.

Answers:
little Isabel; little Andrew; a bedside table; a little boy; tiny little/cute girl; little old lady
rather small, little; small bag
main entrance; a large woman; a great goal
You could also ask students to write a sentence in Spanish to illustrate that their understanding.
e.g. *Una abuela de mi Isabelita es una viejecita, la otra una mujerona, su abuelo es feucho.*

B Students practise forming diminutives, augmentatives and perjoratives.

Answers:
1 *casita, casilla, casona, casucha*
2 *chiquillo, chiquito*
3 *maletica, maletón*
4 *ojitos, ojones, ojazos,*
5 *papelito, papelón, papelucho.*

 C Students listen to the advert and note down the suffixes used. They assess their effectiveness.

---

p. 27, actividad C

1 Compra esta ropita nuevecita para tu bebé – tu pequeñín recién nacido estará muy guapito.

2 No seas el feucho de la fiesta. Ponte estas zapatillas deportivas y verás cómo pasas de parecer un hombretón a parecer un jovencito de andares ligeros.

---

6 Work in groups or in pairs. Students use the language and techniques they have learnt to design an advertising campaign. They should choose a product or idea, decide who the campaign is aimed at, the media they will use, and invent a slogan for their product. Design techniques as well as language should be considered.

H 2.1-2 *Hojas* 2.1 and 2.2 offer additional listening and speaking practice for this spread.

Los pros y los contras

Planner

Key language

un cenicero	ashtray
el destape	taking the lid off/ exposing
la desventaja	disadvantage/drawback
la mentira	lie
la ventaja	advantage
aconsejar	to advise
canturrear	to hum/sing
hacer daño	to harm
lograr	to manage to/achieve
molestar	to annoy
no dejar de	not to let up/leave off
padecer de	to suffer from
sobrepasar	to outweigh
capaz	capable
dañino/a	harmful
desenfrenado/a	uncontrollable
innecesario/a	unnecessary
lujoso/a	luxurious
maligno/a	evil/wicked/malign
fuera de su alcance	beyond their means

Resources

♦ Student Book pages 28 and 29
♦ CD 1, track 19
♦ Vocabulario, Student Book page 31
♦ Hoja 2.3

1a Students look at the poster and describe it in their own words by answering the questions.

1b Students complete the sentences to match the recommendations on the poster.

Answers:
1 *El anuncio recomienda que seamos educados y que preguntemos si molestamos a los que están con nosotros.*
2 *Aconseja que fumemos cigarillos bajos en nicotina.*
3 *Quiere que dejemos la última parte del cigarillo en el cenicero.*
4 *Insiste que no lo probemos si padecemos de alguna enfermedad respiratoria.*

 2 Students listen to the discussion and identify the speakers whose views match most closely the statements 1–12.

---

p. 28, actividad 2

Profesor: Bueno, clase, hoy vamos a discutir el tema de la publicidad o mejor dicho la influencia que ejerce esta sobre nuestra vida. ¿Es una fuerza para el bien o para el mal? En mi opinión las ventajas superan a las desventajas. ¿Qué opináis? A ver Jorge, comienza tú.

Jorge: Bueno pues, creo que, en efecto, nosotros, el público, nos beneficiamos bastante de la publicidad y que somos lo suficientemente adultos como para saber cuándo la publicidad exagera y dice mentiras. Somos capaces de escoger entre lo bueno y lo malo. ¿No crees, Ana?

Ana: Estoy de acuerdo. Las campañas publicitarias a favor de la salud o contra las drogas y demás cosas que nos pueden hacer daño por ejemplo, son beneficiosas para todos, y tienen sus ventajas – pero al mismo tiempo todos somos consumidores y el mundo está saturado de bienes innecesarios y con precios por encima de nuestras posibilidades. Se gasta más dinero en la publicidad que en el producto. Esto es una desventaja. ¿A ver profe, tú qué piensas?

Profe: Es cierto, pero también es bueno poder comparar distintos productos y cuando una

---

> nueva empresa saca un nuevo producto es interesante tener información sobre ello. ¿Tú, Roberto, estás de acuerdo?
>
> **Roberto:** Pues sólo hasta cierto punto porque creo que las grandes empresas siempre tendrán ventaja sobre las pequeñas, pueden utilizar propaganda más cara y trucos más impactantes e ingeniosos. Aunque tengo que confesar que los anuncios más eficaces son los que me dejan canturreando una canción todo el día, los que son muy originales o los que más me entretienen. ¿No es así Marta?
>
> **Marta:** Sí así es pero el aspecto negativo de ésto es que los niños siempre se acuerdan de los mismos anuncios y muchas veces no dejan de pedir cosas que no son aptas para ellos y que son hasta dañinas como los dulces o la comida rápida.

Answers:
Profe = 1, 7, 10; Jorge = 3; Ana = 2, 5, 6, 9;
Roberto = 4, 8; 11 Marta = 12

3a Students read the points of view and identify them as positive or negative.

Answers:
1 *negativo;* **2** *positivo;* **3** *negativo;* **4** *positivo;*
5 *positivo;* **6** *positivo;* **7** *negativo;* **8** *positivo;*
9 *negativo;* **10** *positivo;* **11** *negativo;* **12** *positivo*

3b Students consider which is the most positive and which the most negative point of view. They add ideas of their own. This could be a class discussion with ideas put up on whiteboard.

4a Work in pairs. Students discuss whether the anti-smoking campaign has been successful. They consider whether there should be a government campaign against fast foods, which also damage our health.

4b Students write three reasons for supporting such campaigns (los pros) and threee reasons for opposing them (las contras).

5a Students read the text on publicity campaigns and find the information required.

Answers:
Students form their own answers, which should include the following:
1 *Los anuncios en Navidades contra el consumo de alcohol; Los anuncios que aconsejan contra el consumo de tabaco y drogas.*
2 *Los anuncios de Navidades que animan a comprar muchos dulces y cosas que no necesitamos.*
3 *Suprime la información política y cuando se levante llega aun más pornografía.*
4 *Son 1966 La Ley de Prensa queintordujo una actitud más liberal; 1977 cuando se levantó la censura y llegó el momento de "destape"*

5 *Persuadirnos a comprar; darnos envidia.*
6 *Usan imágenes seductoras o que chocan para llamarnos la atención.*

5b Vocabulary work. Students identify in the text the Spanish equivalents of the words and phrases listed.

Answers:
1 *de una forma u otra;* 2 *sobrepasamos los límites;*
3 *nuestra manera de pensar;* 4 *dañan los dientes;*
5 *Al final, nos incitan comprando…;*
6 *ante todo esto;* 7 *del mismo año;* 8 *abrió el camino;* 9 *no hay más que;* 10 *empero.*

6 Work in pairs. Students discuss the practicalities of censorship on advertising. They give three examples of when they think cnesorship is beneficial and important and three examples of when censorship is not necessary and seems to be limit our right to choose. They discuss various techniques involved.

H 2.3 *Hoja* 2.3 offers additional practice for this spread.

Gramática en acción

Planner

Resources
♦ Student Book page 30
♦ Hoja 2.4

This section can be used to revise and reinforce new grammar structures or to test how much students have retained from the unit.

Recuerda

Subjunctives

Present the formation of the present subjunctive so that students fully appreciate the difference between the indicative and the subjunctive patterns.

A Ask students to identify the changes made to verb endings when a verb is in the subjunctive.

Answer:
endings are swapped around –ar verbs end like –er and –ir verbs and vice versa

B Students write out in full the present subjunctive of *cruzar* and *pagar*.

Answers:
z changes to c in *cruzar:*
cruce, cruces, cruce, crucemos, crucéis, crucen
g changes to gu in *pagar:*
pague, pagues, pague, paguemos, paguéis, paguen

C Students write out in full the present subjunctive of *dormir* and *preferir*.

Answers:
duerma, duermas, duerma, durmamos, durmáis, duerman
prefiera, prefieras, prefiera, prefiramos, prefiráis, prefieran

D Students write out in full the present subjunctive of *decir* and *poner*.

Answers:
diga, digas, diga ,digamos, digáis, digan
ponga, pongas, ponga, pongamos, pongáis, pongan

E Students make learning cards for these six irregular verbs. They put the Spanish on one side and English on the other. Working in pairs they test each other until they know these verb forms by heart.

F Students read the sentences and identify which verbs are in the subjunctive. They translate the sentences into English

Answers:
1 *compres* after *quiero*; I want you to buy me those trainers in the advert.
2 *veas* after *insisto*; I insist that you see this new advert for perfumes
3 *sea* after *esperamos*; We hope that the new advert will be funnier/more amusing.
4 *lea* after *aconseja*; He/she advises me to read the detail in the advert.
5 *sigas* after *quiero*; I don't want you to keep on humming that silly advert all day long!
6 *respalde* after *necesita*; The new publicity campaign against smoking needs the government to back it up/needs the backing of the government.
7 *dejemos* after *pide*; It is asking us all to give up smoking.
8 *fume* after *permite*; My parents do not allow my brother to smoke at home.
9 *hagamos* after *impedir*; But they can't stop us doing it outside.
10 *oiga* after *deja*; Let him hear the new advert.

G Students translate the sentences into Spanish.

Answers:
1 *Los anuncios normalemente quieren que compremos algo.*
2 *Las campañas publicitarias sobre los problemas de salud esperan que sigamos sus consejos.*
3 *El gobierno puede insistir que un anuncio sea retirado.*
4 *Algunas personas quieren que los anuncios den información solamente.*

5 *Otros prefieren que los anuncios les seduzcan y que creen un mundo de fantasía.*
6 *El gobierno debe exigir que todos los anuncios sean una influencia para el bien para los niños.*

H 2.4 *Hoja* 2.4 offers additional practice of using the subjective.

Vocabulario

Page 31

Answers:
1 *compres*
2 *hicimos*
3 *vi*
4 *antiedad*
5 *fenomenales*

Extra

Planner

Skills focus
♦ Developing and justifying points of view

Resources
♦ Student Book page 32
♦ CD 1, track 20

This page is aimed at A-A* students.

1a Students read the two blogs. They identify which text discusses the advertisement for a toiletry product, which is a criticism of an advertisement, which mentions different methods of communication, which mentions sexual content of the campaign, which offers its own opinion of the campaign, which informs us about reaction to the campaign.

Answers:
1 *Los dos;* 2 *20 minutos;* 3 *Los dos;*
4 *Los dos;* 5 *Publicidad.net;* 6 *20 minutos*

1b Vocabulary and comprehension. Students find words in the texts with the same meaning as the words listed.

Answers:
1 *denigra;* 2 *atuendo;* 3 *supuestas;* 4 *desempeñan;*
5 *pretende;* 6 *descaradas;* 7 *rechazo;* 8 *iluso*

1c Students read the statements underlined in the text and explain what they mean in their own words, in Spanish. Do they agree with the statements? This could be developed as a class discussion.

2 Students listen to Raúl and Octavia and identify who says what.

> **p. 32, actividad 2**
>
> **Raúl**: Pues yo diría que hay que entender que esa publicidad va dirigida a un cierto grupo de la población, o sea al grupo específico que va a comprar ese producto. Les hace reír. Entienden que no representa la realidad. Saben que un simple desodorante no tiene ese efecto instantáneo y embriagador sobre las mujeres. Igualmente saben que los anuncios juegan con ideas estereotípicas de forma sofisticada, como rechazo de lo políticamente correcto.
>
> **Octavio**: Esa campaña justifica a través del humor que se puede vilipendie a las mujeres. Quien defiende la dignidad de todos y de todas, no es que carezca de sentido del humor, sino que no aprecia las injurias y ultrajes que ya ni siquiera se toleran en el patio de la escuela de la boca de niños groseros e inmaduros.

Answers:
1 *Octavio;* **2** *Raúl;* **3** *Raúl;* **4** *Raúl;* **5** *Raúl;* **6** *Octavio*

3 Group work. Students choose one of the points of view, either for or against the advertisement for Axe, and prepare to defend their view in a class debate.

Técnica

Developing and justifying points of view

Take students through the points they should bear in mind in developing an argument.

Unit 2 Assessment offers exam practice for this unit.

Unidad 3 Los medios de comunicación

Unit objectives

By the end of this unit students will be able to:
♦ Comment on the popularity of modern technological gadgets
♦ Discuss the current potential usage of the Internet
♦ Talk and write about the benefits and dangers of the Internet and modern technological gadgets

Grammar

By the end of this unit students will be able to:
♦ Use *se* to avoid the passive voice
♦ Use the imperative correctly
♦ Use the subjunctive giving value judgements/ wanting and not wanting

Skills

By the end of this unit students will be able to:
♦ Use strategies for reading
♦ Infer meaning when listening

Resources

♦ Student Book page 33
♦ CD 1, track 21

These exercises introduce the topic and vocabulary of modern technological gadgets.

1 Students read the descriptions 1–3 and match them to the pictures A–C.

Answers:
1 *C*   2 *A*   3 *B*

2 Students write a list of cognates that are related to/have to do with technology. Make sure they understand the term cognate. They can check their lists against the *Vocabulario* on page 41 of the Student Book. Ensure students learn the difference in spelling between English and Spanish cognates and that they pronounce the Spanish words correctly.

 3a Students listen to Raúl, Jesús and Celia and choose a piece of equipment for each of them.

> **p. 33, actividad 3a**
>
> **Raúl:** Pensaba comprar un MP3 porque quería escuchar música mientras me dedicaba a hacer deporte, pero decidí comprar uno que puedo utilizar también como teléfono.
>
> **Celia:** A los 46 años, no voy a empezar a jugar a videojuegos, pero tengo ganas de comprar un aparato para poder escuchar música y con una pantalla lo suficientemente grande como para ver fotos y vídeos.
>
> **Jesús:** No voy a volver a comprar otro aparato. Acabo de encontrar éste que incluye todo lo que quiero. Me puedo conectar a Internet, tiene juegos excelentes, y admite 300 canciones o mil fotos de alta resolución.

Answers:
Raúl A; *Jesús B*; *Celia C*

3b Students discuss whether these gadgets are useful, necessary or for entertainment; whether they have one; what they think of them.

Tecnología: los hechos

> **Planner**
>
> *Grammar focus*
> ♦ Using *se* to avoid the passive
> ♦ The subjunctive for value judgements and emotions
>
> *Key language*
>
> | | |
> |---|---|
> | un aparato | gadget |
> | un auricular | earpiece |
> | la diversión | entertainment |
> | la energía solar | solar power |
> | el fichero | file |
> | una lástima | pity |
> | un mando a distancia | remote control |
> | la mayoría | majority |
> | el móvil | mobile phone |
> | el portátil | laptop |
> | un sondeo | survey |

conectarse	to connect
descargar	to download
emitir	to send out
enchufarse	to plug in
navegar (Internet)	to surf the Internet
recargar	to charge up/recharge
valorar	to value
me choca que ...	I'm shocked that ...
me preocupa que ...	I'm worried that ...

Resources

♦ Student Book pages 34 and 35
♦ CD 1, track 22
♦ Grammar Workbook pages 53, 62

1 By way of an introduction to the spread, students read the descriptions and match them to the objects displayed.

Answers:
1 *C*   2 *A*   3 *E*   4 *B*   5 *D*

2 Students listen to the recording and identify which object is being spoken about. They listen also for an opinion about each object.

---

p. 34, actividad 2

1 Acabo de comprarlo, así que todavía no lo he utilizado, pero me imagino que va a ser muy divertido. No tendré que gritar, y espero que a Tufo también le guste.

2 Es exactamente lo que necesito. A la moda pero a la vez práctico. Voy a poder ahorrar tiempo, dinero y electricidad.

3 Es feo y ridículo. No quiero hablar con un monigote así de tonto. Se lo voy a regalar a mi hermano. Le va a parecer muy simpático.

4 Pensé que era una broma. No puede existir una cosa tan inútil, o si existe, no han de vender muchos. Ni siquiera tiene memoria. ¿Quién necesita desodorante para su ordenador?

5 No. No va a funcionar. Si descuelgas el auricular, se te va a caer el móvil al suelo.

Answers:
1 *remote control wireless dog device – amusing*
2 *solar powered handbag – fashionable and practical*
3 *skype phone monster – ugly and ridiculous*
4 *USB airwick – a joke, who needs it?*
5 *retro handset for mobile – won't work*

Gramática

Using se *to avoid the passive*

Refer students to the relevant grammar section of the Student Book, page 171.
Remind students about the form and purpose of this structure.

A Ask students to identify all the sentences which use *se* this on the page. They should then translate each one as in the example, giving a literal version, and then in correct English.

3 Students read the text and complete the sentences using their own words. They should follow the example given.

Possible answers:
2 *El 62% de los jóvenes ... se conecta al Internet a diario.*
3 *Las chicas ... valoran Internet más para los estudios.*
4 *Los chicos ... tienen otras prioridades.*
5 *El "chat" ... es muy popular entre los jóvenes para comunicarse.*
6 *Las compras en Internet ... no son tan importantes como otros aspectos.*
7 *Las llamadas telefónicas ... son menos importantes que los SMS.*

Gramática

The subjunctive for value judgements and emotions

This follows on from the work covered in Unit 2 page 24 of the Student Book about the use of the subjunctive.

Also, refer students to the relevant grammar section of the Student Book, page 170.

A Students could read through the four examples given here and then make further examples of their own, making sure they can explain what is meant by emotions and value judgements. Students should then give their own translations of the phrases in English.

---

4 Students use the *frases clave* to give their own opinions about the results of the survey from the previous page. They follow the example given.

5 Students read the statements 1–5. They decide whether they agree or not, and then give their own opinions. This is a reading and speaking exercise, not a grammar one, so they do not necessarily need to use the subjunctive in their answers. It should give them an opportunity to see some more examples.

La blogosfera

Planner

Grammar focus

♦ Imperatives – positive, negative, with *usted* and *ustedes*
♦ Subjunctive with wanting/not wanting things to happen

Key language

un bloguero	a blogger
los chaters	a chatter (one who uses SMS style words in text)
un friki	a geek
las mayúsculas	capital letters
una mentira	lie
los newbies	newcomers
la ortografía	spelling
los troles	someone who sends spam or writes abusive messages on blogs
los usuarios títeres	people who use cyber names (not their real name)
los vínculos	links
aportar	to bring to
asegurar que	to ensure that
contravenir	to contravene/break the law
difundir	to spread
impedir	to prevent
molestar	to annoy
permitir	to allow/permit
malsonantes	insulting
para que	in order that

Resources

♦ Student Book pages 36 and 37
♦ CD 1, track 23
♦ Grammar Workbook pages 53, 60

1 Students choose definitions for the ICT vocabulary.

Answers:
a *los newbies*
b *un friki*
c *un bloguero*
d *los chaters*
e *los usuarios títeres*
f *los troles*

 2 Students listen and check each definition.

---

p. 36, actividad 2

a Los **newbies** molestan a los usuarios habituales, no porque quieran provocar problemas, sino porque ignoran las reglas y hacen preguntas tontas.

b Soy un **friki**. Lo que más me gusta son los ordenadores e Internet. También me gustan los videojuegos, y paso mucho tiempo jugando.

c Soy un **bloguero**. Tengo un blog personal donde doy mis opiniones sobre el mundo. Blog es una palabra que viene del inglés y significa web log, que es como una bitácora o diario personal.

d Soy un **chater**. Me gusta mandar mensajes SMS y es más rápido y corto escribir las palabras a mi manera.

e Yo manejo varios **usuarios títeres**. Tengo dos o tres nombres diferentes en Internet y nadie sabe mi nombre real.

f Yo creo que los blogs son tonterías. A veces me aburro y pongo mensajes abusivos en los blogs para divertirme. ¡Dicen que soy un **trol**!

Gramática

Imperatives

Refer students to the relevant grammar section of the Student Book.

Students will already be familiar with the imperative form but now need to fully understand how to form it and which form to use when.

A Students find examples of positive forms and explain how each one is formed.

Answers:
5 *Respeta la ortografía del idioma castellano.*
  Explanation: pos = imperative 2nd person sing. of respetar
7 *Trata de aportar comentarios relevantes al debate*
  Explanation: pos = imperative 2nd person sing. of tratar
10 *Respeta a los otros usuarios.*
  Explanation: pos = imperative 2nd person sing. of respetar

B Students do the same for all the negative imperatives.

Answers:
1 *No contravengas el Código Penal de España.*
   *Explanation: neg = subjunctive 1st person
   present tense of venir = vengo. –ar endings 2nd
   person: vengas*
2 *No hagas comentarios abusivos.*
   *Explanation: neg = subjunctive.1st person
   present tense of hacer = hago. –ar endings 2nd
   person: hagas*
3 *No utilices palabras malsonantes.*
   *Explanation: neg = subjunctive. utilizar 1st
   person = utilizo but the spelling changes: a
   becomes e. –er endings 2nd person: utilices*
4 *No escribas en mayúsculas.*
   *Explanation: neg = subjunctive. escribir 1st
   person present = escribo. –ar endings 2nd
   person: escribas*
6 *No pongas vínculos a páginas de SPAM.*
   *Explanation: neg = use of the subjunctive: poner
   1st person present = pongo
   –ar endings 2nd person: pongas*
8 *No difundas información falsa.*
   Explanation: neg = the subjunctive
9 *No inventes identidades alternativas.*
   Explanation: neg = subjunctive

C Students write out the rules in Spanish.

Answers:
1 *No borres los ficheros en el disco duro derrames.*
2 *No derrames té en el teclado.*
3 *Lleva tus bagels en cajas de CDs.*
4 *No difundas información personal.*
5 *Acuérdate de que el Internet es un foro público.*

3 Students read the "Rules for Blogs" 1–10 and
then match the sentences a–g to the relevant rule.

Answers:
1 *a*   2 *c*   3 *g*   4 *d*   5 *b*   6 *f*   8 *e*

Gramática

*The subjunctive – wanting/not wanting
things to happen*

Revise the use and formation of the subjunctive from
Unit 2. Ask students to explain what they think is
meant by wanting things to happen and not happen
and to give you examples in English. They should
then analyse how to put their examples into Spanish.

A Students find examples of subjunctives in
Activity 4.

Answers:
1 *se llene;* 2 *sean;* 3 *participen;* 4 *se ofendan;* 5 *sea*

B Students work out the meanings of the sections in
bold in Activity 4.

Answers:
1 to stop; 2 to make sure that; 3 to allow;
4 so that/in order that; 5 to make sure that

4 Students complete the sentences 1–5, using the
phrases given in the "Rules for Blogs", following
the example given.

Example answers:
1 *Se prohibe poner enlaces a sitios basura … para
   impedir que el sitio se llene de contenidos basura.*
2 *Respeta la ortografía del idioma castellano …
   para asegurar que los mensajes sean legibles.*
3 *Respeta a los otros usuarios … para permitir que
   todos participen.*
4 *No hagas comentarios abusivos … para que los
   otros usuarios no se ofendan.*
5 *Trata de aportar comentarios relevantes al debate
   … para asegurar que tu texto sea coherente.*

5 Students read the text and write answers to
questions 1–5, using their own words.

6 Students invent a questionnaire to find out what
type of ICT user their fellow students are.

7 Students answer the questions on the Internet and
technology of the future.

8 In pairs, students answer the questions given.

Peligros y beneficios

Planner

Skills focus
♦ Reading strategies

Key language

el aislamiento	isolation
el desarrollo	development
las empresas	companies
la incapacidad	incapacity
la intimidad	privacy
el lavado de cerebro	brainwashing
la marca	make
la piratería	piracy
la prepotencia	arrogance
la privacidad	privacy
advertir	to warn
apoderarse de control of	to take possession/
cortejar with	to court/curry favour
desconocer	to not know
negar	to deny
crédulo/a	credulous

rotundamente	soundly/absolutely
cada vez más	more and more
lejos de	far from

Resources

♦ Student Book pages 38 and 39
♦ CD 1, track 24
♦ Hojas 3.1 CD 4, track 10, 3.2, 3.3, 3.5

Técnica

Using reading strategies

A After reading the list of reading strategies, discuss each of its points with the students and ask for their comments. They should then decide which are the most effective for themselves and which for the whole class.

¡Menos logos, Caperucita!

Cultural note: The expression is '*Menos lobos Caperucita*' meaning 'not so many wolves, Red Riding Hood', or 'Don't cry wolf' (this is a direct link with the text – because the supposed dangers didn't materialise), but making a pun with '*logos*', as the text also refers to the demise of big bad brands! Note the link to the cartoon.

a *There are no numbers, and the people/places are not proper nouns, although there are some there. The point is that even if you don't find any, you have combed through the text once while looking for them.*

b *The title and the picture help you anticipate word play/tough ideas/playful ideas, but here they don't help you directly.*

c *There are lots of cognates, but finding specific ones is again less important than the process of a third reading through of the text.*

d *There is a list prefaced by a colon in the first paragraph. While students were looking for questions, they may have found the initials 'SMS' and added that strategy to their list.*

e *This is probably the most useful, as there are lots of sentence starters or sentence halves.*

f *This is quite useful too because more sophisticated strategies have to come into play, as you could have predicted, given the opaque nature of the title and picture. This leads on to point 'g' which is another warning.*

Now students are familiar with the text and aware of its difficulty, they are ready to tackle factual questions on the points that are less opaque.

H 3.5 *Hoja 3.5 offers additional practice of using reading strategies.*

1 Students read the text and decide which of the 10 statements given below are a reality, which a possibility, and which are not a reality, according to what they have read.

Answers:
1 *Es una realidad.*
2 *No se ha hecho realidad.*
3 *No se ha hecho realidad.*
4 *No se ha hecho realidad.*
5 *Es una realidad.*
6 *Es una realidad.*
7 *Es una realidad.*
8 *Es una posibilidad.*
9 *Es una realidad.*
10 *Es una realidad.*

 2a Students listen and decide which of the statements 1–5 are true (*V = Verdad*) or false (*M = Mentira*).

---

p. 39, actividad 2a

– ¿Son perjudiciales los videojuegos?
– Típicamente los jóvenes que juegan en exceso también demuestran síntomas sociales tales como mal rendimiento escolar, aislamiento. Sin embargo, para los menos extrovertidos, pueden mejorar su autoestima. Además pueda ayudar la coordinación. Por eso, pensamos que jugar con videojuegos puede ser bueno, siempre que se haga en su justa medida.
– ¿Cuál puede ser esa justa medida?
– No la puedo definir, pero podría ser una media hora diaria, aunque hay unos jóvenes que suelen pasar varias horas jugando.
– ¿Es cierto que puede ocasionar enfermedades?
– Pues, la estimulación por la luz de la pantalla puede provocar una crisis epiléptica. También los juegos violentos o machistas pueden producir problemas emocionales. Pero son casos aislados. Una preocupación más común es cuando el niño es incapaz de limitar el tiempo que se pasa jugando. Además de malgastar su tiempo, fomenta su adicción al juego.

Answers:
1 *M*   **2** *M*   **3** *V*   **4** *V*   **5** *V*

2b Students match up the two halves of the seven sentences according to what they have heard.

Answers:
1 *f*   **2** *e*   **3** *d*   **4** *b*   **5** *g*   **6** *c*   **7** *a*

2c Work in pairs. Students discuss whether video games are a waste of time.

3 Students read the article and answer the questions in Spanish.

Answers:

Students answer in their own words but answers should contain the following:

1 Aprovechamos todos los aspectos positivos como la educación.

2 Es un herramienta enormemente poderosa/ tiene muchos beneficios para todos.

3 Es un precio asequible.

4 Permite a todos hacer cosas que hace 20 años no se concebían.

5 Es un lugar público y se presta al abuso.

6 Las estafas en las compras.

7 Gente que entra en información privada y secreta.

8 La piratería y sabotaje,

9 La ciberpornografía.

10 La libertad ertenece a todo el mundo no sólo a los delincuentes en Internet.

4 Students reorganise the statements to form a basis for an essay and respond to the question about technology dominating our lives today. The teacher should specify the length. A possible plan could be as follows:

Introduction

Some of the pointless inventions from the opening spread, leading to restating the question

FOR
♦ expensive phones etc.
♦ predicted problems of the internet

AGAINST
♦ some positive results of technology
♦ the survey results showing it's not happened
♦ young people's attitudes and intelligent use of technology, communication, awareness of own purchasing power, end of music as a commodity, own language, knowledge of world, make own use of technology, set demands on companies

H3.1-3 *Hoja* 3.1, 3.2 and 3.3 offers additional practice for this spread.

Gramática en acción

Planner
Resources
♦ Student Book page 40
♦ Hoja 3.4

Recuerda

Imperatives

A Students read and match up the two halves of the sentences 1–7.

Possible answers:

1 *e*   2 *a*   3 *b*   4 *f*   5 *c*   6 *g*   7 *d*

B Students write their own sentences about security.

Recuerda

Uses of the subjunctive

C Students revise the reminder box and then fill in the form, deciding why the subjunctive is being used in sentences 1–5.

Answers:
1 *wanting*
2 *wanting*
3 *value judgement/emotion*
4 *emotion*
5 *not wanting*

D Students complete the sentences using a verb in the subjunctive.

Point out that the answers can be given in the *tú* form, but don't have to be, except for 4.

Answers:
1 *(comprar) compres*
2 *(saber) sepas*
3 *(enviar) envies*
4 *(poner) pongas*
5 *(gastar) gastes*
6 *(ser) sea*
7 *(pasar) pases*

H 3.4 *Hoja* 3.4 offers additional practice of using the subjunctive.

Vocabulario

Page 41

Answers:
1 *cargándose*
2 *contravengan*
3 *haga*
4 *malsonantes*
5 *audaces*

Extra

Planner

Skills focus

♦ Inferring meaning when listening

Resources

♦ Student Book page 42
♦ CD 1, track 25

This page is aimed at A-A* students.

1a Students read the text (newspaper paragraphs A–C) and match the two halves of the sentences.

Answers:
1 *a* 2 *d* 3 *b* 4 *c*

1b Students match the sentences they have made in Activity 1a to the newspaper paragraphs A–C.

Answers:
1 *C* 2 *A* 3 *B* 4 *B*

1c Students explain in one sentence the danger described in each of the paragraphs A–C.

1d Students read the sentences containing the underlined words and classify the words as technology or offences.

Answers:
Tecnología
redes, herramientas, aplicaciones, avisos, insertar, enlazar, hacer clic, descargan, contraseñas, máquinas, buscadores
Crimen
amenaza, acceso, desconocidos, tácticas, delincuentes, sacar partido, espía, sin su consentimiento, víctima, fisgoneo, cibercriminales, aparentan, truco, artimañas, códigos maliciosos, virus, robar, secuestro, ataques, spam

1e Students answer the questions, justifying their opinions in their own words.

Técnica

Inferring meaning when listening

Take students through the points. Make sure they understand the concept of inference.

 A Students listen to Lidia, Rodolfo and Javier and work out which technological problem each person is talking about.

You could ask students to note down "clue words" which helped them decide.

---

p. 42, actividad A

Lidia: Los sitios basura representan un riesgo cotidiano. El diecinueve por ciento de las búsquedas con criterios como Cameron Diaz o salvapantallas llevan a sitios con virus o archivos infectados.

Rodolfo: Lo más peligroso no es que te roben tu identidad, porque nunca doy mi dirección en Internet por ejemplo, sino que las estupideces que haces en la juventud, estén grabadas para siempre en la red. A menudo vemos ejemplos de celebridades que se arrepienten de esas fotos indiscretas o esos comentarios impulsivos. O cuando buscas trabajo, los jefes pueden descubrir ciertos detalles de tu vida que preferirías esconder.

Javier: Mira, la tecnología cambia la vida poco a poco, de maneras que no podemos predecir, pero tampoco hay que exagerar. Hoy, esté donde esté, mis amigos se pueden poner en contacto conmigo. Eso no significa que no tenga privacidad. Igualmente, alguien podría saber mi localización exacta en cualquier momento: dónde estoy, con quién hablo, qué compro. Si tienen propósitos criminales, eso no es culpa de la tecnología.

Answers:
Lidia – 3; Rodolfo – 1; Javier – 2

---

2 Students write a paragraph on one of the two topics listed: either "Without technology we lose the capacity to survive" or "We have lost our privacy".. They use the vocabulary they have identified in Activity 1d.

Unit 3 Assessment offers exam practice for this unit.

Unidad 4 El cine

Unit objectives

By the end of this unit students will be able to:
- Talk and write about types of film
- Discuss the place of cinema in popular culture and changing trends
- Describe a good film they have seen
- Comment on different ways of viewing films

Grammar

By the end of this unit students will be able to:
- Use the imperfect tense correctly
- Recognise and use a mixture of past tenses
- Use *lo* and *lo que* correctly

Skills

By the end of this unit students will be able to:
- Place written and spoken accents correctly
- Put forward opinions convincingly (agree and disagree)
- Speak from notes
- Infer meaning when reading

Resources

- Student Book page 43

This page introduces the topic.

1a Students look at the definitions A–E and match each one with a genre from the list (on the filmstrip) below. There will be six genre labels not used.

Answers:
A *comedia*   **B** *aventura*   **C** *terror*
D *dibujos animados* (feature length ones)
E *ciencia ficción*

1b Students write down similar definitions for the remaining five genres: thrillers, musicals, romance, westerns and police.

Answers:
In Spanish in students' own words

1c Students give an example for each genre and research its equivalent Spanish title. They should consult www.labutaca.net/films for up-to-date information and titles of films in Spanish.

2a Work in pairs. Students discuss which films have been the greatest box office successes in the past six months and how they would rank them, using the star ratings provided.

2b Class survey. Students discuss which film, in their own opinion, has been the best this year so far. They should give their reasons. What genre of film is it? To reinforce the different genres of film students could play a guessing game. One person thinks of a film and the rest of the class ask questions to find out the title.

- ¿Es una comedia?
  (No).
- ¿Es una fantasía?
  (Sí).
- ¿Se trata de?
  OR
- ¿Quién es el director?

Protagonistas y tendencias

Planner

Skills focus
- Pronunciation: how to work out how to pronounce the word from its written form

Key language

una beca	scholarship
un dote	talent
el guión	script
un largometraje	full-length film
la onda	wave
el protagonista	main character
la raza	race
desarrollarse	to develop
desempeñar un papel	to act a role
dirigir	to direct
fundar	to found
heredar	to inherit
lanzar	to launch
rodar una película	to make a film
rodear	to surround
gemelo/a	twin
implacable	implacable/relentless
ricachón/a	wealthy
a pesar de que	in spite of the fact that

Resources
- Student Book pages 44 and 45
- Vocabulary, Student Book page 51
- CD 1, tracks 26 and 27
- Hojas 4.1 CD 4, tracks 12, 13 and 14, 4.2, 4.3

Unidad 4 El cine

1a Remind students about the work covered on reading strategies in Unit 3. Students then read the text about Gael García Bernal and his first film as a director – *Déficit*.

Vocabulary work. Students look in the text for equivalent phrases at first without resorting to a dictionary, and then using a dictionary if need be.

Answers:
1 *compañía productora*
2 *no sólo ... sino que también*
3 *desempeñar el papel de*
4 *el guión*
5 *se trata de*
6 *a pesar de que*
7 *lo que sea que hagas*
8 *rodar*

1b Students choose the most suitable answer from the multiple choice given.

Answers:
1 *c* 2 *c* 3 *a* 4 *a* 5 *c* 6 *b*

2a Students listen to the recording about women in Spanish cinema to get an overall idea of the context. They then study the questions to give them a clearer focus. They can listen a second time if they are unsure of the answers and then indicate which are the three correct ones.

---

p. 44, actividades 2a y 2c

Hoy celebramos a la mujer española como actriz de cine y destacamos a la actriz madrileña Penélope Cruz.

Su vida comenzó el 28 de abril de 1974. Según ella y toda su familia, Penélope siempre fue una niña enérgica y voluntariosa que pasaba mucho tiempo en casa de su abuela.

Debutó con la película *Belle Epoque* de Fernando Trueba en 1993 y después siguieron otras muchas como *Carne Trémula* de Pedro Almodóvar y la película española *Abre los Ojos*, que ganó varios Goyas – premio español equivalente a los Oscars. De allí se fue a Hollywood donde desempeñó el mismo papel en la versión estadounidense de la película, *Vanilla Sky*, con Tom Cruise.

La fama no la ha cambiado y se sigue comportando igual con sus hermanos Eduardo y Mónica, que son dos gotas de agua. Mónica sigue los pasos de su hermana mayor; después de ser una de los protagonistas de la serie *Un paso adelante*, que tuvo mucho éxito en España, ha participado en varias películas.

Penélope forma parte de un impresionante grupo de actrices españolas – Ana Belén, Carmen Maura, Victoria Abril y Ana Torrent. Ana trabajó con Saura en *Cría Cuervos* y Victoria Abril protagonizó con Javier Bardem *Tu Nombre Envenena Mis Sueños* entre otras muchas.

Su estreno en inglés fue la película *The Hi Lo Country* de Stephen Frears, quien la considera como Venus. Penélope se sintió tan orgullosa de su papel en dicha película que donó todo su salario a un fondo de caridad de la Madre Teresa.

Decididamente ha tenido papeles muy diversos: una monja embarazada con Sida, una novelista, una cocinera brasileña y la amante del ministro nazi Joseph Goebbels. Su película *Fan Fan La Tulipe* triunfó en el Festival de Cine de Cannes.

Answers:
2, 5, 7

2b Students explain why they think the others are incorrect.

2c Students listen again and make notes in order to write a brief resumé in English under the given headings.
There are several Spanish film stars mentioned in this recording, so to follow up, students could research them and present their details at a later time.

2d Students prepare an oral presentation about their favourite film star, using the headings as a basis. They should pay attention to pronunciation and practise their piece before they present it to the class. Students could score each other's presentation for fluency, accuracy and intonation.
Here is a list of who's who in Spanish cinema world. You might suggest students take one each and research and make an oral presentation on them and make a critique of one of their films.

Pedro Almodóvar; Julio Medem; Carlos Saura; Luís Buñuel; Alejandro Amenábar; Alex de la Iglesia; Diego Luna; Antonio Banderas; Salma Hayek; Carmen Maura; Paz Vega; Javier Bardem.

H 4.2 *Hoja* 4.2 offers additional speaking practice for this page.

3a Students read the text on Juan Carlos Rulfo and decide if the sentences that follow are true (*V = Verdad*) or false (*M = Mentira*).

Answers:
1 *M* 2 *V* 3 *V* 4 *M* 5 *M*

3b Students work out the meaning of the title ("Chip off the old block"/ "Like father, like son").

3c Students find in the text synonyms for the words and phrases listed.

Answers:
1 *más importantes;* 2 *dotes;* 3 *becas;* 4 *rodar;*
5 *seleccionada;* 6 *trascender;* 7 *convertirse en;*
8 *de la actualidad*

Técnica

Pronunciation: How to work out how to pronounce a word from its written form.

Accents and stress

Take students through the advice step by step and ensure they understand.

hablo	mesa	independiente
hablas	hablan	mesas independientes
hablar	actitud	corral
jardín	último	jóvenes

A Students then read words 1–6 and decide which ones need a written accent.

Answers:
película; fantasía; romántico

B Warn students that words in Spanish that look like English words can catch them out in oral work. Students practise saying the Spanish words in the list of similar English/Spanish word forms.

 4a Students listen to the interview and make notes on the changes that have occurred in cinema using the headings provided.

> **p. 45, actividad 4a**
>
> – Bienvenidos al mundo del cine. Hoy vamos a entrevistar a alguien que es cinéfila desde hace muchos años. Buenas tardes Señora Vivanco. Me imagino que usted habrá visto bastantes cambios en el mundo del cine a lo largo de su vida ¿verdad?
>
> – Buenas tardes; pues la verdad es que sí, he visto muchos cambios. Cuando era niña, todavía había muchas películas en blanco y negro y hoy solamente se hacen así o en sepia para dar un efecto especial de antigüedad. Además nosotros no veíamos películas para adultos porque había más control y censura en aquél tiempo no como hoy que se pueden ver toda clase de películas de todas las partes del mundo. La verdad es que hay más variedad ahora que antes. Hoy tienden a hacer demasiadas películas de terror que son impactantes pero a veces, se pasan con los efectos especiales, y quedan ridículas. Hasta las pantallas han cambiado de formato y tamaño.
>
> – ¿Y qué me dice usted de los actores y las grandes estrellas?

> – Pues en efecto, mantener a los famosos y famosillos se ha convertido en una industria. Puede existir toda la técnica que quieras para presentar a una persona en la pantalla pero lo que la técnica no puede cambiar nunca es el talento. Los cines han cambiado también hasta tal punto que para una persona mayor como yo es carísimo ir a los cines del centro de la ciudad porque los precios de las entradas se han disparado. También, hay muchos más servicios dentro, se vende de todo y las butacas son mil veces más cómodas. En fin, si tengo que evaluar los cambios, debo decir que el cine ha cambiado mucho y para mejor.

4b Students write a short paragraph (about 50 words) comparing what cinema was like in the days of Señora Vivanco with what it is like today.

H 4.1, 4.3 *Hojas* 4.1 and 4.3 offer additional listening and reading practice for this spread.

Las más taquilleras

> **Planner**
>
> *Grammar focus*
> ♦ Imperfect tense
>
> *Skills focus*
> ♦ Speaking: putting forward opinions
>
> *Key language*
>
> | | |
> |---|---|
> | *el argumento* | storyline |
> | *la bondad* | kindness |
> | *un cinéfilo* | film buff |
> | *el género* | genre/type |
> | *un incendio* | fire |
> | *los intérpretes* | actors/interpreters |
> | *la locura* | madness |
> | *la mentira* | lie |
> | *un obrero* | worker/labourer |
> | *aparecerse* | to appear as a ghost |
> | *nominar* | to nominate |
> | *premiar* | to reward/give a prize to |
> | *sobrevivir* | to survive |
> | *tratar de* | to be about |
> | *ambos/as* | both |
> | *chocante* | shocking |
> | *impactante* | impressive |
> | *en paro/parado* | out of work/on the dole |
>
> *Resources*
> ♦ Student Book pages 46 and 47
> ♦ Vocabulary, Student Book page 51
> ♦ CD 2, tracks 28 and 29
> ♦ Hoja 4.5
> ♦ Grammar Workbook page 41

1a   Students listen and fill in the gaps in the dialogue.

---

p. 46, actividad 1a

– ¿Qué tipo de cinéfilo eres? ¿Qué género prefieres?

– Pues, me encantan las aventuras y películas de fantasía con efectos especiales como Piratas del Caribe.

– ¿Quién es el director?

– Gore Verbinsky, pero no sé quién escribió el guión.

– ¿Quiénes son los intérpretes?

– Johnny Depp, Keira Knightly y Orlando Bloom son los protagonistas.

– Vale. ¿Y el argumento?

– Bueno, trata de las aventuras del capitán Sparrow ...

1b   Using their own points of view in answering the questions, students adapt and practise the dialogue with a partner. Draw their attention to the *frases clave*, which they should use in their answers.

 1c   Students listen to further dialogues, noting down the information required.

---

p. 46, actividades 1c y 1d

1   – ¿Qué tipo de película prefieres?

– Me encantan las comedias. ¿Y a ti?

– Prefiero las películas de fantasía con efectos especiales como El Señor de los Anillos o Spiderman.

– Sí, son impactantes, pero a veces son muy extravagantes. Lo que más me gusta son las películas que tratan de la vida normal como Dame diez razones, ya sean tristes, románticas o realistas.

– ¿Quién la dirigió?

– Creo que el director se llama Brad Silberling.

– ¿Quiénes son los protagonistas?

– Morgan Freeman y Paz Vega.

– ¿De qué trata el argumento?

– Cuenta la historia de una cajera (Paz Vega) que trabaja en un supermercado en un barrio pobre de Los Ángeles. Una noche llega al supermercado Morgan Freeman, actor de cine también en la película, que quiere informarse sobre el personaje que va a desempeñar en su próximo trabajo. La película cuenta la historia de su relación y cómo se ayudan mutuamente ...

---

2   – A mí me gustan todas las comedias románticas como *Tú la letra yo la música* porque son sencillas.

– ¿Quién dirigió esa película?

– El director es Marc Lawrence si recuerdo bien.

– Y los actores, ¿quiénes son?

– Pues, los protagonistas son Hugh Grant y Drew Barrymore.

– ¿De qué trata?

– Pues, trata de Alex Fletcher (Hugh Grant), una estrella de pop en horas bajas. Conoce a una chica (Drew Barrymore) que le ayuda a escribir la letra de una canción y así termina recuperando su autoestima.

3   – Prefiero los thrillers psicológicos y las aventuras de intriga como *El último Bourne*.

– ¿Qué es eso?

– Pues es la tercera película de Doug Liman y Paul Greengrass, basada en la novela de Robert Ludlum en la que Matt Damon desempeña el papel de Jason Bourne, un agente secreto que tiene amnesia. Bourne sigue buscando su identidad por todo el planeta, incluso en Madrid, donde rodaron varias escenas.

1d   Students listen again and decide whether the sentences are true (V) or false (F) or not mentioned (X).

Answers:
Dialogue 1: *1 = F/ de fantasía; 2 = V; 3 = X; 4 = F/ Los Angeles.*
Dialogue 2: *1 = F / romántica; 2 = V; 3 X;*
Dialogue 3: *1 = V; 2 = F/ es la tercera; 3 = F/ en Madrid*

Gramática

Imperfect tense

Take students through the examples to ensure they appreciate the subtleties and nuances of language. Students will meet time clauses such as *acabar de* later.

Refer students to the relevant grammar section in the Student Book, page 166.

A   Students then use the imperfect tense to describe a scene from a film they have seen recently, using the questions as prompts.

2a   Students read the synopsis of the film *Volver* and fill in the form.

Answers:
Título: Volver
Director: Pedro Almodóvar
Género: comedia dramática/drama comedia
Argumento: Se trata de la vida de tres mujeres, una de las cuales muere y empieza a aparecerse a las otras. La película presenta como las otras dos mujeres llevan la muerte de su madre.
Protagonistas: Raimunda (Penélope Cruz), Sole (Lola Dueñas), la madre (Carmen Maura).
Premios: Cinco premios Goyas, premio a la mejor interpretación femenina y al mejor guión en el Festival de Cine de Cannes.

2b Vocabulary. Students read the synopsis and look for synonyms in the text for the phrases listed.

Answers:
1 que sobreviven; **2** un obrero en paro; **3** ambas; **4** los demás personajes; **5** no mueren nunca del todo

2c Students translate the last paragraph of the synopsis of the film into English maintaining a similar register and level of formality.

Possible/suggested translation
Winner of five Goyas, nominated for a Hollywood Oscar and a prize winner at the Cannes Film Festival for the best female artist and best script, Volver *shows a Spain which is spontaneous, amusing, intrepid, supportive and just.*

As the film *Volver* is a very popular cultural topic, please note that a further critical analysis of the film and of its director Almodóvar and his thinking is on the Extra page at the end of this unit.

Técnica

Speaking: putting forward opinions

Remind students about the work covered in Unit 1 pages 18–19 about agreeing and disagreeing. They now add more phrases to their list and consider the different ways of expressing themselves.

A Students match the phrases to one of the three sample ways of expressing an opinion.

Answers:
1 Por un lado ... por el otro; No solamente ... sino también ...
2 Hay que considerar que; No se puede negar que ... Se podría creer que ...; Se supone que ...
3 Creo que ...; No podemos olivdarnos de que ...; A mi modo de ver ...

Remind students about making value judgements and therefore needing to use the subjunctive in the subordinate clause.

B Students discuss more fully than previously the merits and faults of recent films. Encourage them to use more technical vocabulary connected to cinema. Show them a commentary in English to help them appreciate what is required of them if they want to raise their language to a more sophisticated level. They use the phrases from the *Técnica* box and the *frases clave*.

H 4.5 *Hoja* 4.5 offers additional practice of speaking skills.

3a To sum up this section, students write a critical synopsis (150 words) of a film they have seen recently, they use both the advice and the headings given. Remind them that that they are writing a formal piece.

3b Students explain why they would or would not recommend the film. They use the *frases clave*.

¿En el cine conventional o en casa o cómo?

Planner
Grammar focus
◆ Verbs followed by the infinitive or by a preposition
Key language

el ambiente	atmosphere
la calidad	quality
el complejo	complex
la piratería	piracy
acabar de	to have just done something
alquilar	to rent
consistir en	to consist of
contar	to tell
dar miedo	to make you afraid
descargar	to download
hartarse de	to be fed up with
insistir en	to insist on
pensar dos veces en	to think twice about
rendir	to make it/render it
tener ganas de	to feel like doing something
valer la pena	to be worth it
feo/a	ugly
sucio/a	dirty
además	besides
¡no me digas!	You don't say!
hace tiempo	ages ago
¿Qué has hecho?	What have you been up to?

1a Students read the chat and decide who says what. They write down abbreviated answers – B (for Bela) or L (for Lagartija).

Answers:
1 *L;* 2 *L;* 3 *B;* 4 *B;* 5 *L;* 6 *B;* 7 *B;* 8 *L;* 9 *L;* 10 *B*

1b Students read the English expressions and find their Spanish equivalents in the chat text.

Answers:
1 *¿Qué te has hecho?* 2 *pensabas dos veces;*
3 *no me digas;* 4 *ya me harté;* 5 *cosa tuya;*
6 *acertaste;* 7 *fenomenal;* 8 *qué si quiero*

2 Students read the article on the future of cinema and identify in which of the paragraphs A–D the topics listed 1–8 are mentioned.

Answers:
1 *paragraph C;* 2 *A;* 3 *C;* 4 *B;* 5 *D;* 6 *B;* 7 *C;* 8 *A*

3 Class survey; oral work. Students use the vocabulary and expressions they have developed in this spread to discuss

1 how they prefer to watch films, and give their reasons.
2 whether they think cinema will continue as it is now, or, what changes they think there will be in the cinema of the future.

Suggestions by students could be put up on a whiteboard (or similar) to link spoken with written words, reinforcing the work on stress and accents. A count could be taken to identify the most popular media for watching films.

Gramática

Verbs followed by the infinitive or by a preposition

Students need to learn these constructions by heart.

A Students organise the list of verbs according to what follows them.

B Students reread the chat and find examples of the verbs listed in the *Gramática* box.

Answers:
insistieron en ir; me harté de estar; acabo de bajar; puedes ver; dejé de ver; tener ganas de ver; he comenzado a comprarlas; prefiero ir; tienes que pagar; dedicarme a rodar; acabo de alquilar

Gramática en acción

Recuerda

Past tenses

Students read the reminder section about mixed past tenses. First they practise recognising them from reading texts. You could add a listening text as well so that they practise listening out for mixed tenses.

A Students read the text on Gael García Bernal on page 44 again and list the verbs which are in the preterite, perfect and imperfect tenses. This can be done orally or as a written exercise. They should find one imperfect tense; four perterite and two perfect tenses.

B Students translate the verbs into English to show they have understood how the tense affects the meaning and its expression in English.

Answers:
estudiaba – he was studying = *imperfect tense;*
le invitó – he invited him = *preterite tense; lanzó* – launched = *preterite tense; ha fundado* – he has founded = *perfect tense; escribió* – wrote = *preterite tense; fue* – was = *preterite tense; se han ido separando* – they have been growing apart from each other = *perfect (continuous) tense*

C Students now translate sentences 1–10 into Spanish.

Answers:
1 *Cuando era pequeño a mi hermano le gustaba jugar con El Hombre de Acción.*
2 *A todos nosotros nos gustaba ver películas para niños con nuestros padres.*
3 *No había tantas películas entonces que uno podía escoger.*
4 *Solamente íbamos al cine en ocasiones especiales.*
5 *La semana pasada vi una nueva película en tercera dimensión.*
6 *Me encantaron los efectos especiales pero el argumento fue soso.*

7 *Mi padre solamente veía películas de guerra o del oeste.*

8 *Iban a derrumbar nuestro cine local porque nadie iba allí.*

9 *Afortunadamente a alguien se le ocurrió remodelarlo y ahora es muy popular.*

10 *Siempre me ha gustado ir al cine. Nunca he visto una película en el ordenador.*

D In pairs, students tell each other at least six things they did before they left home this morning. They should use the perfect and/or preterite tense.

E Written work. Students write about what they did on one specific day last week. Encourage them to use a variety of tenses.

F Finally, students describe the events of a film they went to or saw recently.

H 4.4 *Hoja* 4.4 offers additional practice of past tenses.

Recuerda

Iba a ...

Students read the reminder section about how to say what they are, or were going to do.

G In pairs, oral work. Person A says what he/she **is** going to do; and Person B says what he/she **was** going to do. They then swap roles and invent further activities they are/were going to do.

Recuerda

Pronouns

Read through this section with students asking them for further examples of their own to make sure they have fully understood how *lo* and *lo que* function in Spanish.

H Students read the text about Gael García Bernal on page 44 again and find the relevant phrases.

Answers:
lo interesante; lo mejor; lo que nos interesa; lo que sea que hogas; lo político; lo más importante; lo que comenta Bernal

Vocabulario

Page 51

Answers:
1 *dijeron*
2 *murió*
3 *éramos*
4 *salaz*
5 *novedosas*

Extra

Planner
Skills focus
♦ Inferring meaning when reading
Resources
♦ Student Book page 52
♦ CD 1, track 30

This page is aimed at A-A*students.

This page builds on activities relating to the film *Volver* on page 47. It would be a good idea to show excerpts of the film *Volver* to the class and encourage students to watch the whole film.

1a Students read the comments made by the director Pedro Almodóvar (five paragraphs). They decide which of the four topics listed applies to each of the five paragraphs.

Answers:
1 *la vida personal de Almodóvar, la vida profesional, y* **Volver**; **2** *la vida personal;*
3 *la vida personal;* **4** *la vida profesional;*
5 *vida personal,* **Volver**, *la filosofía de Almodóvar*

1b Vocabulary work. Students look for certain kinds of words in the text and fill in the columns of the table under the headings given.

Answers:

película	emoción	filosofía
guión	me ha sentado bien	existencia
rodaje	sentimiento pasajero	muerte
dirigir	desajuste	no creyente
personaje	dolor	cielo
talento	ansiedad	infierno
perfeccionista	angustioso	purgatorio
	sereno	el más allá
	inquietud	Sartre

Técnica

Inferring meaning when reading

Make sure the students understand the concept of inference. Take them through the points listed and draw them out with examples from the text on *Volver*.

A Students consider whether the sentences are true. They explain what in the texts has given them that impression.

Answers:

1 *Yes, because when he says his mother was always very close, we know this isn't literally so. Also the film is all about death.*
2 *Yes, although he says it's not up to him to say it, he talks about the film's emotional impact positively.*
3 *Perhaps he's not satisfied because he had lost patience with details and we understand his other films didn't get to the bottom of his worries.*
4 *Yes, because he says he hasn't become any less of a perfectionist, and he obviously puts a lot of his heart and soul into his films.*
5 *Yes, because even though he doesn't believe in God, he still thinks in terms of heaven and hell.*

 2 Students explain what is meant by the opening sentence of paragraph 4 – "It is more important to have patience than talent to direct a film." Do they agree?

 3 Prepare students for the listening task by directing them to the points they are to listen for. Students listen to the words of Almodóvar about *Volver*. They then put the ideas 1–4 in order to match what they have heard.

Answers:
3 2 4 1

p. 52, actividad 3

Supongo que "Volver" es una comedia dramática. Tiene secuencias divertidas y secuencias dramáticas. Su tono imita "la vida misma", pero no es costumbrista. Más bien es de un naturalismo surrealista, si es que eso es posible. Siempre he mezclado los géneros y sigo haciéndolo. Para mí es algo natural.

Aunque la mezcla de géneros sea natural en mí, eso no significa que no esté exento de riesgos (lo grotesco y el grand guiñol son siempre una amenaza). Cuando uno se mueve entre géneros, y atraviesa tonos opuestos en cuestión de segundos, lo mejor es adoptar una interpretación naturalista que consiga hacer verosímil la situación más disparatada. La única arma con la que se cuenta, además de una puesta en escena realista, es con los actores. Las actrices, en este caso. He tenido la suerte de que todas estén en continuo estado de gracia. El gran espectáculo de "Volver" son ellas.

4 Students write about 100 words on the topic "Does a philosophy of life and death have a place in cinema? Films are not art but are meant to entertain us." They should give their own point of view; and mention films that they have seen as examples of the point they are making. Remind them that they can find some help in building their argument in Unit 2 page 32.

Unit 4 Assessment offers exam practice for this unit.

Unidad 5 La música

Unit objectives

By the end of this unit students will be able to:
♦ Comment on different types of music and changing trends
♦ Talk and write about the place of music in popular culture
♦ Talk and write about music they like
♦ Discuss how music defines personal identity

Grammar

By the end of this unit students will be able to:
♦ Use object pronouns (direct and indirect) correctly
♦ Recognise and use the pluperfect tense

Skills

♦ Respond to speaking stimulus materials
♦ Speak from notes with the correct intonation
♦ Transfer meaning: explain in Spanish

Resources

♦ Student Book page 53
♦ CD 1, track 31

This page introduces the topic.

 1 Students listen to the discussion between a grandmother and her grandaughter and note down the order in which they mention the types of music in the lists A and B.

> **p. 53, actividad 1**
>
> **Abuela:** Baja el volumen hija mía. ¡No entiendo por qué no puedes escuchar la música clásica de Mozart en vez de ese ruido tan estrepitoso! No se le puede llamar música.
>
> **Girl:** Pues abuelita para que lo sepas esto sí es música y se llama hip-hop y es más, me encanta.
>
> **Abuela** ¡Qué nombre tan raro! ¿Por qué la música de hoy en día no puede tener nombres tradicionales como Swing o Jazz. Hoy día no cantan, gritan.
>
> **Girl** No es verdad abuela. Seguro que no has escuchado el ritmo pop-rock de Shakira. Tiene una voz fantástica.
>
> **Abuela** No lo creo. No hay nada como las suaves baladas de Julio Iglesias.

Answers:
1 = *7 list A* ; **2** = *4 list B* ; **3** = *5 list A* ; **4** = *4 list A* ; **5** = *1 list B* ; **6** = *6 list A*

2a Students answer the questions, practising using past tenses and the *frases clave*.

2b In pairs, students discuss and then write down five changes in the music scene.

La música – un arte popular

Point out that art form in Spanish is masculine (*el arte*) in the singular and feminine (*las artes*) in the plural.

> **Planner**
>
> *Skills focus*
> ♦ Intonation
> ♦ Sound linking
>
> *Key language*
>
> | | |
> |---|---|
> | *el apoyo* | support |
> | *el barrio* | area of town |
> | *el enemigo* | enemy |
> | *el éxito* | success |
> | *la fuente* | fountain/beginnings |
> | *la ira* | anger |
> | *el mensaje* | message |
> | *la mezcla* | mixture |
> | *la pobreza* | poverty |
> | *el orgullo* | pride |
> | *el soldado* | soldier |
> | *disparar* | to shoot |
> | *inaugurar* | to inaugurate/start up |
> | *lastimar* | to hurt/wound |
> | *liderar* | to lead |
> | *poner en marcha* | to start off |
> | *premiar* | to reward/give a prize to |
> | *salvar* | to save |
> | *trabajar en equipo* | to work as a team |
> | *trascender* | to transcend/go beyond |
> | *prodigioso/a* | talented |
>
> *Resources*
> ♦ Student Book pages 54 and 55
> ♦ Vocabulary, Student Book page 61
> ♦ CD 1, tracks 32 and 33
> ♦ Hoja 5.1 CD 4, tracks 15, 16 and 17

Unidad 5 La música

 1a Students listen to the song by the artist David Bisbal and fill in the gaps in the text.

Answers: see transcript

---

p. 54, actividades 1a y 1b

Soldado de papel
Hay un lugar donde no hay sol,
sólo dolor sin marcha atrás
ni dirección tienes que luchar

No, no han crecido y ya tienen valor
no han vivido y mueren por error
y su juego lo destruye el fuego
¡Son niños!

¿Quién puso en tus manos odio de regalo?

¿Quién con tanta ira te lastima?

¿Cómo pudo la inocencia convertirse en destrucción?

¿Quién te habrá robado el mundo en un disparo?

¿Quién le puso precio a tu vida?

¿Cómo vive la conciencia con tanto dolor?

Dime quién, cómo y por qué, soldado de papel.

 1b Students listen again to the song and write a short paragraph to explain what the song protests about. Students could/should mention that the song protests against: the use of children as soldiers/ children who lose their childhood to armed conflicts/ the unnecessary death of children to war conflicts.

2a Work in pairs. Students discuss the message of the songs listed with a partner. This could be set as a research/writing exercise if preferred.

Some interpretations of the songs may include:

Earth Song, Michael Jackson: the power of destruction of the human race/the current sorry state of our planet/misguided interests of world leaders/ abandonment of God.
Beautiful, Christina Aguilera: there are different kinds of beauty/it is ok not to go by the standard idea of beauty set by the media/acceptance of own self without need to change to seek acceptance.
No son of mine, Genesis: child abuse/ domestic violence.

2b Students reflect on current music trends and artists and discuss whether there is a particular current song that could be classed as a 'protest' song because it goes beyond the topic of the love between a couple.

Técnica

Intonation

Students read the information, then practise the intonation.

Sound linking

 Students read the information on text linking, then they listen to the second part of the recording and then practise saying the examples themselves. Make sure that they understand the two forms of elision and can pronounce the Spanish terms.

A They copy out the examples, marking the *sinalefa* and *entrelazamiento*.

B They listen to the poem 'Martín Fierro' by José Hernández and practise the pronounciation.

---

p. 54, actividad B

Soy gaucho y entiéndaló
Como mi lengua los esplica;
Para mí la tierra es chica
Y pudiera ser mayor.
Ni la víbora me pica
Ni quema mi frente el sol.

Nací como nace el peje,
En el fondo de la mar;
Naides me puede quitar
Aquello que Dios me dio;
Lo que al mundo truje yo
Del mundo lo he de llevar.

Mi gloria es vivir tan libre
Como el pájaro del cielo;
No hago nido en el suelo,
Ande hay tanto que sufrir;
Y naides me ha de seguir
Cuando yo remuento el vuelo.

3a Students read the article "From Barquisemeto to Raploch" for gist and briefly discuss what it is about.

Some examples of acceptable answers would be:
A scheme to get teenagers off the streets by involving them in music.
A successful South American/Venezuelan initiative to bring music to the poor.

3b Students read the article, this time for detail, and then they answer the questions.

Answers:
1 *Acercar la música a los niños menos afortunados para darles esperanza.*
2 *Un director de orquesta con mucho éxito que hoy lidera la Filarmónica de Los Ángeles.*
3 *Porque fue a través del "Sistema" que empezó a tocar y proviene de una familia pobre, demostrando que no se necesita ser de clase alta para tocar el violín o tener éxito en el mundo de la música.*
4 *Recibe apoyo económico del gobierno/23 países han inaugurado programas similares.*
5 *El sentimiento de pertenencia a una comunidad/ la experiencia del trabajo en equipo/la satisfacción que produce la música.*
6 *Que los programas inaugurados en el resto del mundo tengan tanto éxito como en Venezuela.*

3c In pairs, or small groups, students discuss their opinion about the project and whether they would like to belong to a similar one.

4a Students read the blog and make notes on the topics listed.

4b Students choose a musician they admire. They write a similar piece, including the reasons they admire him/her; what it is about the music that they like; and what sort of music he/she plays/ sings. Remind them that verbs of liking take the subjunctive (page 24), and about the expression *lo que* (page 50).

5a Group work. Students discuss the place that music has among the young. They should be encouraged to discuss the positive aspects of different topics such as talent contests, fame, technology, and so forth. They should use structures with *lo*, as suggested in the activity.

5b Students should consider the negative aspects of the issues raised in the previous activity, while still focusing on the use of structures with *lo*.

H 5.1 *Hoja 5.1 offers additional listening practice for this spread.*

De música y músicos

Planner

Grammar focus
♦ Object pronouns – direct and indirect

Skills focus
♦ How to approach speaking stimulus material

Key language

un aficionado/a	fan
una canción	song
un cantante	singer
una cantautora	singer-songwriter
una carrera	career
la estructura	structure
la fecha	date
un ganador	winner
el premio	prize
el triunfo	triumph
debutar	to have a début/begin
gozar de	to enjoy
criollo/a	creole
estrepitoso/a	strident
digan lo que digan	say what they will
no solo ... sino también	not only ... but also
sea como sea	be that as it may
según	according to
sin lugar a dudas	without a shadow of doubt

Resources
♦ Student Book pages 56 and 57
♦ Vocabulary, Student Book page 61
♦ CD 1, tracks 34–35
♦ Hoja 5.2
♦ Grammar Workbook page 23 and 24

 1 Students listen to the programme and decide which of the questions are correct. They correct the incorrect ones. They should look through the *frases clave* to make sure they know what these mean.

Answers:
1 ✗ *Menciona Juanes, Shakira, Carlos Vives y una cubana Celia Cruz.*
2 ✗ *Menciona cinco clases de premios.*
3 ✓   4 ✓   5 ✗ *Era actor.*

p. 56, actividad 1

– Sin lugar a dudas, Colombia está en la cima de la música latina y más aún tras el triunfo del colombiano Juanes, que consiguió cinco Grammy Latinos en una gala de homenaje a Celia Cruz, la "reina de la salsa cubana".

> El cantautor triunfó al llevarse los premios para Grabación del Año, Álbum del Año, Canción del Año, Mejor Solista Vocal y Mejor Canción de Rock.
>
> Pero vamos a ver lo que opinan nuestros reporteros juveniles.
>
> Juanes me flipa y me encanta su nombre verdadero, Juan Esteban Aristizábal – tiene una sonoridad tan profunda – igual que sus canciones.
>
> – Digan lo que digan, Shakira es para mí la mejor de todas las cantautoras – ella también ganó mogollón de premios incluidos varios Grammy y prefiero su estilo rock – además es una guitarrista fenomenal. Y la letra de sus canciones es genial.
>
> – ¿Y qué decís de Carlos Vives – gran actor como era y cantante estupendo como es ahora que interpreta vallenatos antiguos, modernos – un poco de todo? Sea como sea haré todo lo posible para ir a su próximo concierto.

 2a Students listen to another programme and make notes using the questions as prompts.

Answers:
1 *baladas lentas, flamenco pop, rock pop*
2 *la salsa, grunge, garage*
3 *los latinos no deben cantar en inglés sino en español*
4 *es lo mejor del momento*

> **p. 56, actividad 2a**
>
> Buenas tardes, amigos poperos. ¿Qué opinamos de la música favorita del momento? A ver. Sin lugar a dudas las opiniones varían como siempre, pero los votos van para la música lenta de las baladas y de los boleros porque se entiende mejor la letra y son super bailables cuando uno sale de noche.
>
> Una crítica negativa es que los artistas latinos siempre terminan cantando en inglés en vez de conformarse con su lengua materna y mi opinión es que deberían promocionar el español y no el gringo.
>
> Además es cierto que la salsa ha pasado un poco de moda al igual que la música grunge y garage, pero hay que reconocer que el flamenco pop ha ganado popularidad.
>
> De hecho, a mi parecer la fusión del rockpop con un toque de instrumentos regionales es lo mejor del momento. A ver lo que opináis, queridos radioaficionados. Llamad o enviad un mensaje al número de siempre …

2b Students use the words given and on page 47 (Técnica) together with the *frases clave* to write about the current musical scene in the UK as they see it.

3 Students choose an appropriate word to describe the various musical styles.

Gramática

Object pronouns – direct and indirect

If students are secure in using pronouns then they could read through the *Gramática* box on their own. Otherwise, take them through each stage carefully. Pronouns are often overlooked in language but they play a key part in understanding longer sentences.

As students progress in their ability to write more sophisticated language they will need to use pronouns more and more, so they need to have a secure grasp of them.

Refer students to the relevant sections of the grammar section of the Student Book, pages 161 and 162.

A Students write sentences using the verbs given.

Answers:
1 *Siempre veo las emisiones de EastEnders. Yo no, las grabo en un vídeo.*
2 *Siempre escucho la radio por la tarde. Yo no, la escucho por la noche.*
3 *Siempre practico el piano después de clase Yo no, le practico par la mañana.*
4 *Siempre toco la batería en mi habitación. Yo no, la toco en el soltano.*

4a and 4b Students follow the example and complete the dialogues.

Answers:
4a 1 *Se los regaló su padre;* 2 *Nos las regaló su hermana;* 3 *Se la regalaron mis padres*
4b *Iba a dársela yo/Ya se la he dado; Iba a dárselos yo/Ya se los he dado; Iba a dárselos yo/Ya se los he dado.*

5a Students read the text on Juan Diego Flórez and Luis Miguel and complete the sentences in their own words.

Possible answers to include:
1 *dos cantantes jóvenes – estilos diferentes*
2 *Elvis – la música criolla*
3 *a los 23 años*
4 *La Scala – Kew Gardens*
5 *pop o baladas latinas*
6 *vendido más de 52 millones de discos*
7 *pera llenar el Madison Square Garden*

5b Students choose two contrasting singers and give a brief comparative analysis, using the phrases given.

Técnica

How to approach speaking stimulus material

Preparation for oral examination.

Ask students to read through the advice and discuss the ideas before they complete activities A and B.

A Students follow the points listed and prepare to respond to the cartoon and questions.

B In pairs, students take up roles and take it turns to ask and answer the questions in Spanish.

H 5.2 | *Hoja* 5.2 offers additional speaking practice for this spread.

La expresión musical

Planner

Grammar focus
♦ Compound tenses using *haber* (2) – the pluperfect tense

Skills focus
♦ Speaking from notes

Key language

el cante	singing
el compositor	composer
la edad	age
el estreno	first performance/début
el gitano	gypsy
el paisaje	countryside
la penuria	poverty/hardship
la raíz	root
casarse con	to marry
cobrar vida nueva	to get a new lease of life
componer	to compose
contraer	to catch (a disease)
pasar hambre	to go hungry
avanzado/a	advanced
ciego/a	blind
poderoso/a	powerful
casi	almost
de niño	as a child
de regreso	on his return

Resources
♦ Student Book pages 58 and 59
♦ Vocabulary, Student Book page 61
♦ CD 1, track 36
♦ Hojas 5.3, 5.5
♦ Grammar Workbook page 45

1a Students read the obituary of Joaquín Rodrigo and make notes on the four topics listed. Draw students' attention to last point and ask how might this define his personal identity.
They use their notes as a basis for an oral presentation. They should use their own words as far as possible.

1b Students research the musicians listed, or any other Spanish or Latin American musicians of their choice, and prepare an oral presentation, making sure to include the points required.

H 5.3 | *Hoja* 5.3 offers additional reading practice for this page.

Gramática

Compound tenses using haber (2) – the pluperfect tense

Students read through the information. Ask them questions about it to elicit whether they have fully understood both how the tense is formed and when it is used.

Refer students to the relevant grammar section of the Student Book, page 168.

A Students look for examples of the pluperfect tense in the text.

B Students write the sentences in Spanish.

Answers:
1 *Antes de llegar a ser cantante de ópera Juan Diego Flórez había querido centor música de pop como los Beatles.*
2 *Luis Miguel había hecho una gira por Latinoamérica cuando dio este concierto en Málaga.*
3 *No había escuchado de él antes de que apareciera en Nueva York.*

 2a Students listen to the programme about singer-songwriters of protest songs. They then answer the questions.

> **p. 59, actividad 2a**
>
> La canción de protesta tiene una larga historia tanto en España como en Latinoamérica. En los años 60 del siglo pasado cantantes como Joan Manuel Serrat y Joan Baez ya levantaron sus voces.

Al mismo tiempo en Latinoamérica la voz de Soledad Bravo, nacida en España pero educada en Venezuela, empezaba a hacer impacto. Heredó sus convicciones políticas de su padre y en su primer álbum incluyó la canción de Carlos Puebla "Hasta Siempre", un tributo a Che Guevara, que hace poco resurgió como número uno en Francia.

Igualmente las palabras del guatemalteco Ricardo Arjona hablan de la pobreza, el dolor y la desesperación de la gente de su país. Su canción "Jesús Verbo No Sustantivo", que escribió en Buenos Aires, Argentina, lanzó su carrera con Sony. Otra canción "Mojado" de su último álbum "Adentro" habla del sufrimiento de los inmigrantes ilegales en los Estados Unidos.

Por último actualmente es muy famoso el colombiano Juanes, Juan Esteban, con canciones que posan preguntas sobre los temas universales del terrorismo y la violencia, que ha sufrido en su ciudad natal de Medellín.

Los tres logran combinar una mezcla interesante de liricismo y folklore además de ritmos populares como salsa y rock y es por eso que tienen un atractivo universal.

Answers:
1 *En los años 60 del siglo pasado;* **2** *en España;* **3** *a Che Guevara;* **4** *resurgió como número uno en Francia* **5** *la pobreza, el dolor y la desesperación de la gente de su país, y el sufrimiento de los inmigrantes ilegales en los Estados Unidos* **6** *guatemalteco* **7** *Juanes, Juan Esteban* **8** *porque ha sufrido en su ciudad natal de Medellín* **9** *Les tres logran combinar una mezcla interesante de liricismo y folklore además de ritmos populares como salsa y rock y es por eso que tienen un atractivo universal* **10** *Students' own words.*

Técnica

Speaking from notes

Students read through the advice, then put it into practice.

A Students use the notes they made in Activity 1a and give an oral presentation using headings only.

B Students now make further use of their notes to prepare an oral presentation on the musician, singer or group they most admire and whose music they like best. They consider how their choice reflects their personality.

Students record their presentation and listen to it in order to correct their pronunciation and intonation.

H 5.5 *Hoja 5.5 offers additional practice of speaking from notes.*

2b In groups, students ask five classmates what sort of music they prefer. They analyse the personality of each one and write five sentences to explain how their taste in music reflects their personality, following the example given.

3a Students read the text on flamenco and then decide if the statements which follow are made in the text.

Answers:
1 ✓ **2** ✓ **3** ✓ **4** ✗ **5** ✗

3b Students find evidence from the text to back up their decisions.

3c Class discussion: "How do you think flamenco defines the gipsy culture?" Students make use of the ideas in Activity 3a to prompt their thoughts and provide expressions.

Gramática en acción

Planner
Resources
♦ Student Book page 60
♦ Hoja 5.4

Recuerda

Pronouns

This is part one of *Gramática en acción* covering pronouns. Part 2 comes at the end of Unit 10. Students read the reminder about the order of pronouns. Refer them to the overview of pronouns in the grammar section of the Student Book, pages 161–162. Students copy out the table of direct object pronouns on page 161.

A Students rewrite the sentences replacing the underlined words with an appropriate pronoun.

Answers:
1 *Ellos van al concierto.*
2 *Le prometí que iría al concierto.*
3 *Tina la tocó.*
4 *Mi padre se lo regaló.*
5 Mi hermano va a dársela.

Recuerda

The pluperfect tense

Read through the information here and direct students to the Gramática box on page 56 of the Student Book.

B Students translate the sentences into Spanish.

Answers:
1 *Rodrigo se había puesto ciego antes de aprender la música.*
2 *Había aprendido a tocar la batería (los tambores) mucho antes de poder caminar!*
3 *Había dado varios conciertos antes que la gente comenzara a apreciar su estilo de jazz.*
4 *Nadie había oído hablar de ellos hasta los años setenta.*
5 *Se hizo famoso por lo menos veinte años después que había comenzado su carrera como cantante.*

Refer them to the overview of the Pluperfect tense in the grammar section of the Student Workbook, page 168.

Recuerda

Sequencing tenses

Read through this section with students asking them for further examples of their own to make sure they have fully understood how *lo* and *lo que* function in Spanish.

Refer them to page 164 of the grammar section in the Student Book.

H 5.4 | *Hoja* 5.4 offers additional practice for this spread.

Vocabulario

Page 61

Answers:
1 *se ha comenzado*
2 *cobran*
3 *se hizo*
4 *impresionados*
5 *veraniegos*

Extra

This page is aimed at A–A* students.

1a A skimming task to familiarise students with the reading before focusing on detailed understanding of specific sentences. Students skim read the blog and pick out vocabulary that (a) relates to music and (b) introduces or links sentences

Suggested answers:
Música:
industria musical, fan, CD, en vivo, festivales, en directo, conciertos, disco.
Vincular:
Es evidente que..., Y es que..., Hoy en día..., Al contrario de..., No viéndose equilibrado por..., Después de analizar..., Cabe comentar que..., Al fin y al cabo..., Si... ¿cómo es que...?

1b Students read the blog again with closer attention. They then match each opening phrase 1–5 with the appropriate end of the sentence a–e.

Suggested answers:
1 *e*   2 *b*   3 *d*   4 *c*   5 *a*

Técnica

Transferring meaning – explaining in Spanish (1)

Ensure students understand the concept of transferring meaning. The following exercise is aimed at preparing students for discussing texts but also develops their own strategies for understanding and explaining complex ideas in their own words.

Take them through the points listed.

A Students explain in Spanish using their own words the meaning of the phrases underlined in the blog.

Suggested answers:
1 *El modelo de negocio antiguo no funciona porque el consumidor comparte música en formato digital.*
2 *No se venden tantos discos como antes.*
3 *Hoy los consumidores sólo quieren complacer sus deseos.*
4 *Algunas compañías han cambiado su forma de distribuir la música*
5 *Es el mejor ejemplo de una nueva filosofía*

 2a Students listen to the comments on the blog and identify who (A, B or C) says each of the statements listed.

Answers:
1 *C*   2 *B*   3 *A*   4 *C*

p. 62, actividad 2a

A No quiero comprar un disco solo porque está de moda, sino que me gusta escuchar los diferentes tipos de música que me recomiendan mis amigos. Nunca compro CDs, prefiero descargar o compartir canciones.

B Los efectos son negativos para la industria, pero no significa que sean negativos para la música. Precisamente, la música no debería ser un producto que se venda. La música debe ser algo espiritual, democrático, universal. Cualquier músico puede poner su talento en Internet, sin necesidad de que pase por distribuciones de música.

C Te olvidas de otros modelos de negocio como las plataformas de suscripción, la música en las redes sociales, las tiendas online o las empresas de teléfonos móviles que promocionan música y conciertos. Los Arctic Monkeys y Spiralfrog son mejores ejemplos de esto que Prince.

2b Students choose one of the comments and listen again. They take notes to prepare for explaining what is said.

3 Students write an essay in Spanish of about 200 words, answering the question " Do you think there will always be great stars and groups in the world of music?" with their own viewpoint. They use their own ideas and ideas and language from this unit. Remind them to organise their material, using headings and ordering the headings before they start. They could also be reminded to revise the material on page 32 of the Student Book on developing an argument.

Unit 5 Assessment offers exam practice for this unit.

Unidad 6 La moda y tendencias

Unit objectives

By the end of this unit students will be able to:
♦ Talk and write about how their 'look' defines who they are
♦ Comment on different ways we can alter our image
♦ Discuss lifetstyles and leisure activities
♦ Talk and write about the cult of celebrity

Grammar

By the end of this unit students will be able to:
♦ Use the subjunctive mood in past tenses
♦ Use the personal *a* correctly
♦ Use the relative pronouns correctly
♦ Recognise and use time clauses

Skills

By the end of this unit students will be able to:
♦ Write in paragraphs
♦ Transfer meaning: explain in English

Resources

♦ Student Book page 63

This page introduces the topic.

1a Students read the two comments (A and B) and say which is positive and which negative. They make a note of the words and phrases that give this impression.

Answers:
A *positive;* **B** *negative*

1b Work in pairs. Students discuss with a classmate how to they can change their 'look'. They make use of the *frases clave*. Revise the present subjunctive following verbs of wanting; requesting; advising and expressions giving value judgements:
Prefiero que…
Le aconsejo que…
Insisto que…
No quiero que…
Espero que…
Me fascina que…
Me choca que…
Me sorprende que…
Encourage students to disagree with what is written in the comments and with each other to liven up the debate/discussion.

1c Class discussion on what is the 'look' of the moment that they like. Students describe it, explain why they like it; or indeed, if they don't like any contemporary style, they explain why not. Encourage students to disagree with what is written and with each other to liven up the debate/discussion.

2 Students answer the questions.

They should write their answers in Spanish.

Answers:
Students' own words

¿Quién soy yo?

Planner

Grammar focus
♦ The subjunctive mood in past tenses

Key language

las arrugas	wrinkles
el blanco	target
los caprichos	whims/fancies
una cifra	number
la cirugía	surgery
las normas	rules/regulations
el ombligo	bellybutton
la pasarela	catwalk
las pastillas	tablets
las pecas	freckles
la promesa	promise
la talla	size
envejecer	to grow old
fomentar	to promote
restringir	to restrict
rodear	to surround
seducir	to seduce
pasmado/a	overwhelmed

Resources
♦ Student Book pages 64–65
♦ Vocabulario, Student Book page 71
♦ CD 2, track 2
♦ Hojas 6.3, 6.4
♦ Grammar Workbook page 53

1a Students listen to the recording of the four young people talking about what they have bought. They fill in the table.

---

p. 64 actividad 1a

Ronaldo: Para mí lo más importante son **las zapatillas**. Con ellas lo dices todo: eres alegre, extrovertido, deportista. Además estás cómodo y sabes que estás a la moda.

Lucía: Bueno pues lo que cuenta para mí es **el "look" completo**, no solo una prenda. Los pendientes tienen que combinar con el maquillaje que tienen que ir con la camiseta y los vaqueros. Los vaqueros a su vez tienen que pegar con las botas. La imagen completa demuestra que eres una persona organizada. No me gusta ser diferente a los demás.

Ana Luisa: Lo que más me llama la atención hoy en día son **los piercings** ¡son tan feos cuando se llevan en la boca o en la nariz! Las personas que los llevan aparentan tener tienen malas intenciones y hasta dan miedo a la gente mayor. No me gustan nada. En cambio **los productos cosméticos** son súper importantes; cambian tu aspecto. De persona sin carácter te transforman en una persona interesante y con vitalidad. Además puedes cultivar tu propio estilo y destacarte de los demás.

Roberto: A veces se usan demasiado los productos cosméticos, sobre todo de día. No me importa que las chicas se maquillen cuando salen de noche pero durante el día me gusta ver su cara tal como es – natural. Por otra parte, me fascinan **los** discretos **tatuajes** que llevan algunos jóvenes aunque no me gustan los tatuajes que cubren todo el brazo o la espalda como por ejemplo los que llevan algunos futbolistas – son ridículos. Está bien que quieran destacar y cultivar su propio estilo pero no tanto.

Answers:

	La moda mencionada	Opinión
Ronaldo	*zapatillas*	*indican la personalidad y son cómodas*
Lucía	*el "look" completa*	*demuestra que eres una persona organizada*
Ana Luisa	*los piercings*	*feos/dan miedo*
	los productos cosméticos	*cambian el aspecto de una persona*
Roberto	*los tatuajes*	*discretos son buenos/ grandes son ridículos*

1b Students identify who said what.

Answers:
1 *Lucía and Roberto*
2 *Ana Luisa*
3 *Ana Luisa*

4 *Lucía*
5 *Lucía*
6 *Ronaldo*

1c Work in pairs. Students ask each other with which of the four (Lucía, Roberto, Ana Luisa, Ronaldo) do they most identify and why.

1d Written work. Students write a brief paragraph on what they think of tattoos and body piercing?

2 Students read the text and discuss what the phrase in bold means ("therapies and treatments that have become a whole new industry"). They give some examples and comment on them.
Ask students to point out cognates and near cognates to show them how straight forward reading such articles can be.

3a Vocabulary work. Students read the article on "young victims". They make a note of the words in bold. If they do not know hat they mean they look them up in a dictionary.

3b Vocabulary work: synonyms. Students look in the text for words with a simialr meaning to those listed.

Answers:
el debate; resurgido; el largo; indicado; por debajo de; demacradas; han alcanzado

3c Students read the text a second time and match the two halves of the sentences.

Answers:
1 *Todos hablan del*
   d *problema de la talla cero.*
2 *Ya no discuten*
   e *el estilo ni la moda.*
3 *Nos preocupa que*
   f *las chicas sean tan delgadas.*
4 *Madrid decidió*
   a *establecer unas normas de tallas.*
5 *Se espera que*
   c *otros centros sigan su ejemplo.*
6 *Hoy hay mucha inquietud*
   b *por el problema del peso.*

3d Discuss the final paragraph of the text and ask the questions:

¿La cirujía cosmética es antifeminista? (Is cosmetic surgery antifeminist?)

¿El gobierno debe sacar leyes y controles sobre la cirujía estética? (Ought the government introduce laws to control cosmetic surgery?)

Then ask students to write a brief response. Remind them to use sentences including subjunctives by using the following set phrases

Aconsejo que…
Advierto que…
Quiero que…
Me choca que…
Me preocupa que…
Es una lástima que….

Gramática

The subjunctive mood in past tenses

Revise the main uses of the subjunctive in wanting, requesting and advising sentences, in sentences expressing value judgements, doubt or improbability and in *cuando* clauses. Work through the *Gramática* box in the Student Book.

Refer students to the relevant grammar section in the Student Book, page 169, and to the Grammar Workbook, page 53.

A Students write out the verbs in the imperfect subjunctive.

Answers:
1 *pudiera, pudieras, pudiera, pudiéramos, pudierais, pudieran*
OR
pudiese, pudieses, pudiese, pudiésemos, pudieseis, pudiesen
2 *hiciera, hicieras, hiciera, hiciéramos, hicierais,* hicieran
OR
hiciese, hicieses, hiciese, hiciésemos, hicieseis, hiciesen
3 *viviera, vivieras, viviera, viviéramos, vivierais, vivieran*
OR
viviese, vivieses, viviese, viviésemos, vivieseis, viviesen
4 *tuviera, tuvieras, tuviera, tuviéramos, tuvierais, tuvieran*
OR
tuviese, tuvieses, tuviese, tuviésemos, tuvieseis, tuviesen
5 *fuera, fueras, fuera, fuéramos, fuerais, fueran*
OR
fuese, fueses, fuese, fuésemos, fueseis, fuesen

Sequencing of tenses and some uses of the imperfect subjunctive

Refer students to the grammar section in the Student Book, page 170.

B Students translate the example sentences in the *Gramática* box into English.

Answers:
My father is asking me not have a tattoo (done).
My father asked me not to have a tattoo (done).
I do wish I could change my image.
If I were thinner I would be a model.

C Students analyse the verbs in the sentences: they give mood, tense, and why the subjunctive is used.

Answers
1 *Me alegra = present indicative   vayamos = present subjunctive – after value judgement*
2 *Aconsejería = conditional (indicative)   hicierais = imperfect subjunctive – after verb advising*
3 *era = imperfect indicative   pensara = imperfect subjunctive after value judgement*
4 *sorprende = present indicative   haga = present subjunctive after value judgement*
5 *chocó = preterite indicative   fuera = imperfect subjunctive after value judgement*

H 6.4 *Hoja 6.4 offers additional practice of the subjunctive mood in past tenses.*

4a Class discussion. "An image has more power than a thousand words". Students discuss how this statement is reflected in how people behave.

4b Students write 100 to 150 words to express their views about the place of image in youth culture and how it does/does not influence the behaviour of the young. They mention the influence of their friends, the influence of the media; the good or bad example presented by celebrities; and the difficulty of swimming against the tide.

H 6.3 *Hoja 6.3 offers additional reading practice for this spread.*

Mi modo de ser

Planner	
Grammar focus	
◆ The personal *a*	
◆ Time clauses	
Key language	
la altura	height
un apretón de manos	handshake
el argot	slang
las bandas	gangs
el barrio	district
la cancha	court
el diseño	design
el estilo	style

una media de	an average of
el monopatín	skateboard
el mundo	world
el ocio	leisure
un partido	game/match
la salud	health
el sondeo	survey
afiliarse a	to belong to
fracasar	to fail
pisar	to tread
regresar	to return home
rondar	to prowl around
tomar el pelo	to tease
holgado/a	loose hanging
parado	out of work/on the dole
habitualmente	normally/usually
cueste lo que cueste	whatever it costs
'fashionista'	'slave to fashion'

Resources

♦ Student Book pages 66–67
♦ Vocabulario, Student Book page 71
♦ Hojas 6.1 CD 4, tracks 19 and 20, 6.2
♦ Grammar Workbook page 20

1a Students read the six statements and work out what the survey questions would have been.

1b Work in pairs. Students ask a classmate the questions from 1a. The classmate should answer using the statements in 1a, but reflecting the facts in their own country. They then discuss differences between young people's habits in Spain and their own country. Perhaps statements 3 and 6 present the best discussion points because probably only a small minority of 15 to 25 year-olds return home after 6 a.m. in most parts of the UK, while the percentages of young people owning games consoles and computers is likely to be much higher.

2 Students order the leisure activities listed from most popular to least popular, according to what they think is more common in Spain and then they compare their answers with the answers given. You should explain that the phenomenon of *El botellón* is not accepted in Spanish law, but the Spanish police and law enforcement agencies are struggling to keep it under control.

Gramática

The personal *a*

Students read through the examples of sentences requiring the perosnal *a*. Make sure they notice that all three Spanish sentences mean the same thing and that they understand that *a* is only needed when the direct object is a person.

Refer students to the relevant grammar section of the Student Book, page 160, and to the Grammar Workbook, page 20.

A Students make complete sentences using the personal *a* when required.

Answers:
Accept students' own combinations but they need to make sense

Possible answers:
Vi a la víctima de la dieta que la dejó demacrada.
Vi a mis amigos con su ropa nueva.
Escuché el último CD de fusión.
Escuché a mi grupo favorito en concierto.
Presenté mi nuevo tatuaje a mi familia.
Presenté la nueva moda de botas largas.

3a Students read the texts.

3b Students identify from the texts the person described in each of the statements 1–10.

Answers:
1 *Agata;* **2** *Felipe;* **3** *Victoria;* **4** *Agata;* **5** *Sebastián;*
6 *Victoria;* **7** *Felipe;* **8** *Victoria;* **9** *Sebastián;* **10** *Agata*

3c Ask students with which of the young people do they most identify and with which do they least identify. They give their reasons.

Gramática

Time clauses

The tenses used in English are not always those used in Spanish. Where English uses the perfect tense in some time clauses, Spanish uses the present; and where English uses the pluperfect, Spanish uses the imperfect. Most of these time phrases suggest that something that happened in the past still has an ongoing result. Students should be encouraged to look for this as they work through the examples.

Refer students to the relevant grammar section of the Student Book, page 172, and to the Grammar Workbook, page 67.

A Students read the texts again and find five examples of time clauses.

Answers:
Text 1: hace años; hace poco
Text 2: me acabo de afiliar
Text 3: cuando tenga edad
Text 4: llevo años

B Students translate the sentences into Spanish.

Answers:
1 *Me acabo de afiliar a un gymnasio para tratar de perder peso.*
2 *No me interesa la moda desde hace años.*
3 *Mi modo de ser seguía la misma rutina cuando se cambió de repente.*

H 6.1-2 *Hoja 6.1 and 6.2 offer additional listening and speaking practice for this spread.*

La feria de las vanidades

Planner

Skills focus
♦ Write in paragraphs

Grammar focus
♦ Relative pronouns

Key language

el autoestima	self-esteem
la búsqueda	search
las caderas	hips
el corazón	heart
la corriente	current
la época	epoch/age
el esfuerzo	efforts
las lágrimas	tears
la meta	aim/goal
el porvenir	future
los rizos	curls/ringlets
la sangre	blood
el sudor	sweat
emerger	to emerge
hechizar	to cast a spell on
lograr	to achieve
merecer	to deserve
otorgar	to credit/grant
dotados	highly skilled
a pesar de	in spite of
Don Nadie	Mr Nobody
lo odio	I hate it
unos cuantos	a few

Resources
♦ Student Book pages 68–69
♦ Vocabulario, Student Book page 71
♦ CD 2, track 3
♦ Hojas 6.4, 6.5
♦ Grammar Workbook page 26

1a Students read the paragraph about the changing face of fame and answer the questions.

1b Work in pairs. Students write a list of five famous people in their country, and discuss them with a partner by answering the questions 1–4.

2a Students discuss their opinions about the desire of young people to imitate famous people.

 2b Students listen to the speakers and decide who mentions or implies each of the statements 1–6.

> **p. 68, actividad 2b**
>
> **Marga:** Porque tratan de parecerse a ellos, porque saben que la forma en que tal o cual famoso actúa y es, está aceptada o asimilada por la sociedad. Así el camino es más corto y más fácil.
>
> **Maria José:** No todos los famosos dan mal ejemplo, algunos comparten lo que tienen y su éxito no se les sube a la cabeza sino que lo utilizan para causas altruistas y ayudas sociales tanto a nivel económico como a nivel propagandístico ya que tienen el poder de hacer llegar su causa a las masas.
>
> **Alicia:** Lo hacen para ser aceptados ... para ser un tanto populares ... es como esas mujeres que quieren ser como las que salen en las telenovelas. Son muy superficiales, y además no tienen una personalidad propia ni original ya que sólo imitan lo que ven en las telenovelas.
>
> **Nacho:** En realidad creo que es por falta de amor propio, de no saber valorar lo que tienen, y no darse cuenta de que, al fin de cuentas, serán más felices sabiendo por qué son valiosos y no imitando a gente famosa. Creo que la necesidad de aceptación y de reconocimiento es ahora muy fuerte en la sociedad, y buscan una manera sencilla de ser aceptados.
>
> **Iván:** ¿La verdad? Simple, por falta de talento propio.
>
> **Iñaki:** La verdad ... pues no sé, yo no hago eso, si lo hiciera tal vez te respondería pero no sé. Somos muchos los jóvenes con opiniones propias y que no nos dejamos influenciar tan fácilmente. ¡No es oro todo lo que reluce!

Answers:
1 *Nacho;* 2 *Nacho;* 3 *María José;* 4 *Alicia;*
5 *Alicia;* 6 *María José*

Técnica

Write in paragraphs

Take students through the material in the Student Book on how to structure paragraphs and how to develop an argument by linking paragraphs. Some vocabulary is provided to help them identify how to link concepts.

Answers:
A
Introduction:
Parece que cada día ... llegaban a la fama.

Presentation of the situation:
En mi infancia ... o mejor dicho 'famosillo'.

Explanation/information and argument:
a través ... dudoso talento y porvenir.

Evidence to support argument:
He aquí los culpables ... no recuerdo.

B The answers below are for guidance as some of the phrases may fit in more than one category depending on the context.

Answers:
1 Continuing or adding an idea: *quizás la verdad es más compleja/al mismo tiempo/más importante aun es/además*
2 Qualifying an idea: *el mejor ejemplo sería/...*
3 Contrasting or denying: *a pesar de/claro ..., pero ...*

H 6.5 *Hoja 6.5 offers additional practice of writing in paragraphs.*

Gramática

Relative pronouns

Introduce students to the function of the relative pronoun. Like other pronouns, a relative pronoun that has differentiated gendered forms has to agree in number and gender with the noun it refers to. Refer students to the relevant grammar section of the Student Book, page 162, and the Grammar Workbook, page 26.

Answers:
A
1 *Buenafuente, quien ha escrito nueve libros, es un presentador de televisión muy popular.*
2 *El nuevo Gran hermano, que empieza hoy, parece muy extravagante.*
3 *La cantante Chenoa, cuya nacionalidad es argentina, lanzó su primer álbum en 2002 después de su éxito en OT.*
4 *La fama de David Bustamante, la cual (or que) se debe a su paso por OT1, ha resultado en una carrera musical de mucho éxito.*

H 6.4 *Hoja 6.4 offers additional practice of relative pronouns.*

3a Students read the article about David Bisbal and order the paragraphs so that it presents a coherent piece in a logical order. Remind students to revise the *Técnica* section on page 68.

Answer:
3, 1, 2, 4

3b Students read the passage about David Bisbal, and try to think of a brief title for each paragraph.

Answers:
Some suggested titles:
1 *trayectoria discográfica/discografía/éxito discográfico*
2 *¿Quién es?/un joven con talento/presentación*
3 *sus inicios/¿De dónde proviene?/el comienzo*
4 *un joven con principios/conciencia humana/su contribución a la sociedad*

3c Students read the text thoroughly from a grammatical perspective. They identify the relative pronouns within it and what they substitute in each case.

1 *... que fue su debut discográfico ...*
   (su primer álbum)
   ... cuya fama le precede... (Bisbal)
2 *... que emergen de los reality ...*
   (algunos famosos)
   ... que se les otorga ...(la fama)
3 *... que fue uno de los primeros ...*
   (Operación Triunfo)
   ... el cual elegiría ... (el público)
4 *... cuya meta es denunciar ...*
   (un conmovedor tema)
   ...que esto supone para los ...
   (el uso de niños en conflictos armados)

4 "Celebrities/Famous people have a social duty to live an exemplary life."
Students write 150 to 200 words to support, or express their disagreement with the statement given. They should be reminded that their view needs to be justified fully.
Ask students to read out their essays and get the rest of the class to question them about their stance on the subject.

Gramática en acción

Planner
Resources
♦ Student Book page 70

Recuerda

The subjunctive mood in past tenses

Answers:
A
1 *Mi madre me pidió que no pusiera esa falda tan corta.*
2 *Yo esperaba que ella no viera mis piercings nuevos.*
3 *Mi padre prohibió que hiciera un tatuaje.*

4 *Quería que mis amigas me regalasen un bolso de* moda.

5 *¡Ojalá no siguiera esa moda de punkie feo!*

6 *Mi madre me trata como si todavía tuviera ocho años.*

B

1 *Mum asked me not to put on my very short skirt.*

2 *I hoped she would not see my new piercings.*

3 *Dad forbade me to have a tattoo.*

4 *I hoped that my friends would give me a fashionable handbag.*

5 *Believe me, I wouldn't follow this ugly punk fashion.*

6 *Mum treats me as if I were still eight years old*

C

There is more than one logical way of ordering the sentences. It will depend upon the paragraph that the students produce.

D

Carolina tenía el pelo largo, rubio y rizado. Fue a la peluquería y le dijo al peluquero que le cortase el cabello. Emilio, el peluquero, le sugerió que cambiase el color de su pelo. Carolina siempre había querido que su pelo fuese diferente. Siempre había querido parecerse a Victoria Beckham. Decidió que quería tener el pelo corto, oscuro y liso. Cuatro horas después de que entrase en la peluquería, salió una mujer diferente.

E

Students describe their ideal liftsyle and leisure activities. How would they be influenced by the latest fashion and trends? They should use the imperfect subjunctive and include the topics listed.

Recuerda

*The personal **a***

F

Answers:

2, 3, 8

Vocabulario

Page 71

Answers:

1 *se ponen*

2 *hiciera*

3 *ha querido*

4 *cuya*

5 *los cuales*

Extra

Planner

Resources

♦ Student Book page 72
♦ CD 2, track 4

This page is aimed at A-A* students.

Cultural note. Manu Chao is a French born musician of Spanish parents who lives in Barcelona. While enjoying fame and success, he has avoided the clutches of a "celebrity lifestyle" and commercialisation.

1 Students read the text and take notes. They look for evidence of:
Manu Chao's success; freedom in his way of life; the ordinariness of his life; the luxuries in his lifestyle.

Example answers:

vende millones de discos y convoca multitudes
su alto grado de autonomía respecto a la industria musical/Dormir diez horas, pasar un día sin hacer nada son libertades bonitas
hacia un bar donde le conocen
suele escapar hacia latitudes menos agobiantes

Técnica

Transferring meaning: Explaining in English

Take students through the material in the Student Book. It is important that they understand that answering in English is not "the easy option", but tests their ability to understand and to use appropriate English vocabulary and expressions.

A Students read the text again and answer the questions in English.

Answers:

1 *They were kicking a ball around.*

2 *They were waiting for Manu Chao (their leader).*

3 *Because they let a lot of other musicians go.*

4 *He didn't sign for another big company.*

5 *"Slow is bad"*

6 *Taking your time, sleeping, and doing nothing are luxuries.*

B Students read the sentences that contain underlined words/phrases. They use the context to work out the meaning of the underlined words and translate them.

Unidad 6   La moda y tendencias

Suggested translations:
word of mouth
straight away
playing to the gallery in a costly manner
relax
slap

2 Students listen to the words of Manu Chao in interview and take notes in order to answer the questions. They prepare by reading the questions. They explain the motives underlying Chao's choices.

---

p. 72, actividad 2

— Me he pasado demasiados inviernos sin ver el sol. El alma de la gente, las relaciones humanas, todo se entristece y se amarga. Si hay una prerrogativa de star que creo haberme ganado es la de vivir bajo un cielo azul, sin nubes grises. Se trata de algo por lo que nunca voy a pedir disculpas. Oye, hay personas que viven en climas fríos y tienen sol en el corazón. Pero mi opción es esta: Barcelona.

— También viaja a Brasil, donde crece su hijo.

— Yo rechazaba la paternidad, no quería esa responsabilidad. Aún hoy, con 46 años, me niego a reconocerme como adulto: siempre odié la idea del núcleo familiar, los padres y el niño encerrados en su pisito o en su chalé. Tampoco creo que padres e hijos deban estar todo el tiempo juntos. Vi la última vez a mi niño en diciembre, pero sé que está bien y eso me basta. A veces, cuando voy allí, sólo me lo encuentro a la hora de comer: tiene su vida, anda con su pandilla, va a la playa. Allí, igual que en África, los niños son un proyecto de la comunidad entera, los adultos cuidan de todos. A su lado he revivido algo que había perdido: el sentido poético de la existencia, la capacidad para vivir lo onírico, el reino de la fantasía. Veo una chispita en sus ojos que me maravilla: así era yo... Y me alegro de ser padre.

Answers:
1. *En Barcelona, porque necesita vivir bajo un cielo azul.*
2. *No, porque lo vio en diciembre eso basta. No le gusta la idea de la familia nuclear.*
3. *Le gusta, porque su hijo le recuerda cómo era él de joven.*

3 Class discussion. "The life of Manu Chao shows that a famous person can live a normal life."

"Manu Chao wants to avoid fame, but in reality he cannot lead a normal life."

After a class discussion the students write their own viewpoint.

Unit 6 Assessment offers exam practice for this unit.

Unidad 7 El deporte

Unit objectives

By the end of this unit students will be able to:
♦ Talk and write about traditional and 'fun' sports
♦ Discuss reasons for taking part in sport
♦ Talk and write about the links between physical exercise and health

Grammar

By the end of this unit students will be able to:
♦ Avoid using the passive when asking questions
♦ Use the future tense correctly
♦ Form and use of adverbs correctly
♦ Use the prepositions *por* and *para*
♦ Use the subjunctive in the perfect and pluperfect tenses

Skills

By the end of this unit students will be able to:
♦ Check their wrtten work
♦ Use debating skills
♦ Find ideas and information on the Internet

Resources

♦ Student Book page 73

This page introduces the topic.

1a See how many faces and sports the students can recognise immediately.

1b and **1c** Students read the fragments of a newspaper article and put them in order to make a single article. Then they match them to the appropriate sports person. Note that this activity could be continued as homework.

You could further develop this material and ask students to research their favourite sports person or a sports person they consider to be influential and make an oral presentation to the class giving reasons why this person is their favourite/influential and if he or she has influenced their choice of sport.

Answers:
1 *A*   **2** *C*   **3** *D*   **4** *B*

Tradición contra novedad

> **Planner**
>
> *Grammar focus*
> ♦ Avoiding the passive when asking questions
> ♦ Talking about the future
>
> *Key language*
>
> | | |
> |---|---|
> | *una cesta* | basket |
> | *una cometa* | kite |
> | *la destreza* | skill |
> | *un equipo* | team |
> | *un espectador* | spectator |
> | *el frontón* | wall (as in a squash court) |
> | *una jaula* | cage |
> | *la lucha libre* | wrestling |
> | *el portero* | goalkeeper |
> | *un reto* | challenge |
> | *un salto* | jump |
> | *los trucos* | tricks |
> | *una vela* | sail |
> | *alzar* | to raise up |
> | *arriesgar* | to risk |
> | *marcar un gol* | to score a goal |
> | *realizar* | to fulfil |
> | *vistosos* | bright and colourful |
>
> *Resources*
> ♦ Student Book pages 74 and 75
> ♦ Vocabulario, Student Book page 81
> ♦ CD 2, track 5
> ♦ Grammar Workbook pages 48, 62

1a Students read the texts and decide which of the sports they refer to.

Answers:
1 *tórobut;* **2** *levantamiento de piedras;* **3** *jai alai*

1b Now they read the texts again for more detail and find the definitions.

Answers:
1 *all three;* **2** *1;* **3** *1 and 3;* **4** *2 and 3;* **5** *3;* **6** *1*

2a Students listen to the descriptions and identify the three modern sports.

---

p. 74, actividades 2a y 2b

1 Es un deporte que se juega mucho en Europa, pero no tanto en Inglaterra. Se juega con dos equipos de siete, en un recinto cubierto o en la playa. Se utiliza un balón un poco más pequeño que el balón de fútbol, que no se puede tocar con el pie. Se pueden dar tres pasos con el balón en las manos, y sólo se puede tener el balón durante tres segundos como máximo. Se marca un gol cuando el balón entra en la portería.

2 Es un deporte que se ha hecho muy popular en España a causa del éxito que han tenido Miguel Indurain, Óscar Freire y Alberto Contador. Se puede practicar a nivel individual, pero es más normal hacerse socio de un club. Se practica al aire libre, en carreteras o a veces en pistas especiales. Practicando este deporte se alcanzan excelentes niveles de condición física. En concursos o carreras, se trata de completar el recorrido más rápido que los demás.

3 Se juega con dos o cuatro jugadores. La pelota se golpea con una raqueta pequeña. No se ganan puntos cuando la pelota cae al suelo o da en la red. Es un juego que se practica en el interior y en una mesa.

Answers:
1 *balonmano*; **2** *ciclismo*; **3** *ping-pong*

 2b Students listen again for the words given.

Answers:
team – *equipo*; goal – *gol*; small ball – *pelota*; inside – *en el interior*; outside – *al aire libre*; racquet – *una raqueta*; large ball – *un balón*; track – *la pista*; win points – *se ganan puntos*; steps – *pasos*; competition – *concurso*; net – *la red*; to score – *marcar*; race – *la carrera*

You could extend this activity by asking students to describe other sports for a partner to guess.

Gramática

Avoiding the passive when asking questions

Students read through the advice about asking questions using *se*. The construction of the question is likely to influence the way they construct their answer.

Also refer students to page 34 of the Student Book, where they first met the use of *se* to avoid the passive. The passive is also dealt with in the grammar section of the Student Book, page 171 and on page 62 of the Grammar Workbook.

A Students practise asking questions using the prompts provided.

3a Students read the text on kite surfing and try to put into practice the reading skills they learnt in Unit 2. They should try to complete the task without resorting to a dictionary as far as possible. They will find the phrases and words in the text.

Answers:
1 *cada vez más impresionantes*; **2** *ya se han inventado*; **3** *el vuelo de cometa*; **4** *el deporte de moda*; **5** *no es sorprendente*; **6** *se ha vuelto muy popular*

3b Students match the two halves to make a complete sentence.

Answers:
1 *b*   **2** *d*   **3** *a*   **4** *c*

3c Students choose a traditional and a modern sport and write about them.

3d Students then present one of their sports to a partner who guesses the name of it.

Gramática

Talking about the future

This revises the formation and use of the future, immediate future and conditional tenses. It also presents examples of a Spanish present tense used where English uses a future tense.

Refer students also to the grammar section of the Student Book, page 167, and to page 48 of the Grammar Workbook.

A Students complete the definitions for each of the tenses.
They could check their answers at the back of the Student Book to encourage them to find out information for themselves and to get used to using the grammar section for reference.

B Students fill in the gaps in the dialogue using the verbs provided.

Answers:
tenga; iré; haré; me gustaría; viviré; saldré; vuelva; descansaré; tendría; leería

C They then invent a sport for the future and describe it using only the future tense.

¡Participemos en el deporte!

Planner

Skills focus

♦ Debating or discussing; structuring an argument

Key language

el apoyo	backing/support
una carrera	race
la cima	top/peak
el consenso	consensus
el coste	cost
la esperanza	hope
el poder	power
una silla de ruedas	wheelchair
la suerte	luck
una ventaja	advantage
añadir	to add
citar	to cite/quote
darse cuenta	to realise
doparse	to dope oneself/take dope
hacer falta	to lack
jactarse	to boast
alucinante	mesmerising
injusto/a	unjust
a pesar de	in spite of
no sólo ... sino también	not only ... but also
sin lugar a dudas	without a doubt

Resources

♦ Student Book pages 76 and 77
♦ Vocabulario, Student Book page 81
♦ CD 2, track 6
♦ Hojas 7.1 CD 4, tracks 20 and 21, 7.2, 7.3, 7.5

1a Students read the introduction about Oscar Pistorius the Blade Runner. They match up the questions with an appropriate answer.

Answers:
1 *c* 2 *f* 3 *h* 4 *d* 5 *a* 6 *g* 7 *e* 8 *b*

1b Work in pairs. Students then practise, making these questions and answers into an interview.

2 Students read the article about the state of sport today and answer the questions in their own words but basing their answers on the text.

Suggested answers should contain:
1 *España tiene muchos deportistas famosos.*
2 *porque ganan mucho dinero y están en la tele y en revistas*

3 *que hay muchos y dan un buen ejemplo*
4 *es una situación triste*
5 *Students' own words and ideas*

3a Students listen to the points of view about hosting the Olympic Games. They note down the order in which they hear each comment. It would help students to look through the statements first.

---

p. 77, actividad 3a

– A ver, Marco, tú estarías de acuerdo con que los Juegos Olímpicos se celebraran en nuestro país?

– Pues, a mí me parece que por una parte sí sería buena idea por lo que queda después pero por otra parte también comprendo los argumentos en contra porque es verdad que necesitamos hospitales y colegios.

– Vale. Entonces explica primero cuáles son los inconvenientes.

– Lo que más me preocupa es el coste. Creo que va a aumentar demasiado y que al final seremos nosotros los que tendremos que pagar.

– Vaya, ¡qué ideas tan negativas! Cualquier dinero que se gaste estará bien gastado porque se van a construir muchos edificios bonitos y útiles y después todos podremos usar estas facilidades.

– Lo que pasa es que los arquitectos quieren tener toda la gloria y a veces construyen edificios impresionantes pero poco prácticos.

– Bueno, vamos a concentrarnos en los juegos. Alfredo, ¿tú tienes una opinión sobre lo que atrae del deporte?

– Claro que sí. En mi opinión, verlo es una parte esencial del deporte. Los mejores del mundo necesitan los campeonatos para demostrar su excelencia. Además, a nosotros los espectadores nos encanta verlos. Es un espectáculo que verdaderamente vale la pena.

– En cuanto al deporte comprendo que es un escaparate para el élite del deporte pero mi pregunta es si de verdad anima a los jóvenes a participar en el deporte o si les quita las ganas.

– A fin de cuentas si quieren triunfar tienen que darse cuenta de que hay que hacer un esfuerzo en la vida. De nada les sirve pensar que todo se puede alcanzar sin moverse del sofá.

– En conclusión al mismo tiempo que produce negocio y atrae turistas y su dinero, también cuesta mucho construir y preparar un certamen como los Juegos Olímpicos o cualquier Copa Mundial. Por supuesto hay muchos a favor y muchos en contra.

Answers:
D J B E L I F A K G H C

3b Students decide whether each of the viewpoints from Activity 3a is favourable or not.

3c Encourage students to add their own points of view.

3d Students should then respond to the points of view expressed.

3e In pairs, students discuss the question: 'What use are national and international competitions?' They make use of the sentences in the skills box.

Técnica

Debating or discussing: structuring an argument

Students read through this section carefully. Ask them for their reactions and also ask them to give examples of their own.

A useful extension task could be to revisit the previous units and note examples for discussion on the topics. This could be used as a way of revising previous topics.

A Class discussion. Students use the ideas and phrases and prepare for a class discussion on why we play sports.

Some useful extra phrases for discussing and debating:
No tienes razón/te equivocas
Yo tampoco creo que
Francamente
Estoy harto/a de
Me apasiona
Gracias a
Como consecuencia

H 7.5 | *Hoja* 7.5 offers additional practice of debating and discussing.

H 7.1-3 | *Hojas* 7.1, 7.2 and 7.3, offer additional listening, speaking and reading practice for this spread.

Mente sana, cuerpo sano

Planner

Grammar focus
♦ Adverbs
♦ *por* and *para*

Skills focus
♦ Checking your written work

Key language

el aro	basketball ring
el baloncesto	basketball
el buceo	diving (scuba)
un equilibrio	balance
la grasa	fat
la liga	league
el muro	wall
una pista	court
el podio	podium
la prueba	test
una rueda	wheel
el sudor	sweat
agotarse	to run out of/exhaust
animar	to encourage
ascender	to go up
decepcionarse	to feel disappointed
divertirse	to enjoy oneself
entrenar	to train
inscribirse en	to apply/sign up for
quemar	to burn
respirar	to breathe
estándar	standard
a menudo	often
al cien por cien	one hundred per cent

Resources
♦ Student Book pages 78 and 79
♦ Vocabulario, Student Book page 81
♦ CD 2, track 7
♦ Grammar Workbook pages 14, 19

1 Students read the text on Juan Rentería and answer the question.

Answer:
SR = en silla de ruedas (wheelchair basketball)

2a Students answer the questions from the text.

Answers:
1 *Terminamos en tercer lugar.*
2 *Se juega sentado.*
3 *Pues, claro un poco porque me gustaría ganar la liga.*
4 *A 3,05 metros*
5 *en un campamento de verano*
6 *porque tendría que viajar y entrenar mucho*
7 *No tanto – ¡este año voy a hacer buceo!*

2b They then practise the interview in pairs, taking the parts of the interviewer and Juan Rentería.

2c Students answer the questions and then discuss their answers with a partner.

2d Students imagine that they are Juan Rentería and write a few thoughts about the future using the *frases clave* provided as prompts.

Gramática

Adverbs

Tell students to revise how to form adverbs and note the points made.

Refer them to the grammar section of the Student Book, page 158, and to the Grammar Workbook, page 14.

A When they have completed activity 3a they re-write the advice using different types of adverbs/adverbial expressions.

3a Students read the advice about maintaining a balanced lifestyle. They then list the statements in order of importance.

3b Students write down advice for a partner using the prompts provided. These cover the conditional tense, the present subjunctive and the past subjunctive.

 4 Students listen and note down the activities each person does. They list them as sport or relaxation.

> **p. 79, actividad 4**
>
> – Hemos preguntado a varias personas acerca de lo que hacen como deporte o para relajarse.
>
> 1 Yo soy Ana y me gusta hacer gimnasia; sobre todo aerobic porque me relaja todo el cuerpo y al mismo tiempo afina los músculos. Me siento mil veces mejor después de pasar media hora en el gimnasio.
>
> 2 Me llamo Felipe y no hago mucho deporte porque no tengo tiempo después de la oficina y el camino a casa. Prefiero poner la tele y pasar un buen rato viendo programas simples para no tener que pensar en nada.
>
> 3 Pues yo, María Elena, voy a menudo a clase de yoga. Me calma la mente y desaparece todo el estrés del día, necesario porque llevo una vida constantemente agitada; es un deporte y al mismo tiempo una diversión que relaja.
>
> 4 A mí, Sarita, me encanta correr tres o cuatro kilómetros antes de desayunar; me gustaría hacer más pero no tengo tiempo salvo en los fines de semana cuando hago 10 o más kilómetros. Despeja la cabeza y al mismo tiempo me ayuda a pensar y organizar lo que tengo que hacer durante el resto del día.
>
> 5 Me llamo Carlos 'el gordito' y voy tres veces a la semana a bailar salsa porque me divierto y hago ejercicio que lo necesito bastante. Antes no hacía nada más que comer golosinas delante de la tele pero ahora el baile me ha salvado y voy bajando kilos poco a poco.

Answers:
1 *aerobic – relajamiento;* **2** *ver la tele – diversión;*
3 *yoga – relajamiento y diversión;*
4 *correr – relajamiento;* **5** *bailar salsa – ejercicio y diversión*

Técnica

Checking your written work

Students read the advice on what to look for when checking their written work.

A They write an essay of no less than 200 words on "Do you think it is important to play sport in order to enjoy good health?". They use the advice in the skills box to check their work.

Gramática

por and para.

Students read through the *Gramática* box and could be encouraged to offer examples for each of the points made.

Refer students to the grammar section in the Student Book, page 160, and to page 19 of the Grammar Workbook.

A They read the text about marathon running and note each example of the usage of *por* and *para* and then translate each one.

Answers:
el por qué y para qué – the why and wherefore;
por el cual – along which;
para conseguir subir – to manage to climb onto;
por minuto – a minute;
por agotarse – about to expire;
para finalizar – in order to finish

Gramática en acción

> **Planner**
>
> *Resources*
> ♦ Student Book page 80
> ♦ Hoja 7.4

Recuerda

The perfect and pluperfect subjunctive

Students read through the Reminder box.

Remind students that so far they have learnt to use the subjunctive after verbs of (not) wanting, requesting advising; after value judgements; after expressing a wish; in hypothetical clauses; after *cuando* expressing a future; after verbs containing doubt or improbability.

They can find a synopsis of the tenses and uses of the subjunctive on page 170 of the grammar section of the Student Book. Encourage students to use the Index in the front of the Student Book to track down relevant *Gramática* boxes in previous units.

A Students translate the sentences into Spanish.

Answers:
1 *Es un milagro que hayamos aprendido a jugar tan rápidamente.*
2 *Me sorprende que no hayan trabajado como equipo.*
3 *Ganarán cuando hayan adquirido mejor disciplina.*
4 *Si no hubiera llovido habríamos hecho el piragüismo.*

H 7.4 *Hoja* 7.4 offers additional practice of the subjunctive in past tenses.

Recuerda

Tenses using the auxiliary verb

Students remind themselves about all the compound tenses using *haber* that they have covered so far.

Refer students to pages 168 and 170 of the grammar section of the Student Book. Encourage students to use the Index in the front of the Student Book to track down relevant *Gramática* boxes in previous units.

B Students read the text and note the tenses using *haber*. They analyse each one indicating the tense.

Answers:
1 *se han enfrentado – perfect reflexive*
2 *había atraído – pluperfect*
3 *han tenido que – perfect*
4 *se había preparado – pluperfect reflexive*
5 *ha sabido – perfect*
6 *no le ha gustado – perfect*
7 *se haya recuperado, haya podido – perfect subjunctive*
8 *haber ganado – perfect infinitive*
9 *había hecho – pluperfect*

C Students re-use all the tenses identified in the text above and make up an imaginary story. This could be done orally as a shaggy dog story with each student making up a sentence and adding it to the previous one.

Recuerda

Por and para

Students complete the reminders about *por* and *para*. They use the grammar section of the Student Book, page 160 to confirm their answers.

D Students write out the sentences correctly using either *por* or *para*.

Answers:
1 *por;* 2 *para;* 3 *para;* 4 *para;* 5 *para*

Vocabulario

Page 81

Answers:
1 *fuera*
2 *ganaran*
3 *se dieran*
4 *alucinante*
5 *precoz*

Extra

Planner

Skills focus
♦ Finding ideas and information on the Internet

Resources
♦ Student Book page 82
♦ CD 2, track 8

This page is aimed at A-A* students.

1 Students read the article on leisure and answer the questions.

Answers:
1 *estar con los amigos*
2 *los fines de semana o en las vacaciones de verano*
3 *muy pocos*
4 *los jubilados*

2a Students read the sentences with words underlined and decide which of the strategies they would use to discover their meaning.
Refer back to *Técnica* box on "Dealing with unfamiliar words" in Unit 1 Extra.

2b Students explain the words underlined either in Spanish (using their own words) or they translate them into English.

Answers:
(can also be in Spanish in own words):
Everyone has free time.
It's not just something belonging to young people.
the people who
free time becomes something you do mainly at home
summer
aren't bound by working hours
has a major role again

 3 Students listen and complete the sentences by filling in the names.

---

p. 82, actividad 3

Beto: Para los más intrépidos, un deporte de aventura que ofrece la posibilidad de hacer ejercicio físico en grupo en auténticos parques acuáticos naturales: el descenso de cañones.

Ana Laura: El ocio tiene una importante dimensión lúdica, y el hogar es un buen lugar para desarrollarla. Los juegos de mesa divierten, favorecen la comunicación y agudizan el ingenio.

Margarita: El deporte se perfila como actividad que mejora el estado de salud, a pesar de los múltiples trastornos que provoca. Se ha desarrollado una especialidad médica sólo para las personas que practican deportes.

Sergio: El ocio ayuda a combatir el sedentarismo y a mantenerse en forma. Para ello nada mejor que elegir una actividad física acorde con sus gustos, ya sea el footing, el ciclismo o los bailes de salón, y animarse a practicarla en los ratos libres, pero con la idea de disfrutar, no puede tomarse como una obligación.

Chente: Dicen que el deporte es hacer ejercicio, pero para la mayoría el deporte es una actividad pasiva, la de sentarse delante de la televisión con una botella de cerveza y unas patatas fritas. Por cierto, la mayoría de los anuncios que promocionan el deporte, quieren animarte a comer y a beber de forma muy poco saludable.

Answers:
1 *Ana Laura*
2 *Beto*
3 *Margarita*
4 *Sergio*
5 *Chente*

Técnica

Finding ideas and information on the Internet

Students read the advice on searching the Internet

A Students research details about sport and health in Spain and present them to the rest of the class orally.

As they use the recommended websites, encourage them to work through the points in the *Técnica* box. They should try to choose different aspects of the topic to cover a broad spectrum of ideas.

Remind them about the work they did on oral presentations in Unit 5 page 59.

Unit 7 Assessment offers exam practice for this unit.

Unidad 8   Salud y bienestar

Unit objectives

By the end of this unit students will be able to:
♦ Discuss the health risks of drinking alcohol
♦ Discuss the health risks of tobacco and illegal drugs
♦ Comment on diet and eating disorders
♦ Talk and write about work–life balance

Grammar

By the end of this unit, students will be able to:
♦ Recognise and use the perfect infinitive
♦ Use the subjunctive to express doubt and improbability
♦ Use demonstrative adjectives and pronouns
♦ Use the imperfect continuous tense

Skills

By the end of this unit students will be able to:
♦ Listen for detail
♦ Pinpoint information when reading
♦ Explore and compare differnet points of view

Resources

♦ Student Book page 83

This page introduces the topic.

1a By way of an introduction to the unit, students test their lifetsyle choices regarding diet and exercise.

1b In pairs. Students invent scores for questions 2–6, following the example in 1 a–c. They discuss their answers with a partner. Then they invent an overall scoring system and provide some advice to match.

1c Students read the text and say what advice it offers.

Answer:
Prepare an adequate diet and exercise and mix with a bit of discipline and will power.

El alcohol

Planner

Grammar focus
♦ The perfect infinitive

Skills focus
♦ Listening for detail

Key language

el botellón	"booze up"
el cinturón de seguridad	seatbelt
la madurez	maturity
la mezcla	mixture
las "rondas"	rounds of drinks
la seguridad	safety
advertir	to warn
conducir	to drive
convencer	to convince
evitar	to avoid
incitar	to incite
olvidarse de	to forget
pararse	to stop
promover (ue)	to promote
provocar	to provoke
pasado de moda	out of fashion

Resources

♦ Student Book pages 84 and 85
♦ Vocabulario, Student Book page 93
♦ CD 2, track 9
♦ Hoja 8.2
♦ Grammar Workbook page 66

1a Students read the publicity leaflet *¡Vive!* and identify in which section the four ideas listed are expressed.

Answers:
1 *3rd paragraph;* 2 *1st paragraph;*
3 *2nd paragraph;* 4 *1st and last lines*

1b Then they identify positive and negative imperatives. To refresh their memory, they can revise the *Gramática* box on page 36.

Answers:
positive: *evita, reflexiona, piensa, bebe, olvídate, párate*
negative: *no conduzcas, no te montes, no participes*

1c Students read the sentences and decide which text they belong to: *¡Vive!* or *Vida.*

Answers:
1 *Vida;* 2 *¡Vive!;* 3 *Vida;* 4 *Vida;* 5 *¡Vive!;*
6 *own choice*

1d Students compare the health warning with the advertisement and decide which of the two would have most impact on young people.

1e Students use the *frases clave* and the information from the advertisement *¡Vive!* to criticise the advertisement *Vida*.

Gramática

The perfect infinitive

Remind students how to form the perfect and pluperfect tenses. Then take them through the steps for forming and using the perfect infinitive. Ask them to give further examples of their own to compare the English and Spanish translations: gerund – perfect infinitive.

Refer students to the grammar section of the Student Book, page 168.

A Students translate the sentences into English.

Answers:
1 *Rafa said he had put his seatbelt on.*
2 *If I had known, I would not have got into the car.*
3 *I/He/She should have gone to my house in a taxi.*
4 *Having drunk he should not have driven.*

B Students use the perfect infinitive to translate the sentences into Spanish.

Answers:
1 *Haber bebido tanto fue mala idea.*
2 *Haber conducido a casa fue muy peligroso.*
3 *Al haber llegado a la casa, se acostó.*
4 *Debe haber bebido agua.*

Técnica

Listening for detail

Students read through this advice and add it to the advice already given in Unit 1, page 16.

A Students listen to the passage once for gist.

p. 85, actividades A y C

– Al haberse prohibido en muchas ciudades, el botellón ya no es el fenómeno que era hace unos años. Los padres y los vecinos han podido caracterizar a los jóvenes de borrachos, fuera de control. Miguel, de 15 años, nos explica qué significa "botellón".

– Se junta un grupo de jóvenes, todos ponen dinero, y compran bebidas alcohólicas en una tienda o supermercado. Luego beben las bebidas en la calle y montan una fiesta. Tal vez es porque es muy caro beber en un bar. Muchas veces son jóvenes menores de edad, que no pueden entrar en los bares o discotecas.

– Los jóvenes dicen que no hay alternativas suficientes. Elena, de 16 años, nos ha comentado:

– Querríamos tener un sitio donde reunirnos, algún centro nocturno donde pudiéramos decidir cómo divertirnos con responsabilidad. Las únicas opciones "legítimas" cuestan dinero: ir al cine o a un bar. Las autoridades deberían haber pensado en cómo darnos las instalaciones que necesitamos.

B Students read the options and make sure they understand the vocabulary.

C Students listen again for detail and select the correct option.

Answers:
1 *a*   **2** *b*   **3** *b*   **4** *a*

2 Students write arguments for and against the statement.

H 8.2 *Hoja 8.2 offers additional reading practice for this spread.*

Las adicciones: ¿engancharse o liberarse?

Planner

Grammar focus
♦ The subjunctive: doubt and improbability

Key language

la amenaza	threat
la cocaína	cocaine
el declive	slope
la droga dura	hard drug
los drogadictos	drug addicts
la heroína	heroin
la marihuana	cannabis
el porro	"joint" of cannabis
el subidón	the high given by a drug
el toxicómano	drug addict
actuar	to act
aliviar	to alleviate
castigar	to punish
detener	to detain/arrest
liberarse de	to free oneself from
mantener	to maintain
pincharse	to inject oneself

reivindicar	to demand/claim
soler (ue)	to be used to
tener en cuenta	to take into account/ have in mind
deslizante	slippery
de hecho	in fact

Resources

♦ Student Book pages 86 and 87
♦ Vocabulario, Student Book page 93
♦ CD 2, tracks 10 y 11
♦ Hojas 8.1 CD 4, tracks 22, 23 and 24, 8.4
♦ Grammar Workbook page 53

1a Students read the article and decide who says each of the statements.

Answers:
Irma Sánchez: 2, 4, 7; Iván Gómez: 1, 3, 5, 6

1b, 1c Students decide which aspects they agree with and write them out following the example.

They then write down the conclusions they have come to, starting the sentences with *Creo que ....*

Gramática

Subjunctive of doubt and improbability

Ask students to read the *Gramática* box and then to give examples of their own in English to ensure they have grasped the main subtleties of the usage.

A Students write out sentences to say which sentiments they do not agree with using verbs in the subjunctive and the *frases clave*.

H 8.4 *Hoja 8.4 offers additional practice of the subjunctive.*

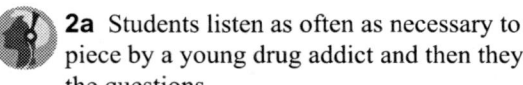

2a Students listen as often as necessary to this piece by a young drug addict and then they answer the questions.

If need be give the transcript to students to work on as a reading comprehension once they have listened to it a few times. They should note down all the vocabulary which has to do with the theme.

---

p. 87, actividad 2a

Confieso que nunca pensé que iba a terminar así. Cuando empecé a fumar a escondidas lo hice para copiar a mis padres y porque en casa había cigarrillos gratis por todos lados. Siempre me decían 'haz como yo digo, no como yo hago' pero ¡qué va! les imité sin problema alguno pensando que así era más sofisticado.

Ya era un poco mayor cuando hace varios años alguien me ofreció un porro y claro pensé que un poco de marihuana o cannabis no me iba a hacer daño. ¡Qué idiota fui! Hay gente que dice que se debe legalizar la marihuana porque es una droga 'suave' que no hace tanto daño como las drogas 'duras' por ejemplo la heroína o la cocaína. Pero no tienen razón porque no comprenden lo que es una adicción. De fumar un porro de vez en cuando es muy fácil pasar a tomar éxtasis, una de las llamadas drogas recreativas, y luego engancharse a la heroína o a cualquier otra droga dura que te dé el subidón que el cuerpo te pide. Así es cómo se empieza a perder el control. Las drogas afectan a tu memoria y fuerza física; deterioran la coordinación de tus movimientos y sentidos hasta que llegas a parecer un zombi.

Hoy, dicen que la adicción al alcohol es la más dañina de todas y es cierto, porque una vez que una persona se ha enganchado, es muy difícil liberarse; necesita a alguien que le ayude. Yo he tenido suerte porque mi mejor amigo de toda la vida nunca me ha abandonado y ahora es mi mentor y guía. Estoy empeñado en liberarme de esta dependencia que me ha llevado al borde de la ruina. Además, aquí en Andalucía donde vivo el estado ofrece bastante ayuda. Existen, por ejemplo, narcosalas supervisadas por médicos.

Answers:
1 *empezó a fumar a escondidas/ alguien le ofreció un porro y claro pensó que un poco de marihuana o canabis no le iba a hacer daño*
2 *como una caída por una pendiente deslizante/ pasarse a tomar extasis, una droga de las llamadas recreativas, y luego engancharse a la heroina o cualquier otra droga dura que te dé el subidón que el cuerpo te pide*
3 *mi mejor amigo de mi vida*
4 *Hay gente que dicen que deben legalizar la marihuana porque es una droga 'suave' que no hace tanto daño como las drogas 'duras' por ejemplo la heroina o la cocaína. Pero no tienen razón porque no comprenden lo que es una adicción.*

2b Class discussion on "The government should legalise 'soft' drugs like marijuana", using the questions listed.

3a Students read the opinions 1–8 about smoking and decide which ones agree with government intervention.

Answers:
3, 7, 8

3b Then they match the statements a–h to the opinions 1–8.

Answers:
a *2* **b** *4* **c** *5* **d** *1* **e** *7* **f** *3* **g** *8* **h** *6*

 4a Students listen to Inma, Pili and Mateo and decide if they are for or against the ban on cigarette smoking in public places.

p. 87, actividad 4a
Inma: Mi abuelo fumaba y murió de un cáncer de pulmón, pero no creo que prohibir el tabaco sea la respuesta. Si todos tenemos la información necesaria, cada uno puede decidir si quiere fumar o no.
Pili: Lo que más me escandaliza es que las compañías inciten a los jóvenes a fumar. Casi nadie empieza a fumar a los veinticinco o treinta años. Y la mayoría de los que fuman quieren dejarlo. Debería ser ilegal, no sólo fumar en lugares públicos sino también el vender cigarrillos a los menores de 30 años.
Mateo: La prohibición sólo hace que fumar sea más atractivo para algunos jóvenes que no quieren conformarse. Lo que deberían prohibir es la publicidad del tabaco en todos los países del mundo.

Answers:
Inma – No; *Pili* – Sí; *Mateo* – No

4b In conversation with each other, students explain their own feelings on the subject.

4c Students write a paragraph giving arguments for and against the banning of smoking in public places.

H 8.1 *Hoja* 8.1 offers additional listening practice for this spread.

Una dieta equilibrada

Planner
Grammar focus
♦ Demonstrative adjectives and pronouns
Skills focus
♦ Pinpointing information
Key language
el aceite de oliva   olive oil
los caprichos   whims
las chucherías   sweets
la grasa   fat
los lácteos   dairy produce
los legumbres   vegetables
el pescado   fish
las verduras   greens
alimentarse   to feed oneself

carecer	to lack
ceder	to give in
gozar de	to enjoy
ponerse de moda	to become fashionable

Resources
♦ Student Book pages 88 and 89
♦ Vocabulario, Student Book page 93
♦ CD 2, track 12
♦ Hoja 8.5
♦ Grammar Workbook page 12

The exercises on page 88 are geared to helping students read the text "Eat to live. Live to eat."

Direct students to page 38 to revise what they have already learnt about reading strategies.

1a Students follow the tasks to help them understand the text.

1b Students find information in the text to complete the chart.

1c Students use the information gathered to answer the question "Is the Spanish diet healthy?"

Técnica

Pinpointing information when reading

Students read the advice and then use the steps to help them understand the text *Comer para vivir. Vivir para comer* about the Mediterranean diet.

H 8.5 *Hoja* 8.5 offers additional practice of pinpointing information when reading.

Gramática

Demonstrative adjectives and pronouns

This consolidates grammar that students will have learnt previously.

Refer students to the grammar section of the Student Book, page 156.

A Students study the text on page 88, *Comer para vivir. Vivir para comer* from which they make a list of the demonstrative adjectives and pronouns, and qualify them.

Answers:
ese *fenómeno = adjective, masculine singular*
éste *es el secreto = pronoun, masculine singular*
este *descubrimiento = adjective, masculine singular*

esta *dieta* = *feminine singular*
estos *dulces* = *(those) adjective, masculine plural*
estas *costumbres* = *adjective, feminine plural*

B Get students to explain the differences in nuances of meaning between the adjectives and pronouns in their list.

Answers:
There are no absolute right/wrong answers. The important thing is to have looked through the text five times. Rather than getting students to write answers down, get them to tell a partner. Give them oral feedback.

2a Students look for synonyms in the text "Los niños quisquillos".

Answers:
la infancia; el rechazo; alimentos; concuerdan; importante; el ambiente

2b Students look for antonyms in the text.

Answers:
antes; el rechazo; el porvenir; cruda; fijos; el riesgo

2c Students read the text and complete the sentences in their own words, but using information from the text.

Answers:
Students' own answers

 3a Students listen to three young people talking about their eating habits.

Students could listen and take notes then discuss the three different attitudes as a whole class or in pairs first before attempting to write their own views on each one.

1 Students write down three points on the diet of each one.
2 They identify whether or not the diet is healthy.
3 Who has the healthiest diet?

---

p. 89, actividad 3a

1 ¡Hola! Me llamo Victoria y comprendo a los que aconsejan llevar una dieta equilibrada pero la verdad es que no soporto las verduras crudas y nunca he probado una ensalada, por más que mis padres insistan. Me gusta estar súper delgada porque la moda insiste en que hay que tener una figura esbelta y a mí me encanta estar a la moda. Como todas las chucherías habidas y por haber; me dan toda la energía que necesito durante el día. Nadie me puede persuadir de lo contrario.

---

2 Buenas tardes – les habla Rigoberto. Me parece que cuando los adultos insisten tanto en que hay que comer tal o cual comida, los jóvenes la van a rechazar porque sí, sobre todo los adolescentes que muchas veces no quieren aceptar los consejos de sus padres. Yo, por ejemplo, como de todo porque mis padres me enseñaron desde chiquito, siempre comíamos en familia y probábamos comidas diferentes todos los días. Nadie me forzó a comer lo que no me gustaba pero cuando veía a los demás comiendo algo nuevo yo quería probarlo también.

3 ¡Vaya! No sé nada sobre qué comida es buena o mala. Lo único que sé es que me gusta comer y siempre tengo hambre. Por suerte no engordo y quemo todas las calorías sobrantes jugando a voleibol todos los días. Creo que si nosotros los jóvenes hacemos suficiente deporte y llevamos una vida feliz, entonces no tendremos problemas con la comida. Como pasta en abundancia, también comida rápida y montones de chucherías pero al mismo tiempo me encanta la fruta y las ensaladas de modo que soy una mezcla de lo bueno y lo malo según el criterio de los especialistas en nutrición; a propósito, me llamo Teresa.

Salud es vida

Planner

Grammar focus
♦ The imperfect continuous

Key language

una cita	appointment
el cuerpo	body
el equilibrio	balance
el éxito	success
el ocio	leisure
el perfil	profile
la sobrecarga	overload
aguantar	to put up with
confundir	to confuse
cuidarse	to look after oneself
darse cuenta	to realise
ignorar	to not pay attention to
prevenir	to prevent
sabroso/a	delicious

Resources
♦ Student Book pages 90 and 91
♦ Vocabulario, Student Book page 93
♦ CD 2, tracks 13 and 14
♦ Hoja 8.3
♦ Grammar Workbook page 43

1a Students read the three texts and decide for which person each category is the most important.

Answers:
1 *Lety;* **2** *Sofía;* **3** *Mariano;* **4** *Sofía;* **5** *Mariano*

 1b Students listen to the recording and decide who is speaking, Lety or Sofía.

> **p. 90, actividad 1b**
>
> 1 El secreto es no exagerar. Es importante no abusar de tu cuerpo, pero tampoco perder la perspectiva de la vida normal. Yo no como mucha carne, pero no soy vegetariana. Hago ejercicio y tengo una dieta muy equilibrada, pero lo más importante es estar a gusto. No tengo filosofía ni doctrina. La vida es para disfrutarla.
>
> 2 Puedes comer bien y estar en forma, pero si no encuentras tu camino, estás perdido. Debes buscar la satisfacción dentro de tu propio ser, no en factores exteriores. Eso me costó muchos años entenderlo.

Answers:
1 – *Lety*   **2** – *Sofía*

1c In pairs, students explain to each other which of the categories in Activity 1a are the most important for them.

H 8.3 *Hoja* 8.3 offers additional reading practice for this page.

1d Ask students to outline the profile of a person who gives no thought to diet, exercise or identity.

2a Students read the text *¿Cómo sacar el máximo provecho a la vida?* and pinpoint ways of saying phrases 1–6 in Spanish.

Answers:
1 *siempre querer tener más*
2 *No olvides la importenía del tiempo libre.*
3 *El secreto es mantener el equilibrio.*
4 *No busques el estres adicional.*
5 *La publicidad nos ofrece cada vez más productos seductores.*
6 *La sobrecarga de trabajo nos quita tiempo.*

2b Point out that the ideas in the phrases 1–4 are mixed up. The task is to correct them.

Answers:
1 *En el trabajo evita una agenda atestada.*
2 *En el tiempo libre evita obsesionarte.*
3 *Durante el dia reserva tiempo para descansar.*
4 *Con la familia aprovecha el tiempo juntos.*

2c Get students to look for examples in the text of how to enjoy life.

Possible answers:
divide el día en tres: dormir, relajar, trabajar;
mantener el equilibrio;
no llenar tu agenda – citas/compromisos sociales/deportes;
decir no al consumismo

3a Students listen to Maritza and complete the chart as indicated.

> **p. 91, actividad 3a**
>
> El despertador suena a las siete. Despierto a mi hija mayor, Ruth, que tiene trece años y se arregla sola para ir al instituto. Más tarde despierto a mi hija pequeña, Nieves, y después de desayunar, vamos caminando al colegio.
>
> No vuelvo a casa, sino que hago las compras para el día.
>
> Llego a casa a las diez y media, y empiezo mis tareas: limpiar, cocinar, lavar, planchar, coser, bricolaje … A veces escucho la radio, pero luego me enfada.
>
> Si viene mi marido a casa, comemos a las dos y media.
>
> Por la tarde, después de recoger la cocina, tengo tiempo para mirar catálogos o hacer compras en Internet.
>
> Luego tengo que recoger a mis hijas y preparar su merienda. Si ven la televisión puedo hacer aerobic. Luego hacen los deberes y yo preparo la cena. A las ocho las niñas se bañan.
>
> Cuando llega mi marido, cenamos, y después recogemos la mesa todos juntos.
>
> Ruth y Nieves se acuestan a las diez, y empieza la parte más tranquila del día. Hablo con mi marido, leo o veo la tele. Luego me acuesto y a medianoche apago la luz y me quedo dormida.

Answers:

Tareas	Actividades	Descanso
14 ticks	5 ticks	6 ticks

3b In pairs, students describe a typical day in their lives including work (*el trabajo*), leisure (*el ocio*), ways of relaxation (*el descanso*) and meals (*la comida*).

Gramática

The imperfect continuous

Students read through the grammar information. Ask them to give examples of their own in English to highlight the similarities with the structure in English

A Students re-read the text on page 90 again and translate all the examples of the imperfect continuous they can find.

Answers:
estaba trabajando (I was working)
estaba viviendo (I was living)
(estaba) durmiendo (I was sleeping)
me estaba poniendo (I was making myself)
Estaba ignorando (I was ignoring)
estaba viviendo (I was living)
Estaba buscando (I was looking for)

B Students rewrite the underlined parts of the sentences 1–3 in the imperfect continuous.

Answers:
1 *Estaba estudiando;*   **2** *Estaba visitando;*
3 *Estaba buscando*

Gramática en acción

Resources

♦ Student Book page 92

Students revise each grammar point and complete the tasks.

Recuerda

The perfect infinitive

Revise the rules for the perfect infinitive

Refer students to page 85.

A Students decide whether the past participle should change or not.

Answers:
1 *no change;* **2** *change to* bebidos; **3** *change to* herida; **4** *no change;* **5** accidentados

B Students write a list of consequences for each picture to tell a story.

Recuerda

The subjunctive for doubt

Use of the subjunctive for expressions of doubt

Refer students to page 86 and to the grammar section of the Student Book p 170.

C Students complete the sentences putting the verbs into the subjunctive.

Answers:
1 *sean;* **2** *deba;* **3** *contribuya;* **4** *tenga;* **5** *esté*

D Students give their own opinions remembering to change the verb into the subjunctive mood if using a phrase of doubt or improbability.

Recuerda

The imperfect continuous

Remind students they can use *estaba* + present participle to make the continuous form of the imperfect.

Refer students to the grammar section of the Student Book, page 167, and to the Grammar Workbook, page 43.

E Tell students to imagine they have had an accident. They must explain to the doctor what they were doing and what happened to them.

Vocabulario

Page 93

Answers:
1 *ayude*
2 *reconozcan*
3 *haberse bebido*
4 *esto*
5 *aquellas*

Extra

Planner

Skills focus
♦ Student Book page 94

Resources
♦ Student Book page 94
♦ Vocabulario, Student Book page 93
♦ CD 2, track 15

This page is aimed at A-A* students.

1a Students read the text about the death of two models and look for words in the text under the headings of fashion, health or death.

Answers:
Moda
una modelo; un desfile; una pasarela; una diseñadora; delgada; el modelaje; la flacura

Salud
la masa corporal; delgada; la flacura; la anorexia;
la mala alimentación; un ataque cardiaco

Muerte
fallecer; sin vida; morir; muerte; desaparición

1b Students consider how they would translate the words listed in the context of the article: a basic meaning in English is given, but is it the best word for the context?

Suggested answers:
as recently as
a few
combined
of international <u>standing</u>
competition
over step the <u>mark</u>
said
ruled

1c Students read the article again and identify the errors in statements 1–4. They then correct the statements.

Answers:
1 *Una hermana murió en la casa de su abuela, la otra se había muerto cuando acababa de participar en un desfile.*
2 *Otra gente dijo que era anoréxica.*
3 *Muchas modelos parecen sufrir el mal de la anorexia.*
4 *Han tomado una medida para proteger a las modelos: prohibir que participen en las pasarelas si no alcancen una masa corporal mínima.*

 2a Students listen to Jimena, Javier and Diana and take notes on their points of view.

> **p. 94, actividad 2a**
>
> **Jimena:** Ha muerto otra modelo, ¡qué tragedia! Se llama Eliana, la hermana menor de Luisel Ramos que murió el año pasado. ¿Cómo puede ser que no hayamos aprendido nada de esa primera tragedia? Si cuando murió, Luisel pesaba apenas 44 kilos y llevaba varios días sin comer nada y tres meses con una dieta a base de lechuga y coca light! Como modelo, estaba obsesionada con la línea y el peso. Y ahora también ha muerto su hermana ha. Tenemos que hacer algo.
>
> **Javier:** Pues, precisamente, la muerte de su hermana nos indica que no se trata de anorexia, sino de otra condición médica que las dos padecían sin saberlo. Murieron de un ataque cardiaco. Las dos hermanas tenían una predisposición congénita y por eso murieron, no por ser modelos.

> **Diana:** Yo digo que sí murieron de anorexia, que provocó un estado de debilidad tan grave que causó un ataque cardiaco. Pero comparto que no tiene nada que ver con el hecho de ser modelo. Para ser modelo, hay que estar delgado, pero también hay que tener un aspecto saludable. No creo que las imágenes de las revistas de moda sean las que causen la anorexia. Es una enfermedad mental, vinculada a la depresión, no un simple deseo de verse mejor.

2b Class discussion. Students explain the three points of view and then discuss which of the three is right.

Técnica

Exploring and comparing different points of view (1)

This section builds on skills introduced on page 32 of the Student Book.

Revise those tips and then take students through the different methods of comparing and contratsing points of view.

You could develop this by asking them to provide outline/heading plans in English for comparing or contrasting topics discussed in this unit, first using one method; then another.

A Students investigate the deaths of Luisel and Eliana. They write a report of 200–250 words and should compare the different circumstances and the different views of the causes of the deaths.

Unit 8 Assessment offers exam practice for this unit.

Unidad 9   Vacaciones

Unit objectives

By the end of this unit students will be able to:
- Discuss different types of holiday and holiday activities
- Comment on the impact of tourism on holiday destinations
- Give opinions on the purposes and benefits of holidays
- Comment on changing attitudes to holidays

Grammar

By the end of this unit students will be able to:
- Use cardinal numbers
- Use continuous (or progressive) tenses
- Use constructions with *si*
- Use impersonal verbs in reflexive expressions

Skills

By the end of this unit students will be able to:
- Write a formal letter
- Organise ideas and facts in order to plan a piece of written work
- Explore and compare different points of view

Resources

- Student Book page 95
- Vocabulario, Student Book page 105
- CD 2, track 16

This page introduces the topic.

1a Students list Spanish-speaking countries and mention any tourist attractions they know there.

Answers:
Bolívia, Perú, Paraguay, Chile, Argentina, Puerto Rico, Costa Rica, Panamá, Colombia, Cuba, Ecuador, República Dominicana, El Salvador, México, Guatemala, Nicaragua, Honduras, Uruguay, Venezuela

1b Students may already know one or two of the destinations and may be able to work out others using common sense. For example, El Salar de Uyuni – salt, white colour. They then complete and check their answers with listening activity 2a.

 2a Students listen to the travel agent to complete and check their answers to Activity 1b.

Answers:
1 *B: Bolivia* 2 *C: México* 3 *D: Chile* 4 *A: Perú*

---

p. 95, actividades 2a y 2b

A Bueno, ¿qué les recomendaría que visitaran en América Latina? Pues, Perú es un destino muy popular porque lo tiene todo: cultura, selva amazónica y, por supuesto, el Machu Picchu y la Ciudad Perdida. Machu Picchu es probablemente el símbolo más conocido del imperio inca y es la atracción turística más visitada y la que genera más ingresos en el país.

B También recomiendo una visita a Bolivia que, aunque tiene muchos parecidos con Perú por su cercanía, tiene lugares únicos y fascinantes como, por ejemplo, el Salar de Uyuni: en la distancia parece nieve, pero es la llanura de sal más grande del mundo. Se extiende 10.582 km2, si no me equivoco, y se puede visitar en coches 4x4, pero se debe ir siempre acompañado por un guía para no perderse. Los turistas más aventureros se alojan en alguno de los hoteles de sal, que son fascinantes porque tanto el edificio como el mobiliario están totalmente construidos de sal.

C Claro, que si buscan unas vacaciones más convencionales un destino muy popular es México donde, aparte de las zonas costeras, se pueden visitar algunos lugares de interés histórico como las ruinas de las pirámides de Chichén Itzá que fueron construidas por la civilización maya y atraen muchísimos turistas que visitan Latinoamérica.

D Hmmm … ¿Algo más relajante y tranquilo? Hmmmm … Déjenme pensar … Si buscan una combinación de relax y herencia histórica … Sí, ¡por supuesto! La chilena Isla de Pascua, en el Océano Pacífico. ¿Han oído hablar de los Moais? ¿No? Bueno, los Moais son más de 600 estatuas gigantes de piedra monolítica que se encuentran distribuidas por toda la Isla de Pascua. Su significado es incierto y hay muchas teorías sobre su origen.

 2b Students listen to the recording again and then answer the questions.

Answers:
1 *Porque es la atracción turística que genera más ingresos.*
2 *Están completamente construidos de sal.*
3 *Los maya* 4 *el océano Pacífico* 5 *600*

Cada cual con su tema

Planner

Grammar focus

♦ Cardinal numbers

Skills focus

♦ Different registers of language

Key language

los aseos	toilets
el barranquismo	canyoning
las cordilleras	mountain ranges
el desagrado	displeasure
la escalada	rockclimbing
el legado	legacy
la pista	pathway/piste
el riesgo	risk
alojarse	to stay in a hotel
deslumbrar	to dazzle
saborear	to taste
alucinantes	fantastic/amazing
borracho/a	drunk
idóneo/a	ideal

Resources

♦ Student Book pages 96 and 97
♦ Vocabulario, Student Book page 105
♦ CD 2, tracks 17, 18 and 19
♦ Hoja 9.3

1a Students read the advert on page 96, and make a list of the activities that are mentioned in it.

1b Oral work. Students then practise speaking by choosing a destination mentioned that they would be interested in visiting. They must also practise the ways of expressing opinions in the *frases clave*.

1c Students team up in pairs and interview their partner about his/her own preferences. Encourage them to use the vocabulary from the *frases clave* in their questions.

 1d Students listen to the tourists speaking, and work out what part of the country they have been visiting according to the advertisement *¡Ven a España!*

Answers:
1 Asturias **2** Alicante **3** Islas Canarias **4** Galicia

---

p. 96, actividad 1d

1 Bueno, en mi opinión la relación calidad–precio es excelente. El hotel era un poco caro pero había gran variedad de tratamientos de belleza para escoger y los masajistas tenían mucha experiencia y eran muy agradables.

Es un placer alojarse allí y descansar de los estreses de la vida cotidiana.

2 ¡Fué fantástico! ¡No os podéis creer la variedad de actividades alucinantes que había! Lo más increíble fue el descenso a los barrancos. ¡Cómo mola, tío!

3 Les llamo para expresar mi desagrado en relación con mi reciente estancia en su hotel. Cuando hice la reserva se me aseguró que el hotel estaba muy bien situado en un lugar idóneo para dejar que los niños se bañasen sin peligro. La realidad es que la cercanía del club náutico suponía un riesgo constante.

4 Pasar las vacaciones borracho, yendo de una discoteca a otra me parece una vergüenza. Yo he utilizado mis vacaciones para relajarme y admirar la belleza natural del país. Debemos aprender a apreciar y proteger los recursos naturales.

Técnica

A Students describe what they think of the advertisement *¡Ven a España!* taking into account the information given in the *Técnica* box.

B Students go on to discuss how different kinds of publicity attract the attention of different kinds of people.

C Students choose the adjectives that they feel best describe the advertisement. Encourage them to choose carefully and be able to justify their answers.

 D They listen to the tourists again and describe the kind of language they use.

 2a Students listen to the programme on Peru and note down the required information.

---

p. 97, actividad 2a

Perú, oficialmente conocido como la República de Perú, está en el oeste de Sudamérica. Es un país de contrastes, tiene regiones de selva, costa y las cordilleras montañosas de los Andes. En el norte, comparte sus fronteras con Ecuador y Colombia y en el sur tiene frontera con Chile. Los 2.414 kms de costa peruana es bañada por el Océano Pacífico, mientras que al este se encuentran Bolivia y Brasil. En total este sorprendente país se extiende 1.285.220 km², unas dos terceras partes de la extensión total de México, lo que lo coloca en el lugar número veinte del ránking mundial de países según su extensión.
Su sistema gubernamental es la república constitucional, donde los ciudadanos eligen al presidente y éste selecciona al primer ministro para que le apoye en su tarea.

> Indios americanos habitaron las tierras de Perú durante milenios, pero hoy en día sus más de 28 millones de habitantes son de etnias y orígenes muy variados, el resultado de los cinco siglos de historia que comenzaron con la conquista española en el siglo XVI.
>
> El español es la lengua más hablada y la lengua materna de la mayoría de los jóvenes, pero coexiste con multitud de idiomas indígenas, el más importante de los cuales es el quechua, que es hablado por un 16% de la población.
>
> La capital de Perú es Lima, que es la ciudad con mayor densidad de población del país, en la que se concentran unos ocho millones de ciudadanos. Otras ciudades importantes son Arequipa, Trujillo, Chiclayo y Cuzco.
>
> La economía del país es moderada, con ingresos per cápita de poco más de 280 dólares al mes, y aunque industrias como la pesca, la agricultura, la minería y los textiles crean empleo, todavía se considera que más del 50% de la población vive en la pobreza. Perú tiene moneda propia, el Nuevo Sol.
>
> Perú es sin duda un país de contrastes, y la carencia de medios económicos coincide con la riqueza de su cultura en la que las celebraciones y tradiciones indígenas se unen a las de la religión católica que domina un país rico en música, danzas, artesanía y gastronomía popular, ingredientes de un folklore únicamente exquisito y abundante.

Answers:
Gobierno: república constitucional
Superficie y comparación: 1.285.220 km2, # 2/3 de México, 20. país más grande del mundo
Población y habitantes: variada, 28 millones
Capital y ciudades importantes: Lima (capital), Arequipa, Trujillo, Chiclayo y Cuzco
Industria: pesca, agricultura, minería y textiles
Cultura: celebraciones y tradiciones indígenas, religión católica, música, danzas, artesanía y gastronomía popular
Otro: Idiomas: español y quechua.
Moneda: Nuevo Sol

2b Students revise the *Técnica* section and listen again if necessary to decide what kind of language is used in the report. A variety of answers may be acceptable providing that they can justify their answer. The more appropriate answers would include *serio*, *formal* and *objetivo*.

Gramática

Cardinal numbers

Remind students that they have already met cardinal numbers on page 11 of the Student Book and information on numbers is gathered on page 173 of the grammar section of the Student Book. This

might be a good moment to point out that there is a Contents list at the begiining of the grammar section, which they can use to find their way to information they need.

Take students through the new material on cardinal numbers in the *Gramática* box.

 A Students listen to the programme on Peru again and note down the information required.

Answers:
1 **Coastline:** *2.414 kms (dos mil cuatrocientos y catorce kms)*
2 **Surface area:** *1.285.220 km2 (un millon, doscientos ochenta y cinco mil, doscientos veinte km2)*
3 **Inhabitants:** *más de 28 millones de habitantes*
4 **Invaded by Spain:** *en el siglo XVI (en el siglo dieciséis)*
5 **Percentage of Quechua speakers:** *16% de la población (dieciséis por ciento)*
6 **Population of capital**: *unos ocho millones de ciudadanos*

---

3 Students study the advertisement and answer the questions orally.

1 *un hotel ecológico*
2 *no hay aire acondicionada; agua reusada; energía soler; comida biológicos; bicicletas*
Answers to the last three questions should be students' own

 4 Students listen to the recording on tourism and the environment and answer the questions in English.

> **p. 97, actividad 4**
>
> ¿El turismo es siempre enemigo del medio ambiente? Pues no, cuando permite a la vez que los visitantes aprecien la naturaleza y que la población local la pueda explotar sin tener que destrozarla. Si el medio ambiente es lo que les proporciona el trabajo, los trabajadores querrán protegerlo.
>
> En Costa Rica está el hotel Punta Islita, único en el mundo. El interés de los turistas hace que el hotel pueda contar con un equipo de biólogos que estudian y protegen las especies en peligro de extinción, como las tortugas que van a la zona a poner sus huevos o las aves tropicales.
>
> No creas que tienes que ser hippie para disfrutarlo: es un hotel de lujo, con un spa completísimo, suites y mini-villas, todo construido con materiales naturales al estilo autóctono.

Answers:
Answers should contain:
1 *When tourists don't abuse it.*
2 *It is for biologists who want to study rare species.*
3 *turtles and birds*
4 *It is a luxury hotel.*
5 *It is built out of natural local materials.*

5 Research and writing, using different registers of language. In this activity, students must do their own research on a Latin American destination of their choice to produce a factual article. Then they need to adapt the facts and the language to produce an advertisement with the objective of attracting tourists to their destination.

H 9.3 *Hoja* 9.3 offers additional reading practice for this spread.

¿El turismo: beneficio o maleficio?

Planner

Grammar focus
♦ Continuous (or progressive) tenses

Skills focus
♦ How to write formal letters

Key language

el costo de la vida	cost of living
la degradación	degradation/spoiling
las instalaciones	facilities
la pérdida	loss
el retraso	delay
aportar	to bring
aumentar	to increase/augment
disculparse	to excuse oneself
incrementar	to increase
lamentar	to be sorry
mejorar	to make better/improve
quebrantar	to break an agreement
ambiental	environmental
asimismo	also

Resources
♦ Student Book pages 98 and 99
♦ Vocabulario, Student Book page 105
♦ CD 2, tracks 20 and 21
♦ Hojas 9.1 CD 4, tracks 25 and 26, 9.2, 9.5
♦ Grammar Workbook page 32

1a Students read the 10 effects of tourism given and decide if they are positive or negative.

Answers:
Positive: *1, 3, 4, 6, 8*
Negative: *2, 5, 7, 9, 10*

1b Work in pairs. Following on from Activity 1a, students try to think of any other effects of tourism to discuss and make a list.

 2a Students listen to Ramón and decide what is his overall opinion of tourism.

> **p. 98, actividades 2a y 2b**
>
> El turismo tiene un lugar importantísimo en mi vida, pues llevo trabajando tres veranos en un cámping, lo que me ha permitido continuar mis estudios.
>
> Además, me está ayudando muchísimo con el inglés. Hablo todos los días con los visitantes y hablar inglés es una ventaja en el mundo laboral.
>
> Personalmente, trabajar en la industria del turismo también me está animando a viajar. No pienso pasarme la vida aquí, pero para viajar tengo que estudiar, aprender más idiomas y conseguir un buen trabajo.
>
> A mi edad, mi abuelo estaba trabajando todo el día en el campo pero yo puedo combinar mi trabajo con los estudios.
>
> Con el dinero que está generando el turismo, se están mejorando el transporte, los restaurantes, los centros recreativos y el patrimonio cultural e histórico de la zona.

Answer:
Positive

 2b Students listen to the recording again and work out which points are <u>not</u> mentioned.

Answer:
4 and 6

 3a Students listen to Jessica's presentation and again decide if her opinion of tourism is positive or negative.

Answer:
Negative

> **p. 98, actividades 3a y 3b**
>
> Mi presentación: El turismo en España.
>
> El turismo en España tiene muchos aspectos que tenemos que considerar. Tal vez el más obvio sea el desarrollo económico. España ocupa el segundo lugar mundial en ingresos

procedentes del turismo, alcanzando los €40 billones anuales. El único inconveniente es que otros sectores de la economía no han tenido el mismo éxito. El turismo ha afectado al medio ambiente. Imagínate una isla como Menorca donde viven cien mil habitantes, pero que recibe cada verano seis millones de visitantes. No llega el agua, no hay donde tirar la basura. El litoral se llena de hoteles. Afortunadamente, el turismo masivo se limita a la costa.

Con la construcción de hoteles, los precios de los terrenos y de las casas se vuelven desorbitados. Los jóvenes que encuentran trabajo en los centros turísticos tienen grandes dificultades en encontrar vivienda.

El comportamiento de los extranjeros no siempre responde a las expectativas de los españoles, pero su influencia se siente en los cambios sociales que se han experimentado recientemente. El horario de las comidas, la dieta, el alcohol, la libertad sexual, todos han ido contagiando las costumbres tradicionales.

Los turistas tratan España no como un país donde viven 40 millones de personas con una historia, una cultura y un estilo de vida, sino como un lugar geográfico con sol y playas. No debemos permitir que España se reduzca a un parque temático artificial.

 3b Students listen again and make a list of points mentioned by Jessica.

Answers:
Some examples may include:
Desarrollo económico
Efecto nocivo en el medio ambiente
Turismo masivo en la costa
Incremento de los precios de la vivienda
Cambios del comportamiento social
Percepción geográfica – no humana – del país

Gramática

Continuous (or progressive) tenses

Students read the notes on the formation and uses of the tenses. They have already seen the present continuous and the imperfect continuous. They are introduced to the preterite continuous and the future continuous here.

Refer students to the grammar section of the Student Book, pages 165 (continuous present) and 167 (continuous imperfect).

 A Students listen to Ramón again and note down the continuous tenses he uses.

Answers:
me está ayudando; me está animando; estaba trabajando; está generando; se están mejorando

---

Técnica

How to write formal letters

Students read the eight points and look for examples in the letter opposite.

H 9.5 *Hoja* 9.5 offers additional practice of writing formal letters.

4a Students read the letter and find as many instances of continuous tenses as they can. There are six examples.

estamos viviendo; estaríemos disfrutando; están perdiendo; está enfureciendo; estaremos sufiendo; está construyendo

4b Students translate the letter with the use of a dictionary if needed. Although word by word (literal) translation should not be encouraged, the translation must carry the same level of formality as the original.

4c Students now reply to the letter. Encourage different levels of detail depending on the ability of the students. But again, it must be a formal letter.

H 9.1-2 *Hojas* 9.1 and 9.2 offer additional listening and speaking practice for this spread

¡Merecidas vacaciones!

Planner	
Grammar focus	
♦ Constructions using *si*	
Key language	
el barro	mud
la cima	peak/top
una encuesta	survey/poll
el entretenimiento	entertainment
la juerga	partying/spree
la leña	firewood
el reino	reign
el relajamiento	relaxation
abordar	to tackle
adelgazar	to lose weight
anhelar	to wish for/desire
curiosear	to rummage
distraerse	to distract/enjoy oneself
perfeccionar	to perfect

realizar un sueño	to realise a dream/make it come true
reflejar	to reflect/think/ponder
renovar	to renew
rumbear	to go out on the town
agitado/a	busy/agitated
desconocido/a	unknown
estresante	stressful
mareado/a	dizzy
previo/a	previous
refrescante	refreshing

Resources

♦ Student Book pages 100 and 101
♦ Vocabulario, Student Book page 105
♦ CD 2, track 22
♦ Grammar Workbook page 58

1a Students listen to the interview and fill in the grid. Ask students to copy the grid into their books and leave eight rows in the grid to complete the task. They could be allowed to provide the information required in English.

p. 100, actividad 1a

Estamos haciendo una encuesta sobre las vacaciones y si no le molesta a usted quisiera preguntarle por qué va de vacaciones y qué beneficios cree que le aportan.

1 Bueno pues, yo busco un lugar tranquilo donde no haya nada que hacer. Necesito dormir mucho porque llevo una vida muy estresante. Tranquilidad y sueño es todo lo que necesito para reponerme.

2 Nosotros vamos a Disneylandia para divertirnos. Las vacaciones son para divertirse nada más. Eso nos distrae y nos aporta cantidad de beneficios como por ejemplo, no tener que ir al cole.

3 Para mí lo mejor de las vacaciones es ir a lugares desconocidos. Me encanta conocer países nuevos. Quiero viajar y satisfacer mi curiosidad. Así me distraigo y me relajo.

4 Estoy de acuerdo; relajarse es lo más importante; olvidarse del trabajo, estar entre amigos y hacer nuevas amistades. Eso es lo más importante para mí; me tranquiliza y me hace feliz.

5 Para mí lo importante es estar con la familia. Con la vida tan agitada que llevo nunca tengo suficiente tiempo para dedicarme por completo a mis hijos y cuando estoy de vacaciones es lo único que hago. Es la mejor terapia.

6 Lo que yo prefiero son unas vacaciones en las que pueda practicar algún deporte porque mi trabajo consiste en estar sentada delante de una pantalla todo el día. Necesito actividad para ponerme en forma. También tengo que comer bien porque en el trabajo solo como comida basura.

7 En cambio yo busco silencio y serenidad para poder reflexionar y encontrar mi verdadera persona interior. Hago yoga y meditación y trato de desintoxicarme en la naturaleza.

8 Sol, mar o montañas, es todo lo que necesito para mis vacaciones. Duermo en la playa durante todo el día y de noche salgo a bailar en las discos y los bares. Una juerga total para alegrar mi vida y después, cuando estoy de regreso en la ciudad, vuelvo a ser una seria abogada.

Answers:
1 *buscar tranquilidad // reponerse*
2 *divertirse, distraerse // no tener que ir al cole*
3 *ir a un lugar desconocido/ver algo distinto // distraerse y relajarse*
4 *olvidarse del trabajo/estar entre amigos/renovar amistades // tranquilizarse/hacerse feliz*
5 *estar con la familia/dedicarse a sus hijos // tónica*
6 *buscar actividades deportivas // ponerse en forma*
7 *buscar silencio/hacer yoga/encontrar su persona interior // desintoxicarse*
8 *dormir en la playa/rumbear/juerga // alegrar su vida seria de abogada*

2 Students read the list of holiday requests (1–8) and match them to the ideas offered (A–H).

Answers:
1 = C; 2 = A ; 3 = D ; 4 = G ; 5 = E ; 6 = H ; 7 = B; 8 = F

Gramática

Constructions using si

Introduce students to the different uses of *si* and the tenses of verbs used in each case. This revises what they have learnt about the use of the subjunctive to express doubt in Unit 8.

A Students read the sentences and by referring to the explanations in the *Gramática* box, decide why certain tenses have been used.

Answers:
1 *The subjunctive is used because it refers to an unlikely situation (to be famous)*
2 *The imperfect indicative is used because the si clause expresses the idea of 'whenever', in the past.*
3 *The conditional is used because it is impossible, or doubtful, that the action referred to can take place.*

B Students decide what would be the most appropriate tense to complete the sentence in each case.

Answers:
1 *puedes*; 2 *hubieras llegado*; 3 *hubiese resultado*

C Students use the sentences in the advert on page 96 in conjunction with the explanations in the *Gramática* box to write their own sentences using the *si* structure.

3a Students read the blog and answer the questions.

Answers:
Students' own answers but should mention:-
1 *realizar un sueño*; 2 *respuesta a deseos/ arquitectura/gastronomía/cursos de lenguas/ excursiones*; 3 *se mareó/altitud/nunca pensó que tomaría coca/aprendió una lección moral;*
4 *simplicidad de vida/panales solares/tecnología;*
5 *ganó más de lo que dio;* 6 *ha aprendido mucho/ ha abierto los ojos/ha visto mucho/ha relajado/ ;*
7 *pobre/superabundadnte y lujosa;* 8 *unas palabras quechua;* 9 *mantenerse en contacto;* 10 *students' own words should mention destrucción de su manera de vivir/cambiar sus ideas de la vida/hacerles desear otras cosas en la vida.*

3b Students write about 150 words giving their opinions on tourism, in response to the blog. They justify their points of view.

Un mundo más pequeño

Planner

Grammar focus
♦ Impersonal verbs – reflexive expressions

Skills focus
♦ Writing skills – organising ideas and facts for a structured response

Key language

el éxito	success
la fiabilidad	reliability
la romería	procession (religious)
el trajín	hustle and bustle/hectic
la viabilidad	viability
aterrizar	to land
conformarse con	to be content with
darse el lujo	to afford
despegar	to take off
gozar	to enjoy
remontarse	to date from
sobrepasar	to exceed
superar	to exceed
ajeno/a	alien
adinerado/a	wealthy
asequible	affordable
a diferencia de	in comparison with

cada vez más	more and more
de antemano	beforehand

Resources
♦ Student Book pages 102 and 103
♦ Vocabulario, Student Book page 105
♦ CD 2, track 23
♦ Grammar Workbook page 63

1a Students read the article and note the advantages and disadvantages of the budget airlines.

1b In pairs, students discuss their views of budget airlines, using the topics listed as a guide.

1c Students use the context of the article to find the words and expressions required.

Answers:
1 *aerolínea;* 2 *aeronaves;* 3 *hoy en día;* 4 *sobrepasa;*
5 *de bajo coste;* 6 *éxito;* 7 *despegó;* 8 *asequibles;*
9 *principales;* 10 *puntuales*

Gramática

Impersonal verbs – reflexive expressions

Students consolidate what they have already learnt about the avoidance of the passive (page 34) and impersonal verbs (page 15) and the personal *a* (page 66).

Refer students to the grammar section of the Student Book, page 172, and to the Grammar Workbook, page 63.

A Students read the article in Activity 1 again and focus on trying to spot the impersonal verbs used.

Answers:
se valora (twice); se pusieron; se vendieron; se realiza; se vuela

B Students make up some sentences of their own using the impersonal expressions given.

 2a Students listen to the people talking about changing attitudes to holidays and make notes.

They fill in the table: on the left the speakers are indentified by their initials. Explain that the initial E refers to "Entrevistadora".
Students may answer in English if preferred.

---

p. 103, actividades 2a y 2b

Entrevistadora

Bienvenidos amigos oyentes a nuestro programa de radio : La Tertulia de la tarde. Hoy vamos a oír opiniones sobre los cambios de actitud de la gente hacia las vacaciones. ¿A ver quién llama?

1 Pues me llamo María Morales y le digo que desde mi infancia he visto enormes cambios en las actitudes hacia las vacaciones. Lo primero de todo he de decir que yo nunca tuve vacaciones; no había dinero para tal extravagancia; no teníamos coche para viajar tampoco y, ni hablar de trenes y aviones, de modo que todos nos conformábamos con quedarnos en el pueblo e ir a la romería de vez en cuando. Hoy todo el mundo va de vacaciones si quiere y puede darse ese lujo. Me parece maravilloso.

Entrevistadora

Gracias por su opinión. ¿Y ahora con quién hablamos?

2 Soy Luís Rubio y entiendo que hace siglos sólo la gente rica y adinerada podía darse el lujo de tomar vacaciones. Estas personas hacían grandes excursiones culturales por Italia o América Latina o se iban a pasar un largo verano a la casa de campo donde podían tomar aire fresco y alejarse del aire contaminado de la ciudad. Ahora mucha gente se toma varias vacaciones al año y la facilidad de buscar destinos interesantes por Internet y conocer la cultura que se va a visitar de antemano, ayuda enormemente a planear el viaje y a gozarlo. ¡Además, ahora lo puedes hacer todo tú solo sin tener que pagar a una agencia de viajes! ¡Me parece fenomenal!

Entrevistadora

De acuerdo, Internet ha cambiado nuestras vidas y actitudes bastante. ¿Bueno y la siguiente persona quién es?

3 Me llamo Victoria González y yo me acuerdo de la primera vez que me monté en avión. ¡Qué nervios tenía! Pero hoy en día todo el mundo se monta en avión, ¡hasta para dar un paseo por el barrio!. Claro la facilidad para viajar hoy en día no se puede comparar con la de antaño, y cada vez hay más gente que se toma largos fines de semana para conocer otras ciudades o simplemente para descansar haciendo senderismo en el campo. Hay tanta variedad de actividades y experiencias hoy que cualquiera puede gozarlas cómo y cuándo quiera. Es impresionante.

Entrevistadora

Gracias; sí la variedad es importante. ¿A ver, el próxima en contribuir a la discusión es ...?

4 Me llamo Alejandro Villegas y soy estudiante. Para mí el cambio más interesante es que la gente joven tiene mucha más libertad para viajar y conocer lugares nuevos que en el pasado. Son intrépidos y tienen un sentido de la aventura que les lleva a cualquier país y a conocer culturas diferentes. Tienen una mente internacional y aceptan más fácilmente las costumbres ajenas. En fin, creo que el turismo universal de hoy ha ayudado mucho a cambiar la insularidad de la gente tanto en su propio país como en el mundo entero. Nosotros los españoles ahora salimos de viaje por todas las regiones cuando antes nunca salíamos de nuestro pueblo natal.

Entrevistadora

De acuerdo; y otra cosa que no ha mencionado nadie es que hoy en día todos tenemos derecho por ley a unas vacaciones pagadas. Además, la necesidad de descansar del trajín laboral diario ha sido aceptada y aprobada, y eso me parece hasta ahora, lo más importante de todo. Gracias a todos por sus contribuciones . . .

Answers should include reference to:-

Quién habla	Cambios	Opinión
MM	no tenían vacaciones /enormes/cualquier puede viajar	maravilloso
LR	solo los adinerados/ internet/investigar de antemano/sin agencia	fenomenal
VG	volar facilmente/fin de semana/variedad	impresionante
AV	jóvenes más libertad/mentalidad internacional	interesante
E	legalización/ descanso aceptado	lo más importante

 2b Students listen again and make notes using initials to identify who mentions items 1–10.

Answers:
1 E = *Interviewer/entrevistadora;* **2** LR = *Luís Rubio;* **3** VG y AV = *Victoria González y Alejandro Villegas* **4** MM = *María Morales;* **5** AV = *Alejandro Villegas ;* **6** VG = *Victoria González ;* **7** LR= *Luís Rubio ;* **8** LR = *Luís Rubio*

2c Discuss the ideas with a partner and add your own ideas.

Técnica

Writing skills – organising ideas and facts for a structured response.

Students read through the *Técnica* box and complete the tasks A–E following the instructions and guidance given.

A Here is a suggested plan for 1a:

*Introduction explaining low cost air travel/
excessive travel
Advantages of budget airlines: personal/social
with justifications
Disadvantages of budget airlines: personal/social
with justifications
Alternatives/feasibility of alternatives
Personal experiences or hypothetical situation
Point of view supported and why
Conclusion/closing statement*

Gramática en acción

Planner

Resources

♦ Student Book page 104
♦ CD 2, track 24
♦ Hoja 9.4

Recuerda

Continuous tenses

Students consolidate their knowledge of continuous tenses. Refer students to page 98.

 A Students listen to the recording while looking at the illustration. Then they note down which statements made by Elisenda are not true according to the illustration.

---

p. 104, actividad A

– Elisenda, ¿has ido a la playa hoy?

– Sí, sí he ido. Estaba llenísima, gente por todas partes, ¡un agobio!

– ¿Algo interesante?

– No, lo de siempre, la verdad: un niño estaba construyendo un castillo de arena, un par de chicas estaban haciendo footing y un bebé estuvo llorando porque se le había caído el chupete y la mamá ... ¡ni caso!

– ¿Estaba la pandilla?

– Sí, estaban jugando al voleibol: chicos contra chicas.

– ¿Y quién ganó?

– No sé. ¡Ah! Y una chiquilla adolescente llena de pecas se estaba embadurnando de crema, parecía que se la regalasen.

– Bueno, lo de siempre, ¿no?

– ¡Ah sí! ¡Qué fuerte! Cuando me iba, un hombre estaba entrando en el agua totalmente desnudo, ¡tal y como vino al mundo!

Answers:
Un niño estaba construyendo un castillo de arena.
Dos chicas estaban haciendo footing.
Chicos contra chicas estaban jugando al voleibol.

B Students correct the false statements according to the illustration.

Answers:
Una niña estaba construyendo un castillo de arena.
Un hombre estaba haciendo footing.
Unos chicos (o dos equipos mixtos) estaban jugando al voleibol.

C Work in pairs. Students describe what everyone else in the scene is doing using the imperfect continuous.

H 9.4 *Hoja* 9.4 offers additional practice of continiuos tenses.

Recuerda

Position of pronouns

Refer students to the grammar section of the Student Book, page 162 and to page 98 for pronouns with gerunds.

D Students practise the use of the continuous tenses and object pronouns by re-writing the sentences following the example.

Answers:
1 *Rita lo está limpiando. Rita está limpiándolo.*
2 *María se lo estaba lavando. María estaba lavándoselo.*
3 *Las estábamos viendo. Estábamos viéndolas.*
4 *Las chicas las están haciendo. Las chicas están haciéndolas.*
5 *Me lo estoy poniendo. Estoy poniéndomelo.*
6 *Nos los estarás diciendo. Estarás diciéndonolos.*

Recuerda

Constructions with si

Students consolidate their knowledge of the sequence of tenses in clauses with *si*.

E Students complete the sentences with the conjugated form of the verb in brackets.

Answers:
1 *fuera/gustaría;* 2 *pueden/quédense;*
3 *pasábamos/tomábamos;* 4 *quisiera/conocería;*
5 *hubieses visitado/hubieses probado*

Vocabulario

Page 105

Answers:
1 *dormía*
2 *planeé*
3 *pudiera*
4 *asequible*
5 *estresantes*

Extra

Planner

Skills focus

Exploring and comparing different points of
view (2)

Resources

♦ Student Book page 106
♦ CD 2, track 25

This page aimed at A-A* students.

1a Students find words in the text to match the
words and phrases listed.

Answers:
1 *campesinos;* 2 *artesanías;* 3 *gastronomía;* 4 *a su
alcance;* 5 *cuencas;* 6 *senderismo*

1b Students read the article and make a count of
positive and negative points. Note they are not
writing down the points, just keeping a tally at this
point. Students will have different tallies depending
on their own understanding and interpretation at
this initial stage, but they should find the article has
many more positives than negatives.

1c Students explain the meaning of the words
underlined and what they tell us about the success of
the project.

Answers:
*Capacitado – los campesinos han tenido una
formación especial*
Beneficio general –trae ventajas más extendidas
*Debidamente valorizados – el turismo aquí respeta
las costumbres locales*
*Los comuneros – miembros de la comunidad
trabajan juntos para desarrollar el turismo, no como
empleados de grandes empresas*
Actividades complementarias – el turismo rural

*necesita combinarse con actividades deportivas o
recreativas si va a ser rentable*
*Organizaciones no gubernamentales – existen
para apoyar a los campesinos y preservar el medio
ambiente, no para sacar ganancias*
*Relevancia social – traen a turistas a los Andes para
apoyar a las comunidades allí*
*Medidas de resguardo – proteger a las comunidades
de los efectos negativos del turismo*

1d Students consider the effects of tourism in remote
places and make a list of positive and negative points.

 2a Students listen to the analysis of ecological
tourism and identify whether there are more positive
or negative points.

---

p. 106, actividad 2

Por un lado el eco turismo busca ser un turismo
sostenible, en armonía con la naturaleza.

A la vez, fomenta el desarrollo económico y la
creación de microempresas en comunidades
pequeñas.

Mantiene la vida silvestre y la biodiversidad en
buen estado.

Trae reconocimiento del país a nivel
internacional.

Trae infraestructuras como carreteras,
aeropuertos y hoteles y también genera
empleos.

Pero por otro lado, hay un riesgo asociado
a la integración de turistas a áreas de gran
valor ecológico.

El desarrollo económico favorece a las grandes
compañías de turismo y la infraestructura no es
lo que requiere la población indígena.

El desecho de residuos supone una amenaza
para el medio ambiente y el proceso de
comercialización cambia a sociedades que
vivían aisladas de los sistemas monetarios.

El contacto entre diferentes culturas muchas
veces afecta a la estabilidad de la vida
tradicional, e introduce la delincuencia.

La demanda de agua, comida y artesanías
lleva a una sobre explotación de recursos.

La demanda de "exotismo" significa que los
indígenas demuestran su cultura de forma
exagerada. Después de la llegada del turismo
la vida no vuelve a ser igual.

Técnica

A Students write about 100 words to show the
complexity of the issue: "Does eco tourism favour
protection of the environemnt and local culture?"
They use the information from the *Técnica* box here
and the material in Units 2 and 8.

Unit 9 Assessment offers exam practice for this unit.

Unidad 10   Entre familia

Unit objectives

By the end of this unit students will be able to:
- Talk and write about the relationship between young people and other family members
- Discuss the role of parents and the importance of good parenting
- Give opinions on the changing models of family and parenting

Grammar

By the end of this unit students will be able to:
- Use exclamations appropriately
- Use possessive pronouns
- Use the subjunctive to express purpose

Skills

By the end of this unit students will be able to:
- Use a monolingual dictionary
- Transfer meaning: explain in Spanish

Resources

- Student Book page 107

This page introduces the topic.

1a Students work in groups to decide which of the images in their own opinion best fits the situation described.

Answers:
Students' answers will vary.

1b Students choose one of the situations and, changing the first person to the third, write a paragraph explaining what happened and the consequences.

1c In pairs, students prepare and act out one of the situations.

Actitudes y conflictos

Planner
Grammar focus
♦ Exclamations

Key language

un botellón	booze up/drinking session
la desgana	lack of enthusiasm
el/la mozo/a	young child
la novia	girlfriend/bride
el novio	boyfriend
los principios	principles
aguantar	to put up with
conseguir	to attain/get
dar la gana	to please
enfadarse	to get angry
enterarse de	to get to know/discover
equivocarse	to make a mistake
hacer caso de	to pay attention to/heed
holgazanear	to laze about
inculcar	to instil values
luchar	to struggle
reemplazar	to replace
regañar	to scold/tell off
borracho/a	drunk
equivocado/a	wrong
antaño	long ago
en lugar de	instead of
ni siquiera	not even
sin permiso	without permission

Resources

- Student Book pages 108 and 109
- Vocabulario, Student Book page 115
- CD 2 tracks 26, 27 and 28
- Hojas 10.1 CD 4, tracks 27, 28 and 29, 10.3
- Grammar Workbook page 13

Gramática

Exclamations

Remind students about exclamation marks and accents.

Refer students to the grammar section of the Student Book, page 163.

A Students write their own exclamatory phrases for each situation.

Possible answers:
¡Qué conejo más lindo! ¡Qué niño tan romántico!
¡Qué tierno! ¡Qué conejo tan travieso!
¡Qué niña tan ingrata!.

1a Students listen to the parents and match each one with one of the situations illustrated.

---

p. 108, actividad 1a

1   Fuiste a un botellón. Un amigo mío os vio allí, borrachos en la calle. No lo pude creer cuando me lo dijo. Si vas a una fiesta es para divertirte, no simplemente para beber.

2   Ya te dije que no me gusta que tu novio suba a tu dormitorio. Esperaste hasta que yo saliera y le invitaste a subir. Si crees que no me enteré, estás equivocada.

3   Te pusiste las zapatillas de tu hermano. Sabías que las acababa de comprar y que le costaron mucho dinero. Te fuiste todo el día con tus amigos, y él se pasó toda la mañana buscando sus zapatillas.

Answers:
1 *a*   2 *c*   3 *b*

 1b Students then listen to the young people and identify which situations they are referring to.

---

p. 108, actividad 1b

Carlos: Si él siempre se pone mi ropa – cogió mi chaqueta y nadie le dijo nada. Yo tenía prisa, tenía que ir a terminar un trabajo para el instituto. No son los únicos zapatos que tiene. No entiendo por qué se enfadó tanto. ¿Por qué no me llamó al móvil en lugar de perder el tiempo?

José: Lo que pasa es que salí con unos amigos a pasear, eso fue todo. Era tarde, eso sí, pero nadie tenía ganas de volver a casa. Estábamos en un lugar donde hay como una plaza pequeña donde se reúne la gente. Creo que había un café o algo por el estilo, con mesas y todo, pero estaba cerrado. Algunos amigos estaban allí y nos invitaron a tomar una cerveza.

Nacha: No lo hice a propósito. Él vino a la casa porque sabe que no te cae muy bien, y quería hablar contigo. Como tú no estabas, no supe qué hacer. ¿Qué ibas a pensar? Entonces le invité a subir a mi dormitorio – es mi habitación y, al fin y al cabo, no debes decirme lo que puedo y lo que no puedo hacer allí.

Answers:
Carlos B; José A; Nacha C

2 Students choose one of the situations listed that cost them a parental reprimand. They describe their version of events.

3a Students read the letter for gist and decide in which paragraph each idea is mentioned.

Answers:
a *3*   b *4*   c *1*   d *2*

3b Students apply more detailed reading to decide which of the accusations are made about young people.

Answers:
perezosos, ingratos, egoístas, degenerados, desobedientes

3c Students decide how each accusation is justified in the text.

Answers:
Perezosos: no estudian ni trabajan.
Egoístas: quieren tener todo/no contribuyen a la sociedad.
Degenerados: pasan de todo/se dedican al sexo, a las drogas y a la violencia/no conocen la responsabilidad.
Desobedientes: no hacen caso a nadie.
Ingratos: no hacen caso a sus padres a quienes deben todo/quieren todo pero no contribuyen a la sociedad.

 4a Students listen to the recording for gist and decide whether the speakers agree with Delia's opinion of today's youth.

---

p. 109, actividad 4a

Nuria: Yo creo que Delia tiene una visión demasiado negativa de los jóvenes de hoy. Por supuesto que hay algunos jóvenes que viven de los padres, pero eso se debe a la falta de oportunidades y al precio inasequible de la vivienda y el coste de la vida en general. Hay muchísimos jóvenes que se interesan por lo que pasa a su alrededor, aunque algunos son un poco inmaduros. Pero a mí me parece que a Delia se le ha olvidado que ella también fue joven. El abismo generacional siempre ha existido y la resistencia al cambio es normal.

Miguel: Creo que Delia no conoce a muchos jóvenes: quizás haya tenido una mala experiencia con los que conoce y por eso generaliza en sus acusaciones. Hay muchos jóvenes emprendedores que buscan salir adelante a base de esfuerzo y trabajo. Algunos son muy creativos, y eso sumado a su esfuerzo hace que lleven adelante proyectos de nuevos negocios, formen empresas y den trabajo a otros jóvenes. Pero sobre todo, yo creo que los jóvenes de hoy tenemos más esperanzas y ganas de vivir en un mundo mejor.

Marta: Hace falta tener en cuenta que hay muchos jóvenes que para nada se pueden identificar con la opinión de la juventud de esa carta. ¿Qué me dices de todos los jóvenes atletas que trabajan para superarse? Empiezan desde muy niños y trabajan muy duro. También están los que se preocupan por la ecología y actúan diariamente para contrarrestar el impacto del hombre en el

---

medio ambiente: estos trabajan para crear un mundo mejor para las generaciones futuras. ¿No es una contribución a la comunidad? Y también están los jóvenes que desempeñan labores altruistas. Por ejemplo, yo he sido voluntario en instituciones para niños desamparados y discapacitados desde que tenía 14 años, junto con otros chicos igual de jóvenes.

Me enfada el veredicto de Delia, creo que nos juzga a todos por igual y los estereotipos siempre son injustos.

Antonio: Creo que Delia debería aceptar que la sociedad cambia y que los cambios no son siempre negativos. Reconozco que la juventud de hoy tiene mala fama pero desde que el mundo es mundo, los jóvenes han intentado romper con lo conocido y salirse con la suya. Seguro que ella no es ni la mitad de tolerante que los jóvenes de hoy. Nuestra mentalidad es mucho más amplia, y tenemos una mente más abierta, capaz de aceptar nuevas posturas y nuevas ideas. Antes, era muy raro que un joven estuviera a favor del aborto o la homosexualidad porque los padres les hacían creer que eso era malo. Afortunadamente ahora hay jóvenes de mente más abierta. Además, tenemos una mente más desarrollada y somos capaces de adquirir nuevos conocimientos más rápidamente. Por ejemplo en el caso del uso de las computadoras y otras tecnologías.

Answer:
Los jóvenes no están de acuerdo con Delia.

 4b Students listen again to the recording and make notes of the positive values of youth as they are mentioned.

5 Students reflect on the strengths and weaknesses of the young people of today and yesterday and they present their views to the rest of the class for open discussion.

6 Students write a letter in defence of young people using the ideas given on these two pages. Remind students to attempt the use of the imperfect subjunctive by revising the grammar box and its examples.
Encourage students to revise the subjunctive from all units and to practise using it wherever possible. See units 2, 3, 6, 7, 8 in particular.

H 10.1, 10.3 *Hojas* 10.1 and 10.3 offer additional listening and reading practice for this spread.

Padres e hijos

Note: The words *padres* and *hijos* is used in generic form to mean parents and children rather than fathers and sons.

Planner

Grammar focus

♦ Possessive pronouns

Key language

las normas	house rules
el roce	friction
las tonterías	nonsense
la vejez	old age
callar(se)	to keep quiet
compartir	to share
dar de comer a	to feed
dejar en paz	to leave in peace
discutir	to argue
disfrutar de	to enjoy
escandalizarse	to get upset
evitar	to avoid
interesarse por	to be interested in
llevarse bien/mal	to get on well/badly
mentir	to lie
pelear	to fight/quarrel
reprochar	to reproach
tomar en serio	to take seriously
apático/a	apathetic
a pesar de	in spite of

Resources

♦ Student Book pages 110 and 111
♦ Vocabulario, Student Book page 115
♦ CD 2, track 29
♦ Hojas 10.2, 10.4
♦ Grammar Workbook page 28

 1a Students listen to the discussion between the five young friends and decide whether they are talking about family or friends.

p. 110, actividades 1a y 1b

Sara: Muchos de ellos no se interesan más que por la ropa y los zapatos. Si quiero hablar de algo serio – de política o de lo que pasa en el mundo – no encuentro a casi nadie de mi edad con quien pueda tener un diálogo inteligente. Soy una persona muy seria y a veces me encuentro muy sola.

Irene: Yo no les digo nada de lo que hago. Si no, discutimos – por las notas, por el sexo, por tonterías. Sé que no les gustaría lo que hago, así que mejor no se lo digo. Es mejor callar que decirles mentiras. No quiero que me pidan explicaciones ni que me hagan reproches. No les pido nada, e insisto en que me dejen en paz.

Alfonso: Me paso la vida en la calle. Me divierto un montón, y allí somos todos iguales, compartimos todo y hablamos el mismo lenguaje, no como en casa. Hoy en día tenemos muchos tipos de relaciones. Lo más normal es no tomártelas demasiado en serio hasta que conoces a alguien especial.

Salvador: Yo trato siempre de respetar sus límites, sus normas. Llego a la hora, como en casa, no les contesto. Pero no me gusta que me hagan interrogaciones del estilo: "Adónde vas? ¿Con quién andas?". Realmente pasamos muy poco tiempo juntos, y así hay menos roce, menos contacto y menos posibilidad de pelearnos. No digo que nos llevemos mal, sino que sabemos evitar el conflicto.

Virginia: Puedo hablar de casi todo con ellos. A veces no les gusta lo que digo, pero saben que si quiero algo, voy a hacerlo de todas formas. A veces se escandalizan, pero también son comprensivos. Creo que puedo hablar con ellos porque no me ponen límites.

 1b Students listen a second time and note whether they are positive or negative comments.

Answers:
Sara: *amigos, negativo;* **Irene:** *familia, negativo;*
Alfonso: *amigos, positivo;* **Salvador:** *familia, más positivo que negativo;* **Virginia:** *familia, positivo*

1c In pairs, students use the *frases clave* to explain to each other how they get on with their family or friends.

2a Students read the text about Montse's family. They match each generation to the appropriate description.

Answers:
1 *sus padres*
2 *los jóvenes de hoy*
3 *sus abuelos*

2b Students decide who is speaking for each of the sentences.

Answers:
1 *su abuelo*
2 *su madre*
3 *Montse*

2c Students back up their answers with evidence from the text.

Gramática

Possessive pronouns

Students revise possessive pronouns.

Refer them to the grammar section of the Student Book, page 157.

Answers:
A
1 *de la mía*
2 *el suyo*
3 *al nuestro*
4 *a la nuestra*

H 10.4 *Hoja 10.4 offers additional practice of possessive pronouns.*

3 Students substitute the underlined words with the correct form of the possessive pronoun.

Answers:
1 *la suya*
2 *los suyos*
3 *la suya*
4 *la mía*
5 *la tuya*

4a Students read the qualities necesssary for good parenting listed on the cards, and add some more of their own.

4b In pairs students compare their lists and discuss the differences. They may need to change the nouns into adjectives – i.e. *tolerancia – tolerante*. Then they play a card game. Students read the card game instructions. They take it in turns to place the cards in a diamond shape to reflect their own opinions. They follow the example and explain why each card is in the place they have put it in and if their partner wants to move it they must explain why. They use the *frases clave*.

5 Students prepare a debate on the themes:

"Problems between the generations are normal and universal."

"Problems between generations are provoked by specific changes in society."

H 10.2 *Hoja 10.2 offers additional speaking practice for this spread.*

La familia de hoy

 1c Students listen and decide who is speaking: Paula or Gregoria.

Planner

Grammar focus

♦ The subjunctive to express purpose

Skills focus

♦ Using a monolingual dictionary

Key language

el decenso	decline
el marco	framework
la pelotera	fight/quarrel
las raíces	roots
el respaldo	backup
la soledad	solitude/loneliness
la tasa de nacimiento	birthrate
conjugarse	to conjugate/manage together
convivir	to live together
cuidar de	to look after
destruir	to destroy
hacer falta	to lack
largarse	to run away
sobrellevar	to manage/survive
sobrevivir	to survive
ambos/as	both
atacado/a	attacked
descarado/a	rude
minado/a	threatened
monoparental	single family
pasajeras	passing/fleeting
antaño	yesteryear/long ago
en aislamiento	isolated/in isolation
fuera del hogar	outside the home
por supuesto	of course

Resources

♦ Student Book pages 112 and 113
♦ Vocabulario, Student Book page 115
♦ CD 2, tracks 30, 31 and 32
♦ Hojas 10.1 CD 4, tracks 27, 28, and 29, 10.5

1a Students read the two views on family life today in Spain. They then decide whether or not Paula and Gregoria would be in agreement on the points listed.

Answers:
1 *No están de acuerdo.*
2 *No están de acuerdo.*
3 *Sí, están de acuerdo.*
4 *Sí, están de acuerdo.*
5 *Sí, están de acuerdo.*
6 *Sí, están de acuerdo.*

1b Students decide whether the opinions listed are made by Gloria or Gregoria.

---

p. 112, actividad 1c

El materialismo intenta sustituir al amor, e inevitablemente lo destruye. Los padres sólo piensan en trabajar para poder comprar cada vez más cosas a sus hijos. Para demostrar que les quieren, les compran un móvil o les regalan una moto.

Como resultado, se vive para hacer dinero, se olvida de la importancia de pasar tiempo con la familia. Hoy en día se valora más lo que se tiene que lo que se siente ... las emociones.

Las oportunidades de comunicación se pierden: televisión o trabajo sí.... pero no la familia.

El materialismo es el valor del siglo XXI, pero no es un valor espiritual. Conduce a una falta de amor y de diálogo, y termina en divorcio.

Answer:
Paula Echevarría

Gramática

The subjunctive to express purpose

Ensure students can identify the difference between clauses implying result and those implying purpose.

They could provide examples in English.

A Students identify whether the sentence expresses result or purpose and decide which form of the verb is required.

Answers:
1 *cuide = purpose. My husband doesn't want me to go out to work so that I can look after his elderly parents.*
2 *tuviesen = purpose. I have never gone out to work so that my children would have someone at home when they come back from school.*
3 *faltan = result. Young people today are quite rude so they are often disrespectful of older people.*
4 *aprendan = purpose. We should be stricter with them so that they learn to be more respectful.*
5 *estuvieron = result. My brothers were very naughty when they were little so they were always fighting.*

Técnica

Using a monolingual dictionary

Introduce students to situations where a monolingual dictionary is useful.

A Students use a monolingual dictionary to find out the meaning of some of the words mentioned above. Some students may already be familiar with some of the meanings so you may need to be selective when you choose which words they should look up.

B Students try to work out the meaning of the Spanish colloquial idioms by use of translation and common sense.

Answers:
charlar por los codos = to be a chatterbox
llamar al pan, pan y al vino, vino = to call things by their name (to call a spade a spade)
llevarse como el perro y el gato = not to get along, to argue all the time (to fight like cat and dog)

H 10.5 *Hoja* 10.5 offers additional practice of using a monolingual dictionary.

2a Students listen to the interview as often as is necessary and complete the phrases. Students will write their own answers. For students who find this task difficult, it might be helpful to give them a copy of the transcript. Let them at least try to do it without first.

---

p. 113, actividad 2a

– Buenas tardes doctora; bienvenida a nuestra tertulia de la tarde. Mi primera pregunta es la siguiente: ¿cree usted que el núcleo familiar ha cambiado mucho en los últimos treinta años o sigue igual que siempre?

Doctora: Pues a mi entender ha habido cambios radicales en la sociedad sobre todo para la mujer española. Según lo que observo en la vida cotidiana, la mujer sigue desempeñando el mismo papel de siempre – ama de casa, madre, amante, costurera, cocinera, enfermera cuando la familia tiene la gripe, psicóloga cuando hay problemas y incluso más hoy en día porque en muchos casos sale a trabajar y a ganarse el pan diario.

– Pues sí, y ¿usted piensa que la familia de hoy requiere las mismas cosas de siempre?

Doctora: No, en realidad me parece que la familia hoy en día es más complicada que hace veinte años. Los niños tienen más libertad y menos respeto hacia los adultos pero al mismo tiempo, han perdido la estabilidad de la familia de antaño cuando los abuelos vivían cerca o en la misma casa.

– Vale y ¿usted cree que lo que hace falta hoy es estabilidad?

Doctora: Claro hay mucho más movimiento por el mundo y muchas familias están separadas y por supuesto son menos estables en ese sentido pero creo que la estabilidad emocional es de suma importancia para que una familia sobreviva los cambios sociales actuales.

– ¿Qué quiere decir con eso?

Doctora: Bueno hay muchas familias cuyas relaciones cambian rápidamente y los niños no siempre comprenden esos cambios pero, si viven sintiendo el amor de ambos padres aun cuando no hay armonía total, ese amor les ayuda a sobrellevar los cambios en las relaciones familiares.

– Es cierto y no importa si la familia es monoparental o si hay varias personas como cabeza de familia, lo que más importa es el amor y la armonía que se siente en la familia. ¿Verdad?

Doctora: Así es. Siempre ha habido peleas y riñas en las familias pero antes no se fracturaban tanto. Hoy es mucho más probable que una pelotera termine en separación sea por parte de los adultos o por parte de los adolescentes que se marchan de casa.

2b Work in pairs. Students discuss what families were like 50 years ago, compared with today. They discuss their ideas with a partner and write down five aspects of the traditional family and five ways in which it has changed.

3 Students learn to evaluate each other's responses to key questions on the unit.

4 Students listen to Freddy's response and evaluate it.

---

p. 113, actividad 4

– ¿El matrimonio es importante?

– Pues, yo creo que las relaciones personales son más importantes que el hecho de casarse. Vivir solo … tener pareja … encontrar a alguien que te quiera …: todas estas circunstancias son posibles, y no quiero decir que una sea mejor que otra. Creo que es importante pensar bien en si vas a tener hijos, teniendo en cuenta las responsabilidades que conlleva, y que no lo hagas sin pensar. Pero casarse no significa automáticamente que vayas a ser un buen padre, y divorciarse tampoco implica que seas un ogro …

Example answers:

Ideas, opinions, relevance (10)	Fluency, spontaneity (10)	Range of language (5)
A high mark	A high mark	A high mark
Thinking on his feet, but following an idea through logically, looking at things from different points of view.	Thinks on his feet, uses strategies to give himself time. Good use of sentence starters, gives reaction then digs out a justification.	Clearly focused on slipping in subjunctive. Good use of sentence starters, opinions etc. Sentences with "if". He knows it is an assessment situation and has made sure he puts in language that will help get a good mark.

5 Students write a response to the key question.

H 10.1 *Hoja* 10.1 offers additional listening practice for this spread.

Gramática en acción

Planner

Resources
♦ Students' Book page 114
♦ Hojas 10.3, 10.4

Students revise each grammar point then complete the tasks.

Recuerda

Different types of pronouns

Students consolidate and build upon their knowledge of pronouns.

Refer students to the grammar section of the Student Book, page 161.

A Students translate the sentences into Spanish.

Answers:
1 *Pablo, ¿ quieres venir a casa con nosotros para merendar?*
2 *El chico con quien me encontré en Málaga acaba de enviarme un email.*
3 *Hay un concierto en el pueblo donde nací (yo).*
4 *Le presté mi ipod porque había olvidado el suyo.*
5 *He pagado mi entrada para el concierto pero no voy a pagar la suya.*
6 *Mis abuelos vivían en un mundo en el cual el tiempo no avanzaba.*
7 *El amigo de quien hablaba ya se ha vuelto famoso.*
8 *El problema al cual te refieres es muy serio.*
9 *La casa que queríamos comprar ya se ha vendido.*
10 *La casa de mis abuelos, la que está en Barcelona, es demasiado pequeña.*

Recuerda

The subjunctive to express purpose

Students consolidate their knowledge of purpose clauses. Refer them to page 112 and the grammar section of the Student Book, page 170.

B Students decide whether the verb should be indicative or subjunctive and then translate the sentences into Spanish.

Answers:
1 *indicative: Perdí el ultimo bus de modo que llegué a casa mucho después de la medianoche.*
2 *subjunctive: Abrí la puerta silenciosamente para que mis padres no me oyeran.*
3 *indicative: Al subir las escalera me tropecé con el perro e hice tanto ruido así que toda la casa se despertó.*
4 *subjunctive: Intenté pedir excusas/decir que lo sentía/para que mis padres estuviesen menos enfadados.*
5 *subjunctive: Sabía que mi hermana había dejado el perro allí a fin de que tropezara con él.*
6 *indicative: Al fin y al cabo mis padres comprendieron que había aprendido una lección de modo que no se alborotaron/preocuparon/escadalizaron más.*

H 10.3-4 *Hoja* 10.3 and 10.4 offer additional practice of the subjunctive to express purpose.

Vocabulario

Page 115

Answers:
2 *hemos tenido*
3 *se comprenda*
4 *holgazanas*
5 *parlanchina*

Extra

Planner

Resources

♦ Student Book page 115
♦ CD 2, track 33

This page is aimed at A–A* students.

1a Students read the adult education book on "Love in family life". They put the sentences (1–5) in order to match the text.

Answer:
3, 2, 5, 1, 4

1b Students select three sentences from the text to sum up its argument.

Suggested answer:
La sociedad tradicionalmente ha establecido que mujeres y hombres tengan diferentes funciones, tareas, responsabilidades, gustos e intereses.
Aunque hay diferencias biólogicas, hay sabemos que la mayoria de las formas de actuar de hombres y mujeres son aprendidas y por lo tanto pueden cambiar.
Afortunadamente, las sociedades avanzan y cada vez es más claro que los comportamientos pueden ser no exclusivos de un género o de otro.

2a Students listen to the recording from the book "Love in the family" and make a note in English of the names of the members of the family, who they are, what they do and what they say.

> **p. 116, actividad 2a**
>
> Lupe preparaba el desayuno mientras su marido, José regresaba del partido de beisbol al que había ido temprano con su hijo Pablo, de once años. Cuando ellos se fueron por la mañana, su hija Noemí, de diez años, había llorado un buen rato porque ella también quería jugar al béisbol y su papá no la había llevado. Ahora jugaba con Chucho y Luisa, sus hermanos menores, pero se veía triste.
>
> Cuando José y Pablo llegaron, todos se sentaron a desayunar y mientras Noemí y Lupe les servían, ellos platicaban de los equipos, del siguiente partido y de la carrera que el papá anotó.
>
> Noemí comenzó a llorar de nuevo.
>
> - ¿Qué le pasa a esta niña? – preguntó José.
>
> - Ella quería ir a jugar contigo – le respondió Lupe en voz baja.
>
> - Pero mi hijita, el béisbol es para hombres, le dijo José a Noemí , tratando de calmarla.

> - El otro día vi en la tele un partido en el que jugaban mujeres – exclamó Chucho.
>
> - Sí, pero han de ser muy feas – dijo Pablo.
>
> - ¡Eso no es cierto! – gritó enojada Noemí.
>
> Ella se levantó de su silla y le dió un empujón a su hermano. Ambos empezaron a pelear. José les regañó y pidió a los niños que se fueran a jugar.
>
> Cuando se quedaron solos, Lupe y José platicaron preocupados sobre los deseos de Noemí. Lupe propuso buscar un lugar para que la niña jugara a beisbol y José se quedó pensativo.

Answers:
Lupe: *Mother, getting meal. Talks to husband afterwards to negotiate a solution*
José: *Husband, returns from playing baseball. Says baseball is for men. Sends children outside.*
Pablo: *Son, says women baseball players must be ugly*
Noemí: *Daughter, wants to play baseball, cries.*
Chucho: *Son, says saw women baseball on TV*
Luisa: *Daughter*

2b Students consider what advice they would give to Pablo, Lupe and Noemí.

Técnica

Transferring meaning – explaining in Spanish (2)

Take students through the material in the *Técnica* box and make sure they understand the concepts.

Then the students carry out the activities A–C.

Unit 10 Assessment offers exam practice for this unit.

Unidad 11   Amistades

Unit objectives

By the end of this unit students will be able to:
♦ Describe the characteristics and roles of friends
♦ Discuss the different values that are important to friends and conflicts about them
♦ Talk and write about the importance of friends
♦ Comment on friendship versus love

Grammar

By the end of this unit students will be able to:
♦ Use time clauses correctly
♦ Use the passive
♦ Use the imperative in all its forms (revision)

Skills

By the end of this unit students will be able to:
♦ Understand how to do cloze tests
♦ Respond to a literary text

Resources

♦ Student Book page 117
♦ CD 3, track 2
♦ Hoja 11.2

This page introduces the topic.

1 Ask students to think about personality adjectives that they already know, particularly those that describe positively young people. A list of adjectives in English is provided so that they have a starting point that will give them numerous possibilities for each of the letters outstanding in the acrostic, with many cognates to get them started. Students should be encouraged to think of additional adjectives. Revise the use of a monolingual dictionary from page 112 and encourage students to work on widening their vocabulary.

Answers:
brave – *valiente;* charming – *encantador;*
daring – *atrevido;* enthusiastic – *entusiasta;*
happy – *joviales;* hard-working – *trabajadores;*
normal – *normales;* original – *originales*
outstanding – *sobresalientes;*
passionate – *apasionados;* seductive – *seductores;*
tenacious – *tenaces;* versatile – *versátiles;*
vibrant – *vivaces;* well-mannered – *educados;*
wise – *sabios*

 2a Students listen to the young people discussing the role of friends. They take notes on the views of each one.

> **p. 117, actividad 2a**
>
> **Rodrigo:** En mi opinión los amigos deben estar siempre a tu lado para respaldarte en cualquier situación difícil. Siempre deben creer que tienes razón y ser leales.
>
> **Sarita:** Creo que los amigos deben decirte la verdad aunque no sea lo que quieras oír. Es mejor que sean honestos contigo.
>
> **Susana:** Los amigos nunca deben tener secretos. Deben consolarte cuando te peleas con otros amigos o con tu familia.
>
> **Pablo:** En mi opinión, los amigos deben compartir los mismos gustos en música, ropa y estilo de vida. Siempre deben estar acuerdo con tus ideas sobre la moda.
>
> **Paco:** Para mí, deben aconsejarte cuando necesites ayuda con los problemas del corazón, sobre todo si creen que te has equivocado de pareja y vas a cometer un error grave.

Answers:
Rodrigo = deben ser leales y darte la razón, para respaldarte
Sarita = deben ser honestos porque es mejor que te digan la verdad.
Susana= deben consolarte cuando peleas.
Pablo = deben compartir tus ideas de la moda.
Paco = deben ser guías en cuestiones del corazón para evitar que cometas un error.

2b Students write five sentences expressing their views of friendship.

H 11.2 *Hoja 11.2 offers additional speaking practice for this spread.*

Amistades y conflictos

> **Planner**
>
> *Skills focus*
> ♦ Adapting information from texts

Key language

los celos	jealousy
las chucherías	sweets/rubbish
la generación	generation
el mensaje	message
la paga	pocket money
el rechazo	rejection
apagar	to switch off/put out
costar	to cost
depender de	to depend on
enfrentar	to confront
gastar	to spend money
hacer frente a	to face up to
negar	to deny
rebelarse contra	to rebel against
simbolizar	to symbolise
tardar en	to take time to
comunicativo/a	communicative
a la moda	fashionable
de hecho	in fact

Resources

♦ Student Book pages 118 and 119
♦ Vocabulario, Student Book page 125
♦ CD 3, tracks 3 and 4
♦ Hojas 11.2, 11.3, 11.5

 1a Students listen to the descriptions and decide which icon is being described.

p. 118, actividad 1a

1 En mi cumpleaños nunca pido regalos, prefiero que me den dinero.

2 No entiendo por qué es aceptable que se ponga un arete, un pendiente o algo en el lóbulo de la oreja pero mis padres se escandalizan si me lo pongo en el ombligo.

3 Sé que te hace daño – te lo advierten en el paquete – pero somos lo bastante adultos como para decidir.

4 Emborracharse – es normal, ¿no?

5 Tu tatuaje es muy bonito, ¿es de verdad? ¿Te dolió mucho?

6 Puedo hacer nuevos amigos por el mundo entero y comunicarme con ellos.

7 Es el último grito de la moda – tengo que comprar una.

8 Siempre estoy en contacto con la pandilla.

9 No como en mi casa, pero no paro de comprar chucherías.

Answers:
1 D   2 A   3 H   4 E   5 G   6 C   7 I   8 B   9 F

1b Students read the texts and complete the grid. Suggestion for a way to test memory and comprehension: ask students to close their books and explain what one of the characters on this page has said in the written texts.

Answers:

Los iconos mencionados	El icono más importante	Razones
Héctor dinero, beber, ropa, tecnología	dinero	Rebelan contra sus padres, pero no contra la sociedad: el consumismo. Todo lo que hacen para rebelarse cuesta dinero.
María Elena ropa, piercings, cigarrillos, móvil	móvil	Pertenece a los jóvenes. Son muy comunicativos.
Marco Antonio dulces, tatuajes, piercings	dulces / chucherías	Para recordar que son niños. No quieren hacer lo que les mandan, pero no quieren actuar como adultos responsables.

H 11.2 *Hoja* 11.2 offers additional speaking practice for this spread.

1c Students say what their own icons are and why.

Técnica

Adapting information from texts

Students read this boxed information and complete the tasks.

A Students practise organising information taken from a text. Help them separate a list of points taken from the text into ideas and examples, taking care to avoid giving conflicting points of view. Different answers are possible. For example, *la tecnología* could be considered as an example.

Possible answers:
Ideas: *la rebeldía, la tecnología, la comunicación, el consumismo*
Examples: *el alcohol, el tabaco, el móvil, la ropa, Internet, los dulces, el dinero, los tatuajes*

B Students read the examples and complete the grid.

Answers:

Algunos dirían que …	Pero se podría decir que …
los jóvenes no quieren que les traten como niños.	*los jóvenes no quieren actuar como adultos.*
los jóvenes quieren tomar sus propias decisiones.	*los jóvenes no quieren que les digan qué tienen que hacer.*
los jóvenes quieren rebelarse.	*los jóvenes son muy conscientes de su imagen y quieren sentir que pertenecen a un grupo y no son diferentes de los demás.*

C and **D** Students complete the tasks using their own words and examples.

Example answers (D):
1   *A los jóvenes no les interesa trabajar.*
2   *A los jóvenes les importa mucho impresionar a sus amigos.*
3   *A los jóvenes les fascina la moda.*

H 11.5   *Hoja* 11.5 offers additional practice of adapting information from texts.

2 Students listen to the programme discussing the causes of conflict among young people. They note five causes that are mentioned and a possible solution for each one.

Class discussion: Continue the debate and ask students to argue the toss between how far should they be conformist and how far should they challenge society. What are their moral values? Do they hold political views? What is their attitude to war? What other more mundane causes of conflict are there, such as cheating in an exam?

---

p. 119, actividad 2

–   Buenas noches amigos oyentes. Nos hemos reunido aquí para discutir un tema importante: ¿Cuáles son las causas de los conflictos entre los jóvenes y qué soluciones podemos ofrecerles? Invito al doctor Rodríguez a que comience el debate – ¿Doctor ?

Doctor R: Me parece que las principales causas son las diferencias en valores que desarrolla la gente joven en la transición de adolescentes llenos de hormonas a jóvenes adultos que han adquirido o no, un sentido moral y que van ocupando su lugar en el mundo adulto. Déjeme dar unos ejemplos: las drogas pueden causar conflictos entre un grupo de jóvenes porque mientras que unos no tendrán problema en engancharse otros las rechazarán por completo. En ese caso, la única solución práctica me parece a mí, sería buscar un grupo

---

de amigos que compartan tus ideas de rechazo a las drogas y además tratar de ayudar a los que han cogido el camino erróneo de drogarse.

–   Vale, pero ese es un caso extremo, ¿verdad?

Doctor R: Pues sí, pero otra causa puede ser el racismo o la inmigración o el paro. Estos también son problemas que enfrentan a nuestros jóvenes. La única solución a mi parecer, es la educación. Hay que educar a los jóvenes para que comprendan los enormes problemas de la sociedad y así puedan hacer frente al mundo de los adultos.

–   ¿Está bien Doctor pero hay otros conflictos más mundanos no?

Doctor R: Claro, una de las causas principales de conflictos entre jóvenes son los celos. Puede ser una cosa trivial como un nuevo par de zapatillas o el hecho de que un estudiante saque mejores notas o sea mejor deportista que otro. De cosas tan insignificantes como estas pueden surgir conflictos, en seguida vienen los insultos y el siguiente paso puede ser sacar los cuchillos. Vuelvo a insistir que la única solución es la educación porque siempre habrá unos más pobres, más inteligentes o más dotados que otros, y si no enseñamos a los jóvenes a conformarse con su situación entonces siempre habrá conflictos.

–   Usted es un poco pesimista en mi opinión. ¿A ver, ustedes que opinan? ¿Hay que enseñarles a ser conformistas? ¿Ésta les parece una solución adecuada?

Answers:
Causas mencionadas: *drogas; racismo; inmigración; paro; celos.*
Resoluciones: *rechazarlos o ayudar a los que se enganchan; educarles a comprender; conformarse con su situación.*

3 Students use the information on the spread to write a reply to each of the questions.

"What is is that unites young people/brings young people together?"

"What provokes conflict between them?"

They write 100–125 words on each one.

H 11.3   *Hoja* 11.3 offers additional reading practice for this spread.

Mis amigos y yo

Planner

Grammar focus

♦   Time clauses

Skills focus

♦ Dealing with cloze (gap-filling) tests

Key language

el aula	classroom
el piropo	compliment
la varicela	chicken pox
acercarse a	to go towards
afiliarse a	to belong to/sign up for
arreglar	to arrange
cuchichear	to whisper
darse de cuenta de	to realise/dawn on
echarse a reír	to burst out laughing
empeñarse en	to undertake/be
determined to	
enterarse de	to get to know/find out
hacer caso de	to pay attention to
integrarse	to integrate
proponerse	to propose oneself/put
oneself	
forward for	
querer decir	to mean
simpatizar	to get on well
sonreír	to smile
tartamudear	to stammer
tomar el pelo	to tease
tramar	to plot
decepcionado	upset
malvado/a	wicked/evil
sensato/a	sensible
a solas	alone
vale la pena	it's worth it

Resources

♦ Student Book pages 120 and 121
♦ Vocabulario, Student Book page 125
♦ CD 3, track 5
♦ Hojas 11.1 CD 4, tracks 30 and 31, 11.2, 11.4
♦ Grammar Workbook 67

 1a Students listen to Javier talking about the importance of friends and answer the questions.

> **p. 120, actividad 1a**
>
> Bueno lo que pasa es que soy el chico nuevo de por aquí y me gustaría hacer amigos rápidamente, no me gusta estar a solas en mis horas libres. Me encantaría tener muchos, pero muchísimos amigos, chicas y chicos, pero en realidad no sé cómo comenzar a buscarlos. Además, cuando los encuentre no tengo la menor idea de cómo empezar una conversación. No me importa si les gustan los deportes o si son súper inteligentes, o altos o gordos, lo único que me importa es que tengamos los mismos gustos musicales porque la música es mi pasión. Creo que voy a unirme

> a un club o mejor tocar en un grupo y así es probable que encuentre a gente de mi edad y con mis mismos gustos.

Answers:
1 = 5 problems; *es un chico nuevo; quiere hacer amigos rápidamente; no le gusta estar solo; no sabe cómo buscar a sus amigos; no sabe cómo empezar la conversación.*
2 = 3 ideas; *que tengan los mismos gustos de música; afiliarse a un club; tocar con un grupo*
3 *should be students' own answers*

1b Students match the two parts of the sentences.

Answers:
1 = *f* ; **2** = *b* ; **3** = *e*; **4** = *a* ; **5** = *c* ; **6** = *d*

Técnica

Dealing with cloze tests

Take students throug the material in the *Técnica* box.

A Students consider which points they used in arriving at their answers in Activity 1b.

B Students complete the sentences.

Answers:
1 = *cariñosa;* **2** = *ayudemos;* **3** = *comunicativos;*
4 = *cuyo;* **5** = *audaces*

---

2 Students read Javier's secret diary and answer the questions.

Answers:
Students formulate their own answers.
Suggestions:
1 *Porque el grupo roquero no le aceptó en seguida.*
2 *Los otros chicos le tomaron el pelo/tenía miedo de entrar en el aula.*
3 *Se empeñó en hablarle durante el recreo.*
4 *Le ofreció un chicle/se le acercó en el patio.*
5 *Se hicieron amigos.*
6 *Que siempre se puede escoger a los amigos.*

H 11.1 *Hoja* 11.1 offers additional listening practice for this page.

3a Students read the texts A–D and decide which of the two replies below best matches two of the letters (two letters will be left without replies).

Answers:
B *1 and* **C** *2*

3b Students follow the example of the two replies and write two more for the other two letters. They use their own words.

Gramática

Time clauses

Revise the material on page 67 and develop students' understanding of time clauses.

A Students read the texts in Activity 3a again and identify six time clauses.

Answers:
Llevo tres años; cuando llegué; antes de que me pasó esto; desde hace años; cuando vaya a la Universidad; hace poco

H 11.4 *Hoja 11.4 offers additional practice of time clauses.*

H 11.2 *Hoja 11.2 offers additional speaking practice for this page.*

Con el corazón en la mano

Planner

Grammar focus

♦ The passive

Key language

el corazón	heart
un embarazo	pregnancy
el fracaso	heartbreak/disaster
la locura	madness
acabar de	to have just
atar	to tie up
enamorarse	to fall in love
disfrutar de	to enjoy
preocuparse	to worry
tener ganas de	to want
tener suerte	to be lucky
cauteloso/a	cautious
ensimismado/a	wrapped up in yourself/conceited
extraño/a	strange/weird
a menudo	often
a primera vista	at first sight
buen sentido del humor	good sense of humour
mediante	by means of

Resources

♦ Student Book pages 122 and 123
♦ Vocabulario, Student Book page 125
♦ CD 3, tracks 6 and 7
♦ Hoja 11.4
♦ Grammar Workbook 62

1a Students test themselves and see what they score.

1b Work in pairs. Students discuss which is more important love or friendship. How would they describe them? They use a dictionary to find five adjectives to describe each emotion.

 2a Students listen to Erica and decide whether the statements 1–8 are true (V), false (M) or are not mentioned (NM).

---

p. 122, actividades 2a y 2b

Quería empezar a salir otra vez después de la muerte de mi primer esposo, y me inscribí en una agencia en Internet. Buscaba a alguien serio, pero con sentido del humor también. Así conocí a Juan Manuel. Hablamos por teléfono y salimos a comer juntos. La primera vez que presenté a Juan Manuel a mi familia fue en Navidad. Ya habíamos decidido vivir juntos.... Pasado un tiempo, nos casamos.

Los dos teníamos hijos y nietos, y queríamos integrar a las dos familias. Todos estaban de acuerdo.

Para mis nietos Juan Manuel es su abuelo. Lo admiran, y él mima a los más jóvenes; se pelean por sentarse a su lado en la mesa. Le llaman "abuelito", aunque mide un metro 90.

En casa fue bastante fácil acomodarnos el uno al otro. Como mi marido se acostumbró a vivir solo, sabe lavarse la ropa y cocina muy bien, aunque suele cocinar lo que a él le gusta, sin tener en cuenta las calorías ni el colesterol.

Answers:
1 *V* **2** *V* **3** *F* **4** *NM* **5** *F* **6** *F* **7** *NM* **8** *F*

 2b Students listen again and make notes comparing her life with Juan Manuel and the personal profile she has presented to "Encuentros 60+".

Answers:
1 *She's not outgoing or sociable. Her husband died and she's lonely.*
2 *She's looking for someone serious.*
3 *She says she wants to have fun and a social life but she got married and settled down and is very family orientated.*
4 *She says she likes eating well yet watches the calories.*

2c Students write a more realistic profile for Erica.

2d Students imagine what kind of profile Juan Manuel might have written and write it themselves.

3a Students read the letter and discuss what is, in their opinion, the best age to have children.

3b Students reflect about the things that one ought to consider before having children and make a list.

 3c Students listen to Alicia, Sara and Elena and decide who gives Elisa each piece of advice.

> **p. 123, actividad 3c**
>
> **Alicia:** Puede ser que sientas que falta algo en tu vida y por eso crees que el amor de un hijo va a llenar ese espacio. Si quieres que tus hijos te respeten y te admiren, consigue un buen trabajo y un buen hombre antes de tenerlos y el resto es coser y cantar; bueno, casi. Creo que sería un error tener un bebé en estos momentos porque tú misma admites que no quieres estar atada.
>
> **Sara:** Quizás deberías buscar trabajo de niñera o algo parecido. Así tendrías la oportunidad de cuidar a bebés y niños y tener una experiencia realista. Sé que no es lo mismo que tener tus propios hijos pero te daría una idea de cómo va a ser.
>
> **Elena:** Sabes que puede ser un problema así que yo te recomiendo que busques otro método anticonceptivo en el que no tengas que pensar cuando estés con tu novio. Estudia, consigue un buen trabajo y entonces piénsalo otra vez.

Answers:
1 *Elena;* 2 *Alicia;* 3 *Sara;* 4 *Elena;* 5 *Alicia;* 6 *Alicia*

3d Group work. Students discuss the questions and justify their opinions.

Gramática

The passive

In this unit students are introduced to the passive in a variety of tenses and are reminded of expressions that can be used to avoid the passive.

Refer students to the the grammar section in the Student Book, page 171, and to page 62 of the Grammar Workbook.

Take students through the material in the *Gramática* box.

A Students translate the sentences into Spanish.

Answers:
1 *A menudo somos influidos por nuestros contemporáneos.*
2 *La chiquita era mimada por sus padres.*
3 *Los conflictos son causados muchas veces por problemitas estúpidos.*

4 *Los jóvenes son rodeados todo el tiempo de tentaciones.*

H 11.4 *Hoja 11.4 offers additional practice of the passive.*

---

4 Students write their own answer to Elisa's letter (minimum of 200 words).

Gramática en acción

> **Planner**
>
> **Resources**
> ♦ Student Book pages 124
> ♦ Hoja 11.3

Recuerda

The passive and how to avoid it

Point students to the grammar section in the Student Book, page 171.

Remind them that they looked at ways of avoiding the passive on pages 34 and 74 of the Student Book. In this unit they have considered how to form the passive and in what contexts to use it.

A Students identify the tense of the passive verb and translate the sentences into English.

B Students rewrite the same sentences in Spanish avoiding the passive voice.

Answers for A and B:
1 *perfect tense, In my opinion young people have been blamed/slandered/'rubbished' too much by the popular press.*
La prensa popular ha calumniado demasiado a los jóvenes en mi opinión.
2 *Preterite tense, The couple/newlyweds were given a welcome at the hotel reception. La recepción del hotel dio una bienvenida a los novios.*
3 *immediate future tense, This young man is going to be criticised by his enemies if he's not careful. Sus enemigos van a criticarle a este chico si no tiene más cuidado.*
4 *pluperfect tense, Javier had been put in an invidious position by his teacher. Su profesor le puso a Javier en una posición injusta.*
5 *present tense, Marisa is seen by everyone as a magnificent example of honesty. Todos ven a Marisa como ejemplo magnífico de la honestidad.*

Recuerda

Revision of commands

Refer students to Unit 3, page 34, and to the grammar section in the Student Book, pages 170–171.

Here students are reminded the forms of the imperative, including negative imperatives, and the position of relative pronouns in commands.

C Students translate the sentences into Spanish.

Answers:
1 *Habla con calma para no meterte en una pelea.*
2 *Ten cuidado de no insultar a tus amigos.*
3 *Sentémonos a hablar sobre esto.*
4 *No te dejes involucrar en un conflicto/ una discusión.*
5 *Cállate y escúchame mientras te doy unos buenos consejos.*
6 *Por favor no fumar/no fumes aquí dentro.*
7 *No me escribas hasta que estés dispuesto a pedirme perdón.*

H 11.3 *Hoja 11.3 offers additional reading practice on the imperative.*

Vocabulario

Page 125

Answers:
1 *fueron mimados*
2 *fue rodeada*
3 *cállate*
4 *algún*
5 *menores*

Extra

Planner

Skills focus
♦ Responding to a literary text (1)

Resources
♦ Student Book page 126
♦ Vocabulario, Student Book page 125
♦ CD 3, track 8

This page is aimed at A-A*students.

Técnica

Responding to a literary text (1)

Introduce students to the skills required to approach a literary text.

A Students read for gist and write a summary in English of what happens.

B Students use context to try to discover meaning of words before having recourse to a dictionary.

Answers:
contraption, a soul without a master, boys, a hard squeeze/handshake

C Students read the text again and write a description of Tomás in their own words. They say why the other students are afraid of him.

D Students explain what the last line of the text means. They consider whether they will be good friends and seek phrases in the text that have influenced their viewpoint.

 1a Students listen to the recording from *La Sombra del Viento* and decide whether the statements (1–8) are true (V), false (M) or not mentioned (NM).

> **p. 126, actividad 1a**
>
> Nos habíamos conocido muchos años atrás en una pelea durante mi primera semana en los jesuitas de Caspe. Su padre había venido a buscarle después de la clase, acompañada de una niña presumida que resultó ser la hermana de Tomás. Se me ocurrió hacer una gracia imbécil sobre ella y, antes de que pudiese parpadear, Tomás Aguilar cayó sobre mí como un diluvio de puñetazos que me dejó varias semanas condolido. En aquel duelo de patio, rodeado de un coro de críos sedientos de combate sangriento, perdí un diente y gané un nuevo sentido de las proporciones.
>
> Tres semanas más tarde, Tomás se me acercó durante el recreo. Yo, muerto de miedo, me quedé paralizado. Este viene a rematarme, pensé. Empezó a balbucear y al poco comprendí que lo único que quería era disculparse por la golpiza, porque sabía que había sido un combate desigual e injusto.
>
> – Soy yo el que tiene que pedirte perdón por haberme metido con tu hermana – dije-. Lo hubiera hecho el otro día, pero me partiste la boca antes de que pudiese hablar.

Answers:
1 *V;* **2** *F;* **3** *V;* **4** *F;* **5** *V;* **6** *NM;* **7** *V;* **8** *V*

1b Students now write a story told from Tomás' point of view of how he and Daniel met and became friends.

Unit 11 Assessment offers exam practice for this unit.

Unidad 12 Matrimonio y cohabitación

Unit objectives

By the end of this unit students will be able to:
♦ Discuss changing attitudes towards marriage and cohabitation
♦ Comment on separation and divorce
♦ Discuss the benefits and drawbacks of staying single
♦ Talk and write about the changing roles within the home

Grammar

By the end of this unit students will be able to:
♦ Use the subjunctive to express possibility and impossibility
♦ Use the subjunctive in a broader range of expressions
♦ Use the subjunctive in relative clauses
♦ Use prepositions accurately

Skills

By the end of this unit students will be able to:
♦ Work out the meaning of words
♦ Respond to a literary text

Resources

♦ Student Book page 127
♦ CD 3, track 9

This page introduces the topic.

1a Discussion in pairs. Students discuss the cartoon. They mention all that is stereotypical in the picture and imagine a scene more typical contemporary scene.

1b Students write down five adjectives to describe the differences

 2a Students listen to the recording and decide which of the phrases are mentioned.

---

p. 127, actividad 2a

– No me permitáis todo. Ya sé que no lo puedo tener todo, pero os voy a poner a prueba.

No temáis ser firmes conmigo. Prefiero que me pongáis normas, porque así me siento segura.

No dejéis que coja malas costumbres. Cuento con vosotros para detectarlas y evitarlas.

No me hagáis sentir pequeña. Me hace querer actuar como si fuera grande y tonta.

No me corrijáis delante de extraños. Presto más atención si lo hacéis cuando estamos solos.

No me hagáis sentir que mis errores son pecados. Altera mis valores.

No me protejáis de las consecuencias de mis acciones. A veces tengo que aprender sufriéndolas.

No me regañéis ni me aconsejéis demasiado. Me tendré que proteger fingiendo ser sorda.

2b Work in pairs. Students discuss the questions with a companion; they use their own words and explain their reasons orally.

Casarse, separarse o divorciarse

Planner

Grammar focus
♦ Further uses of the subjunctive

Key language

el autoestima	self-esteem
el cambio	change
el consejo	advice
la culpa	blame
las disculpas	excuses
el lazo	tie
el rencor	rancour/ill-feeling
la riña	quarrel
arreglar	to arrange
convertirse	to convert/become
descuidar	to neglect
empeñarse en	to insist on something/ be determined
encerrarse	to close up/shut away
lograr	to manage (to)
negar	to deny
reñir	to quarrel
romper	to break
enojado/a	annoyed

<table>
<tr><td>

Planner

Resources

♦ Student Book pages 128 and 129
♦ Vocabulario, Student Book page 135
♦ CD 3, track 10
♦ Hojas 12.1 CD 4, tracks 32 and 33, 12.2, 12.3
♦ Grammar Workbook page 53

</td></tr>
</table>

1a Students read the texts on divorce and search for the meaning of the words in the list.

Answers:
*se vuelven/se convierten en; acaban/terminan;
requiere/necesíta; soportar/adaptarte;
jamás/nunca; te hace falta/debes;
una fase/una etapa; motivo/causa;
aconsejamos/recomendamos*

1b Students decide which of the two texts includes each statement.

Answers:
1 *1   5   8*
2 *2   3   4   6   7*

1c Students choose the most important points to advise the two people.

H 12.1, 12.3 *Hoja* 12.1 and 12.3 offer additional listening and reading practice for this page.

Gramática

Further uses of the subjunctive

Students read this information, much of which is revision. Students are introduced to the subjunctive in clauses expressing possibility or impossibility. Ask them to give further examples of their own in English.

A Students give the grammatical explanation for the uses of the subjunctive in these sentences.

Answers:
1 *possibility*
2 *impossibility*
3 *emotion/value judgement*
4 *value judgement*
5 *not wanting*
6 *improbability*

B Students complete the sentences using ideas from the text 2 on page 128.

2a Students read the text *Consejos para los recién casados* and list the positive and negative imperatives.

2b Students find similar ways of giving each command.

2c Students use their imagination and write the letter of advice as if they were a grandparent.

 3a Students listen to the recording and make notes.

<table>
<tr><td>

p. 129, actividad 3a

Mónica: Mis padres se separaron y yo empecé a portarme muy mal, les hacía sufrir mucho. A mi madre le decía cosas horribles. Le echaba la culpa de que iba a suspender mis exámenes y al final dejé de estudiar.

Edgar: Después del fin de semana, que pasaba en casa de mi papá, mi madre me sometía a un interrogatorio. Me preguntaba cómo era la nueva novia de papá, si tenían lavaplatos o si salían de copas por la noche. Quería saberlo todo.

Inma: Mi papá siempre tenía mejores cosas que hacer que prestarme atención. Llegaba tarde a casa, cuando yo ya había preparado la cena en lugar de ver la tele. Tampoco había hecho los deberes.

</td></tr>
</table>

3b Students explain to a partner the situation regarding one of the young people. They say what advice they would give them and what advice they would give their parents.

H 12.2 *Hoja* 12.2 offers additional speaking practice for this spread.

Hacerlo por tu cuenta

<table>
<tr><td colspan="2">

Planner

Grammar focus
♦ Prepositions

Key language

</td></tr>
<tr><td>el alquiler</td><td>rent</td></tr>
<tr><td>la carroza</td><td>float</td></tr>
<tr><td>la hipoteca</td><td>mortgage</td></tr>
<tr><td>un marinovio</td><td>partner (cohabiting)</td></tr>
<tr><td>el portal</td><td>web page</td></tr>
<tr><td>ahorrar</td><td>to save</td></tr>
<tr><td>alcanzar</td><td>to reach</td></tr>
<tr><td>alegrar</td><td>to make happy</td></tr>
<tr><td>aguantar</td><td>to put up with</td></tr>
<tr><td>atropellar</td><td>to run over</td></tr>
<tr><td>compartir</td><td>to share</td></tr>
<tr><td>convenir</td><td>to suit</td></tr>
<tr><td>convivir</td><td>to live with</td></tr>
<tr><td>flipar</td><td>to be amazed</td></tr>
<tr><td>hacerlo por tu cuenta</td><td>to go it alone</td></tr>
<tr><td>matar</td><td>to kill</td></tr>
</table>

quebrar	to break up
salir del armario	to come out (gay terminology)
sobrar	to be extra/over
soltero/a	single
al borde de	on the edge of
mediante	by means of

Resources

♦ Student Book pages 130 and 131
♦ Vocabulario, Student Book page 135
♦ CD 3, track 11
♦ Hoja 12.4
♦ Grammar Workbook page 18

1 Students read the texts and say to whom the sentences refer: Joaquín, José, Ana, or Leila.

Answers:

1	*José*	6	*Joaquín*
2	*Joaquín*	7	*Ana*
3	*Ana*	8	*Leila*
4	*Leila*	9	*Ana*
5	*José*	10	*Leila*

1b Oral work. Students read the texts again. They analyse the situation of each speaker and decide whether living alone has advantages or disadvantages. They give their reasons, using the *frases clave*.

 2a Students listen to the interview and complete the sentences.

> **p. 131, actividad 2a**
>
> Buenas tardes – le habla Margarita Posada de Córdoba. Quisiera responder a los comentarios que se han hecho en este programa acerca de la crítica situación en la que se encuentra la institución del matrimonio en Europa.
>
> A mi modo de ver, el Estado no tiene nada que ver con mi decisión de quedarme soltera o de casarme por lo civil o por cualquier religión que me dé la gana – la decisión es mía y solamente mía.
>
> En cuanto a vivir sola – para mí tiene miles de ventajas. Lo primero de todo, puedo vivir mi vida como yo quiera; no tengo que considerar otros puntos de vista ni compartir los gastos con nadie. Claro que he vivido con más gente cuando era estudiante y lo hice por la compañía y para conocer gente pero en seguida me di cuenta de que ese estilo de vida no era para mí. Cuando vives con otros tienes que respetar sus deseos ya sea a la hora de elegir los programas de la tele o la comida. Hay quienes dicen que es mejor porque compartes los gastos de la vivienda pero yo a

> esos les contesto que lo importante para mí es poder controlar mis gastos como yo quiera y no tener que pensar en nadie más. Dicen que soy egoísta pero a mí me gusta estar a solas, y por el momento me va bien así.

Suggested answers – but accept all reasonable answers of students' own making:

1 *puede hacer lo que quiere.*
2 *tener compañía/conocer a gente.*
3 *tomar sus propias decisiones sobre el matrimonio/su vida.*
4 *controlar sus propios gastos.*
5 *la gente dice que es egoísta.*
6 *por el momento va bien.*

2b Written work. Students use the expressiosn herad in the interview (Activity 2a) to write a reply to the question "Is it better to live alone as bachelor or spinster or to live with someone whether in marriage or as cohabiting partners. They write 200–250 words.

It would be a good idea to make the transcript available for students to use for this task or at least allow them to listen to the recording as many times as they need to.

Gramática

Prepositions

Students will need time to look through all the examples.

Refer students to the grammar section of the Student Book, page 159.

A Students identify the preposition and explain its use in the examples.

2 *de* usually means 'of' or 'from' but here means 'out of';
3 *de* – as before but here means 'about';
4 *al* usually means 'at', but here means 'on the edge of' (idiomatic expression);
5 *en* usually means 'in' but here means 'on which' (needed in Spanish but not in English);
6 *de* usually means 'from', but here means 'of' (different word order in English);
7 *a* usually means 'at', but here is used as the personal a (note no need for 'for' in 'to look for');
8 *de* usually means 'of' or 'from', and here is used to mean 'possession of my parents' [house] (different word order in English);
9 *para* usually means 'in order to'/'for'; here means 'to get married';
10 *de* usually means 'for' or 'from' , but here means 'that'.

H 12.4 *Hoja* 12.4 offers additional practice of prepositions.

Todo cambio en casa

Planner

Grammar focus

♦ The subjunctive in relative clauses

Skills focus

♦ Working out the meanings of words

Key language

la crianza	upbringing/rearing
la contrapartida	contrast
la década	decade
una enfermera	nurse
el género	gender
la juventud	youth
el papel higienico	toilet paper
el pañal	nappy
la percha	coat hanger
el rechazo	rejection
las tareas	tasks
el tetero	baby bottle
hacer caso de	to take notice of
interrogarse	to interrogate/ask oneself
regañar	to tell off
ambos/as	both
celoso/a	jealous
discapacitado/a	disabled
encargado/a	responsible
igualitario/a	equal
laboral	work
monoparental	single family
debido a	owing to

Resources

♦ Student Book pages 132 and 133
♦ Vocabulario, Student Book page 135
♦ CD 3, tracks 12 and 13
♦ Hojas 12.2, 12.4, 12.5
♦ Grammar Workbook page 53

1a Students read the leaflet and decide which courses relate to the topics listed.

Answers:
1 = *curso 8;* **2** = *curso 4;* **3** = *curso 7;* **4** = *curso 1;*
5 = *curso 5;* **6** = *curso 3;* **7** = *curso 6;* **8** = *curso 2*

1b Students use their imagination and invent a series of courses for "The New Woman".

2a Students listen to the recording and decide who (Amalia = A; Beatriz = B; Carlos =C) mentions the topics 1–10.

---

p. 132, actividad 2a

Amalia: !Hola! me llamo Amalia y tengo catorce años. Lo que pasa es que paso la mayor parte de mi tiempo libre cuidando a mi mamá que es discapacitada. Es cierto que la seguridad social nos da algo de ayuda pero la mayor parte de las cosas las hago yo y no es justo porque nunca puedo salir con mis amigos. Parece como si mi juventud estuviera desapareciendo ante ojos mientras hago de enfermera.

Beatriz: Soy Beatriz. Soy madre soltera y encuentro muy difícil educar a mis tres hijos varones y adolescentes, sin la ayuda de alguien que haga de modelo masculino. No me hacen caso y salen cuando les da la gana y hasta me insultan si les regaño. Todos nos critican porque somos una familia monoparental.

Carlos: Quisiera decirles que acabo de ser padre de una linda bebita y no hay nada que no haría en casa para que mi compañera y mi hija estén cómodas y felices. Ahora siento que mi vida está completa incluso cuando me toca levantarme a medianoche para darle el tetero o cambiarla de pañales. Soy Carlos un hombre nuevo y dichoso con un solo problema; tengo que trabajar largas horas, también los fines de semana, para poder pagar la renta y alimentar a mi familia. Por lo tanto casi no les veo. Quisiera poder ser amo de casa.

Answers:
1 = B; **2** = C; **3** = A; **4** = A; **5** = A; **6** = B; **7** = B;
8 = C; **9** = C; **10** = B

2b Work in pairs. Students discuss with a partner the situation of each person in the recording. Are these situations just, normal or unusual? They justify their opinions.

2c Students give them each advice using the conditional after the phrase *Yo que tú …*

Gramática

The subjunctive in relative clauses

Point students to the grammar section of the Student Book, page 170 and to the Grammar Workbook, page 53. Students read through the material and complete task A.

Answers:
1 *Busco una pareja que sea perfecta.*
2 *Necesito a una pareja que ayuda a fregar los platos.*
3 *No encuentro a nadie que iguale tal descripción.*
4 *Es posible que no exista.*

H 12.4 *Hoja* 12.4 offers additional practice of the subjunctive.

---

3 Students listen to the radio programme and decide which person is making the complaint.

P. 132, actividad 3

– En el programa de hoy tenemos dos jovencitos, jóvenes y guapos los dos, que se casaron hace un año y no dejan ya de pelear. Lupita, Lupita, Lupita, ¿qué os pasa, eh?

– Hola, ¿sabes qué? Me trata como su madre. Tengo que aguantar que llegue tarde sin avisar, y si le pregunto de dónde viene ... ¡hmm! Tengo que hacer las compras, cocinar, hacer las camas, todo ... y eso cuando trabajo más que él. Y gano más. A veces creo que eso es parte de su problema.

– Creo que tenemos que conocer a Rogelio. Rogelio, por favor ...

– Tú siempre quieres saber todo lo que hago, pero cuando llego a casa, casi nunca estás. Trabajas hasta las nueve de la noche, y no te voy a estar esperando en casa como un mono, como un angelito, viendo la televisión. ¡Te diré dónde voy, si quieres! Voy a la casa de mi mamá para comer algo sabrosito y caliente.

– Rogelio, aquí tenemos a tu madre, que te tiene algo que decir, muchachón ...

Answers:
1 *Rogelio*
2 *Rogelio*
3 *Lupita*
4 *Lupita*
5 *Lupita*
6 *Rogelio*

4a Students read the article at speed and write a heading to summarise the theme of each section.

Técnica

Working out the meaning of words

Take students through the advice in the *Técnica* box.

A Students then re-read the article and find the words listed.

Answers:
1 *se ha incluido/incluirse; referimos/referir; establecemos/establecer*
2 *igualitarias; el porcentaje; la liberación*

H 12.5 *Hoja 12.5 offers additional practice of working out the meaning of words.*

4a Students write an essay of 200–250 words. They use both their own ideas and those of the article (in Activity 4a) to answer the question: "How have the rcles of men and women in the home changed and how do they continue to change? What is your view of these changes?"

H 12.2 *Hoja 12.2 offers additional speaking practice for this spread.*

Gramática en acción

Planner

Resources
♦ Students' Book page 134
♦ Hoja 12.4

Recuerda

Making better use of the subjunctive

Students revise the uses of the subjunctive and are encouraged to use it.

Point students to the grammar section of the Student Book, page 170.

A Students identify the subjunctive in the sentences and explain why it is being used in each one.

Answers:
1 *doubt*
2 *wanting*
3 *impossibility*
4 *emotion*

B Students make sentences, changing the verb to the subjunctive.

Example answers:
Quiero que mi padre vaya a pagar el móvil.
No creo que sea mi verdadero padre.
Dudo que mis padres puedan vivir juntos.
Es imposible que mi madre tenga un nuevo novio.
Es ridículo que mis padres me regañen.

C Students provide subjunctives to improve Rosa's sentences.

Example answers:
– *¿Existe un modelo típico de familia?*
– *No creo que **exista**. Es importante que los individuos **decidan** cómo quieren vivir.*
– *¿La familia tradicional va a desaparecer?*
– *No, no es probable que **desaparezca**. Pero podemos impedir que su importancia **disminuya**.*

H 12.4 *Hoja* 12.4 offers additional practice of using the subjunctive.

Recuerda

Negative imperatives

Students revise the negative imperative.

Refer them to the grammar section of the Student Book, page 170.

D Students translate the negative imperatives.

Answers:
1 *No te preocupes.*
2 *No llores.*
3 *No te vayas.*
4 *No lo lleve.*

E Students suggest what they would say to the people in the illustrations.

Possible answers:
A *No le eches agua.*
B *No nades aquí.*
C *No copies.*
D *No lo compres.*

F Students explain, using the subjunctive, why the people in pictures A, B, C and D should take their advice.

Possible answers:
Es peligroso que nades porque es probable que te coma un tiburón.
No es justo que copies porque no quiero que saques mejoras notas que yo.
Es importante que no compres este coche porque dudo que funcione.

Vocabulario

Page 135

Answers:
1 *sigan*
2 *nos empeñemos*
3 *tengamos*
4 *ninguna*
5 *encuentre*

Extra

This page is aimed at A-A* students.

1a Group work. Students divide into groups of three and read aloud the extract from *Como agua para chocolate* by the Mexican author Laura Esquivel. One student narrates the story and the others take the roles of Mamá Elena and Tita. The popular novel *Como agua para chocolate* by the Mexican author Laura Esquivel, has also been made into a film by Alfonso Arau. You could show scenes from the film or suggest students watch the film on DVD.

1b Students decide whether the words listed describe Mamá Elena or Tita. They find words or sentences in the text to justify their decision.

Answers:
Tita:
tímida
callada
rebelde
voz temblorosa
Con voz apenas perceptible
por primera vez en su vida intentó protestar

Mamá Elena:
tiránica
autoritaria
años de represión
orden

 2 Students listen to a further extract from *Como agua para chocolate*, describing what happens when Pedro arrives with his father. Students make notes as they listen and then explain what happened and why.

---

p. 136, actividad 2

Se presentaron en la casa. Mamá Elena los recibió en la sala, se comportó muy amable y les explicó la razón por la que Tita no se podía casar.

– Claro, que si lo que les interesa es que Pedro se case, pongo a su consideración a mi hija Rosaura, sólo dos años mayor que Tita, pero está plenamente disponible y preparada para el dormitorio.

Al escuchar esas palabras, Chencha por poco tira encima de Mamá Elena la charola con café y galletas que había llevado a la sala para agasajar a don Pascual y a su hijo. Disculpándose, se retiró apresuradamente hacia la cocina, donde la estaban esperando Tita, Rosaura y Gertrudis para que les diera un informe detallado de lo que acontecía en la sala. Entró atropelladamente y todas suspendieron de inmediato sus labores para no perderse una sola de sus palabras.

— ¿Ay sí, no? ¡Su 'amá habla d'estar preparada para el matrimonio como si juera un plato de enchiladas! ¡Y ni ansina, porque pos no es lo mismo que lo mesmo! ¡Uno no puede cambiar unos tacos por unas enchiladas así como así!

Cuando Tita estaba acabando de envolver las tortas que comerían al día siguiente, entró en la cocina Mamá Elena para informarles que había aceptado que Pedro se casara, pero con Rosaura.

Answers:

Pedro y su padre vienen a pedir la mano de Tita. Mamá Elena explica que no se puede. Dice que Pedro se puede casar con Rosaura, la hermana mayor. Pedro acepta.

Suggest students look at aspects of the family in modern Mexico: The "Quinceañeras", or "Pedida de Mano".

Técnica

Responding to a literary text (2)

Students consider how to relate to the content of a literary text.

They read the advice and complete the tasks A, B and C.

Unit 12 Assessment offers exam practice for this unit.

Exam practice

Introduction

Each of the four Exam Practice sections is designed to be used after the students have worked through three units of material, which is the equivalent of one Topic of the AQA AS specification. If you require interim practice, you will find unit-by-unit material available on the accompanying Assessment copymasters.

The mark scheme given below will help you and your students to obtain a good idea of how they are progressing in terms of AS level grading, but it is important to bear in mind that the marks to grades boundaries are not constant. In fact they are decided individually by AQA for every single examination. This, and the fact that each Exam Practice section can only give results based on one quarter of the AQA AS specification, means that in order to obtain more accurate grade predictions we recommend that your students also work through past papers and that you use the official mark schemes to obtain their predicted grades. These can be found online at: http://web.aqa.org.uk/qual/gce/languages.php.

Assessment mark scheme for AQA Unit 1

The AQA Unit 1 examination consists of listening, reading, a Cloze test and an essay. Each Exam practice section has the following totals for Unit 1 tasks:

Listening 15
Multiply this by 2 to obtain marks out of 30, as in AQA Unit 1 examination.

Reading 18
Multiply this by 2 to obtain a mark out of 36 then make an adjustment by subtracting one mark to give a total of 35 marks, as in the AQA Unit 1 examination.

Cloze test 5
Multiply this by 2 to obtain marks out of 10, as in the AQA Unit 1 examination.

Essay
For marking the essay, use the official AQA writing mark scheme, as explained in section 3.1 of the AQA A level specification, to obtain the following marks: 35 marks divided up in the following way:
♦ 20 for content
♦ 5 for vocabulary
♦ 5 for structures
♦ 5 for accuracy

Note that there is no need to multiply the essay mark by 2.

Total for Unit 1 30 + 35 + 10 + 35 = 110 marks

The marks-to-grades boundaries given below are averages taken from the four AQA Unit 1 examinations from the current specification that were available at the time of going to press. Please note that, as explained above, they are only an indication of progress towards a final grade.

Unit 1 AS grade boundaries	
A	88–110
B	80–87
C	72–79
D	65–71
E	57–64

Assessment mark scheme for Unit 2

The AQA Unit 2 consists of an oral examination. For marking this, use the official AQA speaking mark scheme as explained in section 3.2 of the AQA A level specification to obtain the following marks:

Oral
50 marks divided up in the following way:
♦ Discussion of stimulus   10
  (5 for response to stimulus + 5 for ensuing discussion)
♦ Conversation   25
  (10 for fluency + 10 for interaction + 5 for pronunciation)
♦ Both parts   15
  (grammar)

Total for Unit 2   50 marks

Unit 2 AS grade boundaries	
A	43–50
B	38–42
C	33–37
D	29–32
E	25–28

page 137

This page summarises the Exam Practice section for students. It explains how the topics are covered and emphasises that the activities they will have to complete are the same as those they will encounter in the AS exam.

Information boxes include how the tests compare with the exam; what the test marks mean; tips on how to revise; and guidance on tackling past papers once they have completed the course and the exam practice sections.

1 Media

Reading

Resources

♦ Student Book pages 138–139

1 Students read the article and write down whether the following statements are true (*V = verdaderas*), (*F = falsas*) or are not mentioned (*NM*). *(6 marks)*

This activity relates to Unit 1, Televison, unit objective 3 Benefits and dangers of watching TV.

Answers:
1 = *V;* **2** = *V;* **3** = *V;* **4** = *F;* **5** = *F;* **6** = *NM*

2 Students read the article on how to create a blog and look for synonyms in the text. *(6 marks)*

This activity relates to Unit 3, Communication Technology, unit objective 2 Internet – its current and potential usage

Answer:
1 *cronológicamente*
2 *lectores*
3 *usuario*
4 *aspectos éticos*
5 *citar las fuentas*
6 *convertirte en todo un profesional*

¿Tienes dependencia al móvil?

3 Students read the comments in the speech bubbles made by six different people and decide whether each one is dependent on a mobile phone (*sí*), not dependent on a mobile phone (*no*) or whether they do not make this clear (*¿?*). *(6 marks)*

This question relates to Unit 3, Communication technology, unit objective 1 Popularity of modern technological gadgets

Answers :
Miguel – no
Javier – no
Ana – sí
Marisa – no
Paco – ¿?
Rosa – sí

4 Students read the sentences and fill in the gap with the correct form of the word in parentheses. *(5 marks)*

1 *parezcan* (Unit 2. Understand and use the present of subjunctive)
2 *suelen* (Unit 1.Use verbs like soler and poder (+ infinitive))
3 *ningún* (Unit 1. Use a range of negatives)
4 *influenciar* (Unit 1. Use verbs like soler and poder (+ infinitive))
5 *chatees* (Unit 3. Use the imperative correctly)

Total for questions 1–3 (main reading tasks) = 18

Total for question 4 (cloze) = 5

Listening

Resources

♦ Student Book pages 139–140
♦ CD 3, tracks 15 and 16

 5 Students listen to the piece on advertising and answer the questions. *(7 marks)*

> **p. 139, actividad 5**
>
> Me gusta bastante ver o leer publicidad cuando los productos me interesan o cuando realmente tengo la intención de comprar algo. Es útil a la hora de comparar los productos que hay en el mercado y conseguir un buen precio. Además estamos en contacto directo con las novedades y con los nuevos productos que salen a la venta. También hay muchos anuncios que realmente me fastidian y me ponen nervioso ya que no tienen ningún sentido y cuando los ves, lo último que deseas hacer es comprar ese producto. Para mí, un anuncio bueno es el que da un mensaje claro de forma creativa. Otro aspecto que tampoco me gusta de algunos anuncios publicitarios es la imagen que dan de los jóvenes y de la gente mayor. Muestran a los jóvenes como gente que siempre sigue la moda y que solo se preocupa por su apariencia. La verdad es que esta imagen no tiene nada que ver con la gente que yo conozco. En cuanto a la gente mayor, siempre los retratan como personas totalmente ajenas al mundo de hoy en día, como personas que no entienden lo que pasa a su alrededor.

Answers:
1 *(1)You can compare prices/get a good price.*
(1 mark)
(2) You can find out more about new products.
(1 mark)

2 *They have a clear message in a creative way.* (1 mark)

3 *Young people (1) who are shown as too concerned about how they look (2) and the elderly (3) who are portrayed as out of touch with today's world (4).* (4 marks)

 6 Students listen to eight people giving their opinion on mobile phones and the Internet. They select the appropriate response (A, B or C) to match what each speaker has said. *(8 marks)*

This question relates to Unit 3, Technology, unit objective 3, Benefits and dangers of the Internet and modern technological gadgets.

---

p.140, actividad 6

1 A mi modo de ver, las ventajas son más evidentes que las desventajas; por ejemplo con el móvil te mantienes en contacto con tu familia todo el día si quieres e Internet te ayuda con los deberes.

2 No comparto tu opinión porque ya no es posible escapar ni de la gente ni del trabajo y eso me preocupa mucho. Te pueden contactar dondequiera que estés con mensajes o problemas y te sientes obligado a responder al instante y todo esto te causa cada vez más estrés.

3 En cuanto a mí, yo estoy contentísima porque puedo hablar a larga distancia cuando quiera y es muy barato. Imagina, hace sólo 20 años tenía que reservar hora para llamar a Colombia y ahora sólo tengo que marcar el número y tengo a mi gente al otro lado y por si fuera poco cuando tenga el nuevo modelo podré verles también.

4 Yo creo que es una cosa buenísima porque cuando me estaban amenazando en el cole pude llamar al 900 20 20 10 y enseguida tuve con quien hablar, me dieron consejo y me consolaron.

5 Los jóvenes pasan todo el día pegados al móvil o al ordenador y eso no puede ser bueno ni para los ojos ni para los oídos, ni tampoco para los dedos, con tanto teclear.

6 Y el lenguaje que han inventado es incomprensible – ya no se respeta la gramática y ni el castellano puro que se hablaba en mis tiempos.

7 Yo por lo menos estoy muy agradecida porque significa que puedo trabajar desde casa o incluso en el extranjero si quiero y me parece que es un beneficio enorme.

8 Y parece mentira pero puedes hacer mil cosas por Internet – hacer compras y operaciones bancarias, reservar billetes de avión o tren y hasta comprar entradas para ir al cine.

Answers:
1 = A; **2** = B; **3** = C; **4** = B; **5** = A; **6** = A; **7** = A; **8** = C

Total for listening = 15 marks

Writing

Resources

♦ Student Book pages 140

7 Students write an essay of 200–250 words answering one of the questions A, B or C. To score full marks.they will need to show that they have heeded all 10 pieces of advice.

Oral

Resources

♦ Student Book page 141

8 Discussing the printed questions should take about half of the five minutes allotted. A further two and a half minutes should be spent on follow-up questions relating to the sub-topic of communication technology. Suggestions are given below, but it is important to react to what students say and pursue the conversation naturally, rather than simply ask pre-prepared questions one after another.

Possible follow-up questions:
- *¿Cuántas horas pasas delante de la tele?*
- *¿Piensas que se ve demasiado la televisión?*
- *¿Crees que deberíamos preocuparnos por la 'telebasura'?*
- *Para los niños, ¿cuáles son las ventajas e inconvenientes de la televisión?*
- *Si pudieras crear tu propio canal de televisión, ¿qué programas incluirías?*

9 Students choose one of the topics – Technology or Advertising – and prpeare answers to the questions with a view to discussing the topic.

Note that a list of discussion questions on 'La televisión' can be found on a Unit 1 Assessment copymaster.

Unit Assessments 1-3 offer additional assessment on the topic of media.

2 Popular culture

Reading

Resources

♦ Student Book pages 142–143

1 Students read the article and write down whether the following statements are true (*V = verdaderas*), (*F = falsas*) or are not mentioned (*NM*). *(6 marks)*

This question relates to Unit 4, Cinema, unit objective 3 A good film they have seen

Answers:
1 = F; 2 = F; 3 = V; 4 = V; 5 = NM; 6 = NM

2 Students read the article and answer the questions in Spanish. *(6 marks)*

This question relates to Unit 6 Fashion, unit objective 2. Comment on different ways we can alter our image?

Answers:
1 *Las mujeres ... con curvas/entradas en carnes/ que no estaban delgadas.* (1 mark)
2 *Que no ganaría (porque tiene muchas curvas).* (1 mark)
3 *Las mujeres extremadamente delgadas. (1 mark)*
4 *1 de cada 100 adolescentes/tanto mujeres como hombres.* (1 mark)
5 *Any 2 of :*
El autor aconseja ... (1) aceptarse a si mismo (2) hacer ejercicio (3) tener una alimentación sana. (2 marks)

3 Students read the views on fashion and indicate whose views statements 1–6 reflect. M = la_Margarita; L = Luis_elgrande; V = Valencia_90. (6 marks)

This question relates to Unit 6 Fashion/Trends, unit objective 1, How your 'look' defines who you are.

Answers
1= L; 2= V; 3 = L; 4 = V; 5= M; 6 = M

4 Students read the sentences and complete them in writing using the correct form of the word in parenthesis. *(5 marks)*

Answers:
1 *eran* (Unit 4 use the imperfect tense correctly)
2 *opinaba* (Unit 4 use the imperfect tense correctly)
3 *había* (Unit 5 recognise and use the pluperfect)
4 *hiciera* (Unit 6 use the subjunctive mood in past tense)
5 *hubiera ido* (Unit 6 use the subjunctive mood in past tense)

Total for questions 1 – 3 (main reading tasks) = 18

Total for question 4 (cloze) = 5

Listening

Resources

♦ Student Book page 144
♦ CD 3, tracks 17 and 18

 5 Students listen to "The history of cinema in two minutes". They write the appropriate date and number for each question. *(7 marks)*

This question relates to Unit 4, Cinema, unit objective 2, The place of cinema in popular culture and changing trends.

> **p. 144, actividad 5**
>
> La historia del cine empezó oficialmente el 28 de diciembre de 1985 cuando los hermanos Lumiere mostraron en una sesión pública sus films a los espectadores del Salon Indien de París. Ya en el siglo XX el cine se convirtió en toda una industria.
>
> Entre 1909 y 1912 todos los aspectos de la naciente industria estuvieron bajo el control de un trust estadounidense que fue finalmente desmantelado dando lugar a que los productores independientes pudieran crear sus propias compañías.
>
> Como las películas eran mudas, a veces aparecían unos rótulos en medio de las escenas que iban explicando la acción o los diálogos. A veces un pianista daba un toque musical al espectáculo.
>
> Las películas cómicas conocieron una época dorada en los años veinte. A Chaplin se unieron otros dos cómicos, Harold Lloyd y Buster Keaton.

El 6 de octubre de 1927 sucede un hecho revolucionario en la historia del cine: el cine empieza a hablar. La productora Warner Brothers lanzó El cantor de jazz, de Alan Crosland, la primera película sonora. El cine sonoro pasó a ser un fenómeno internacional de la noche a la mañana.

En los años 40 se desarrolla la técnica del color en las películas. En la década de 1950 el uso del color se generalizó tanto que prácticamente el blanco y negro quedó relegado a películas de bajo presupuesto.

Después de la segunda Guerra Mundial, la llegada de la televisión supuso un desafío a la industria del cine que aún hoy perdura. A finales de la década de los 50 la audiencia de cine cayó en unos 40 millones de espectadores anuales.

En España, la transición política posibilitó el despegue de un nuevo cine sin censura que influyó en la aparición de la llamada "movida madrileña". Pedro Almodóvar enriquece la escena cinematográfica a través de sus films posmodernos y de esperpento, género este último que también trabajó Berlanga. La primera película de Almodóvar aparece en 1980 con el título de "Pepi, Luci, Bom y otras chicas del montón"

Answers:
1 *28 de diciembre de 1895*
2 *De 1909 a 1912/Entre 1909 y 1912/3 años*
3 *En los años 20*
4 *En 1927*
5 *En la década de los 40/En los 40*
6 *40 millones*
7 *En 1980*

6 Students listen to the interview with David Bisbal and answer the questions in English. *(8 marks)*

This question relates to Unit 5, Music, unit objective 4, How music defines personal identity

p. 144, actividad 6

David Bisbal ha resultado ser el mayor éxito de todas las ediciones del programa televisivo Operación Triunfo. En esta entrevista exclusiva nos habla de su carrera.

Periodista: Desde que salió al mercado tu primer disco, Corazón Latino, en 2002 no has parado de cosechar premios ¿Cómo vive David Bisbal tanto éxito siendo tan joven y con una carrera profesional relativamente corta?

David Bisbal: Bueno, la verdad es que no me puedo quejar. Las cosas han ido bien, pero eso sí, trabajando durísimo; no queda otra; estoy feliz.

Periodista: ¿Crees que sin Operación Triunfo habrías conseguido este éxito?

David Bisbal: Quién sabe si algún día habría llegado una gran oportunidad, pero sin duda, Operación Triunfo fue lo mejor que me pudo pasar.

Periodista: ¿En qué crees que reside la clave del éxito de David Bisbal?

David Bisbal: Pues no sabría decir, pero está claro que hay que trabajar muchísimo, rodearse de un gran equipo de trabajo y a la vez humano, hay que saber tomar a veces decisiones difíciles, saber decir sí o no en los momentos apropiados, tener claras las ideas y objetivos y, sobre todo, creer en lo que haces y amar tu trabajo, eso es lo que yo hago. Si a eso le sumas un poquito de disciplina y vida sana, disfrutas de tu trabajo.

Periodista: ¿Llevas la cuenta de los conciertos que has dado desde que se lanzó al mercado tu primer disco?

David Bisbal: La verdad es que no, tendría que echar mano de los datos que tenemos en nuestra oficina, pero más de 300 sí van...

Periodista: De todas las canciones de tus discos, ¿cuál es la más especial para ti y por qué?

David Bisbal: Hay muchas canciones que significan mucho para mí, pero sin duda hay una que canta todo el público conmigo en cada concierto que doy, sea donde sea, "Dígale".

Periodista: De los numerosos premios y reconocimientos que has recibido (el Ondas, un Grammy Latino, el World Music Award, el Bilboard...), ¿a cuál o a cuáles le tienes especial cariño y por qué?

David Bisbal: Todos significan mucho para mí, ya que son reconocimientos de la industria discográfica, y eso reconforta y te da más energía para seguir trabajando, pero quizás mi primer premio en solitario en España, el Ondas. Por fin la industria española me reconocía, y eso fue algo maravilloso.

Periodista: Y a largo plazo, ¿qué metas te planteas tanto en el terreno profesional, como en el personal?

David Bisbal: En el profesional, seguir trabajando para poder ofrecer buena música en la mayor medida que pueda, yo disfruto con lo que hago. En lo personal, me va muy bien con mi pareja, vamos despacio y espero que sea la mujer de mi vida.

Answers:
1 *Possible answers: (1) To work hard (2) To have a good team (2) To be able to make difficult decisions (3) To have clear ideas and objectives (4) To love your job (5) To have discipline (6)To have a healthy life*
2 *Around 300*
3 *Because the audience always sings it along with him*
4 *Because he was recognised by the Spanish industry*
5 *To carry on working to be able to offer good music*

Total for listening = 15 marks

Writing

Resources

♦ Student Book page 144

7 Students write an essay of 200–250 words answering one of the questions A (music), B (fashion) or C (cinema). To score full marks.they will need to show that they have heeded all 10 pieces of advice.

Oral

Resources

♦ Student Book page 145

8 Students look at the adverts posted for groups needing musicians and prepare to discuss the five questions.

Discussing the printed questions should take about half of the five minutes allotted. A further two and a half minutes should be spent on follow-up questions relating to the sub-topic of communication technology. Suggestions are given below, but it is important to react to what students say and pursue the conversation naturally, rather than simply ask pre-prepared questions one after another.

Possible follow-up questions :
- *¿Hay tipos de música que nunca escuchas ? ¿Por qué ?*
- *¿Qué instrumento te gustaría tocar y por qué?*
- *¿Puedes estudiar y escuchar música al mismo tiempo?*
- *¿Crees que el flamenco es la música que define mejor a España?*
- *¿Qué opinas de los programas de la tele que buscan a nuevos cantantes, como Operación Triumfo?*
- *¿Crees que la música de hoy tiene un estilo propio?*

9 Students choose a topic, either A Cinema or B Fashion and prepare answers to the questions, which they will discuss in conversation.

Note that a list of discussion questions on "La música" can be found on a Unit 4 Assessment copymaster.

Unit Assessments 4-6 offer additional assessment on the topic of popular culture.

3 Healthy living/lifestyle

Reading

Resources

♦ Student Book pages 146–147

1 Students read the passages in which four different people describe their diet. They link the appropriate person to the statements 1–6.

T = Teresa; R = Rafa; F = Fernando; S = Sonia
(6 marks)
This question relates to Unit 8, Health and well-being, unit objective 3, Diet, eating disorders

Answers:
1 = *S;* **2** = *R;* **3** = *F;* **4** = *T;* **5** =*F;* **6** = *S*

2 Students read the article on ecological hotels and answer questions in Spanish. *(6 marks)*
This question relates to Unit 9; Holidays, unit objective 4, Changing attitudes to holidays

Answers :
1 *Que están de moda/que hay muchos/que hay millones de páginas.*
2 *Porque hay hoteles convencionales que usan esta etiqueta para otorgar una apariencia ecológica pero superficial.*
3 *Con etiquetas ecológicas fiables/que ofrecen un turismo responsable.*
4 *Porque usa madera, algodón y lana en vez de plástico y tejidos sintéticos/porque usa champú biodegradable/porque los desayunos son de cultivo biológico.*
6 *No, porque solo hay tres hoteles ecológicos (en la lista de requisitos verdes).*

3 Students read the views on the dangers of high-risk sports and find synonyms or phrases with a similar meaning for those given 1–6. *(5 marks)*
This question relates to Unit 7, Sport, unit objective 1. The difference between traditional and 'fun' sports

Answers
1 = *murió*
2 = *ileso*
3 = *caudal*
4 = *estadísticas*
5 = *ir con ojo*
6 = *titulados*

4 Students read the sentences and complete them in writing, using the correct form of the word in parenthesis. *(5 marks)*

Answers:
1 *cogido* (Unit 8, use the perfect infinitive)
2 *perderás* (Unit 9, use of constructions with si)
3 *comiendo* (Unit 9, use of continuous tenses)
4 *funcione* (Unit 8, use of the subjuntive to express doubt and improbability)
5 *haya* (Unit 7, use the subjuntive with the perfect tense)

Total for questions 1 – 3 (main reading tasks) = 18

Total for question 4 (cloze) = 5

Listening

Resources

♦ Student Book page 148
♦ CD 3, tracks 19 and 20

 5 Students listen to the radio programme about family holidays and answer the questions in English. *(8 marks)*
This question relates Unit 9, Holidays, unit objective 1, Types of holiday and holiday activities

---

p. 148, actividad 5

Presentador: Hoy en nuestro espacio de ocio y tiempo libre tenemos a Rafael López que nos va a dar unos cuantos consejos a la hora de planear un viaje en familia. Buenas tardes Rafael.

Rafael: Hola, buenas tardes. Vamos a ver está claro que cuando realizamos un viaje en solitario o con nuestra pareja es bastante sencillo planificar todo. Y es que ponerse de acuerdo dos personas puede ser realmente fácil pero que una familia entera se ponga de acuerdo suele costar bastante más. Lo primero que hay que decidir es si es mejor ir a la playa o la montaña. Por ejemplo, tener hijos cambia radicalmente el itinerario del viaje, es evidente que según la edad el niño que tenga una visita a un museo le puede resultar de lo más aburrido. Por eso que hay que buscar lugares que ofrezcan actividades para los niños.

En el norte de España por ejemplo existen grandes praderas con paisajes de ensueño donde el verde y el aire puro se hacen notar. Un sitio ideal para el descanso donde los más pequeños tendrán un espacio amplio donde correr y divertirse fuera del peligro de los vehículos y la vida urbana. Además se pueden realizar excursiones con actividades diversas relacionadas con el montañismo.

> Pero si por el contrario tienes decidido ir a un lugar más cercano y eso de la montaña no te va mucho, puedes escoger ciudades pequeñas como Cádiz, Almería o Málaga que no tienen el ajetreo de grandes urbes como Madrid o Barcelona. En Andalucía disfrutarás del encanto y la amabilidad de la gente, de unas playas preciosas y un clima magnifico .
>
> También hay que pensar en el alojamiento y la verdad que si vas familia lo ideal es alojarse en algún apartamento o casa de campo donde descansar y tener todo más controlado.

Answers :
1 *Whether to go to the beach/seaside or the mountains* (1 mark)
2 *Places that offer activities for kids* (1 mark)
3 *Any 3 of : Lots of greenery and fresh air/ideal to relax/big space for the kids to run and have fun/ no danger for the kids/excursions for trekking in the mountains* (3 marks)
4 *Any 2 of: It has kind people/beautiful beaches/ great climate* (2 marks)
5 *An apartment or country house* (1 mark)

 6 Students listen to the new item about stress in Spain. They select the correct answer from the multiple choices to match the information they hear. *(7 marks)*

This question relates to Unit 8, Health and well-being, unit objective 4, The work/life balance

> **p. 148, actividad 6**
>
> Cada vez son más las personas que sufren estrés en nuestra sociedad. Cuando a nuestro cuerpo se le exige una carga extra de energía por presiones en el trabajo o por estrés emocional, el organismo agota las reservas de energía y nos vuelve vulnerables a padecer depresión, insomnio o irritabilidad.
>
> En España 3 de cada 4 trabajadores sufren de estrés por culpa del trabajo. El número de trabajadores en España es de unos 15 millones y el estrés es el culpable del 4% de todas las bajas laborales al cabo del año. El estrés afecta más a los hombres que a las mujeres, sobre todo aquellos que tienen entre 30 y 45 años y esto se debe a que son mucho más competitivos.
>
> Comer de forma equilibrada es fundamental para mantener en orden tu cuerpo y tu mente y evitar que el estrés afecte a tu estómago, tus defensas y tu sistema nervioso. Hacer ejercicio es algo indispensable para combatir el estrés. Y no solo eso, te ayuda a sentirte mejor y eleva tu autoestima. Está comprobado que ir al gimnasio, salir a correr o apuntarse a clase de meditación o aromaterapia reduce los niveles de estrés.

> Ir al gimnasio parece la opción preferida por los hombres pero las mujeres optan por el yoga que se ha convertido en la opción más de moda para controlar la mente y relajarse. Los ejercicios te ayudan a tranquilizarte y dejar a un lado la ansiedad acumulada. Muchas personas afirman que han aprendido a controlar las emociones y a mantener la calma y por lo tanto la presión en el trabajo ha disminuido.

Answers:
1 = B; **2** = B; **3** = A; **4** =A; **5** =A; **6** = C; **7** = B

Total for listening = 15 marks

Writing

Resources

♦ Student Book page 148

7 Students write an essay on one of the topics A (smoking ban), B (youth travel) or C (sports facilities: formal letter). Remind students that they need to bear in mind the ten points for guidance presented for essay writing in the Exam Practice 1 and 2. To score full marks they will need to show that they have heeded all ten pieces of advice.

Oral

Resources

♦ Student Book pages 149

8 Students look at the holiday advert and prepare to discuss the five questions.

Discussing the printed questions should take about half of the five minutes allotted. A further two and a half minutes should be spent on follow-up questions relating to the sub-topic of communication technology. Suggestions are given below, but it is important to react to what students say and pursue the conversation naturally, rather than simply ask pre-prepared questions one after another.

Possible follow-up questions :
- *La última vez que tuviste vacaciones,*
  ¿dónde fuiste?
- *¿Qué es lo positivo del turismo?*
- *¿Crees que el turismo puede tener un efecto*
  negativo en el medio ambiente?
- *¿Cuál es tu opinión de las aerolíneas de bajo coste?*
- *¿Crees que ir vacaciones está al alcance de todo el*
  mundo hoy en día?

Note that a list of discussion questions on 'Las Vacaciones' can be found on a Unit 3 Assessment copymaster.

9 Students choose a topic, either A (Sport) or B (Health and Well-being) and prepare answers to the questions, which they will discuss in conversation.

Unit Assessments 7-9 offer additional assessment on the topic of healthy living.

4 Family/relationships

Reading

Resources

♦ Student Book pages 150–151

1 Students read the article on marriage in Argentina and match the opening of the sentences (1–6) with the appropriate ending (a–i). *(6 marks)*

This question relates to Unit 12, Marriage and partnerships, unit objective 4 Changing attitudes towards marriage and cohabitation.

Answers:
1 = a; 2 = d; 3 = e; 4 = f; 5 = g; 6 = h

2 Students read the comments (1–6) and match them with section in the list (a–n) where they may find the help they need. *(6 marks)*

This question relates to Unit 11 Friendship, unit objective 1, Characteristics and roles of friends

Answers:
1 = b; 2 = h; 3 = m; 4 = a; 5 = e; 6 = n

3 Students read the text on sexual relations in adolescence and decide in which paragraph (1–4) the statements (a–g) occur. *(6 marks)*

This question relates to Unit 10 Relationships within the family, unit objective 1, Role of parents and the importance of good parenting

Answers:
a = 4; b = 1 c = 2; d = 3; e = 4; f = 1

4 Students read the sentences and complete them in writing using the correct form of the word in parenthesis. (5 marks)

Answers:
1 *suyas* (Unit 10 use of possessive pronouns)
2 *sea* (Unit 10 use of the subjunctive to express purpose)
3 *encontré* (Unit 11 recognise use time clauses correctly)
4 *para* (Unit 11 use the imperative in all its forms)
5 *tenga* (Unit 3 use the subjunctive in relative clauses)

Total for questions 1 – 3 (main reading tasks) = 18

Total for question 4 (cloze) = 5

Listening

Resources

♦ Student Book page 152
♦ CD 3, tracks 21 and 22

5 Students listen to Miguel telling the story of his best friend. They identify which seven sentences in the list a–n are true. *(7 marks)*

This question relates Unit 11, Friendship, unit objective 3, The importance of friends.

---

p. 152, actividad 5

Periodista: Buenas tardes. Hoy tenemos en el programa a Miguel, un joven de veintiséis años que nos va a hablar de la amistad a través a su propia historia personal.

Miguel: Buenas tardes, gracias.

Periodista: Bueno Miguel, tú tienes un amigo muy especial, ¿no?

Miguel: Sí, y tanto, un amigo que se ha convertido en mi cuñado pero bueno, voy a empezar por el principio.

Conocí a Roberto en el colegio cuando tenía 13 años. Yo era nuevo en la clase y él había repetido curso y era un año más mayor que el resto. Nos hicimos amigos desde el primer día y siempre nos sentábamos juntos. Roberto me presentó a sus amigos del curso superior y enseguida pasé a formar parte del grupo. En poco tiempo nos hicimos inseparables. Siempre íbamos juntos a todos los sitios y quedábamos también los fines de semana para hacer los deberes o jugar al fútbol. Hablábamos de todo, sobre todo de chicas, pero nunca le contábamos a nadie más nuestros secretos o conversaciones. Después de dos años, a mi padre lo volvieron a destinar a otra ciudad y nos mudamos a Madrid. Así que perdimos prácticamente el contacto. En aquella época no usábamos Internet y a mí lo de escribir cartas siempre se me dio bastante mal.

Bueno pasó el tiempo y de repente un día que estaba en el aeropuerto esperando para coger un vuelo de fin de semana a Londres, voy y me lo encuentro trabajando en la cafetería. No me lo podía creer. Los dos nos reconocimos inmediatamente. Roberto estaba estudiando su carrera en Madrid y llevaba un año y medio en la ciudad. Era como si no hubiera pasado el tiempo, nos pusimos a hablar de todo otra vez y nos pasamos los móviles. Esta vez fui yo quien le presenté a mi grupo de amigos y también a mi hermana. Como se pasaba el día en mi casa, terminaron en una relación. Y bueno, ahora aparte de ser mi mejor amigo es también mi cuñado. Se casaron el año pasado.

Answers :
1 = a; 2 = b; 3 = d; 4 = f; 5 = g; 6 = l; 7 = n

6 Students listen to the news item on the falling birthrate in Spain. They write down the numbers required. *(8 marks)*

This question relates to Unit 10, Relationships, unit objective 4, Changing models of family and parenting.

P 152, actividad 6

Y volvemos al espacio de noticias.

Aunque España ocupa el quinto lugar en cuanto a la tasa de natalidad dentro de la Unión Europea, la natalidad ha caído un 5% por primera vez tras una década de crecimiento constante. En el año 2009 nacieron en España alrededor de 25.000 niños y niñas, y el número no ha aumentado en 2010.

Para muchos analistas, la causa directa de eso es la crisis económica que ha derivado en el crecimiento del paro y la bajada de salarios.

El gobierno intentó luchar contra la bajada de la natalidad en España a finales de 2007, introduciendo el "cheque bebé", una ayuda de 2500 euros por cada nuevo nacimiento. La ayuda se incrementó a 3500 euros para las madres solteras.
Además, la edad media de las mujeres españolas cuando tienen su primer hijo es de 29 años y no ha dejado de crecer desde 1995.

El descenso de la natalidad ocurrió en todas las Comunidades Autónomas, con la única excepción de Asturias, que pasó de 7,8 a 7,9 nacimientos por cada mil habitantes. Aunque por otro lado, es la Comunidad Autónoma que menor tasa de natalidad tiene de toda España, es decir es la última de las 49 provincias.

Además de reducirse el número de nacimientos, en el 2009 también disminuyó la cifra de matrimonios. En ese año, el número de bodas que se celebraron se redujo un 10,8% en comparación con 2008.

Sin embargo, continuaron creciendo las uniones entre personas del mismo sexo, en total 3.412, 218 más que el año anterior.

Answers:
1 *5%*
2 *25,000*
3 *2500*
4 *3500*
5 *29*
6 *49*
7 *10.8%*
8 *3,412*

Total for listening = 15 marks

Writing

Resources

♦ Student Book page 152

7 Students write an essay of a minimum of 200 words answering one of the questions A (reasons for the falling birthrate in Spain), B (ideal relationship) or C (meaning of friendship). To score full marks. they will need to show that they have heeded all 10 pieces of advice given.

Oral

Resources

♦ Student Book page 153

8 Students look at the statistics relating to the increasing divorce rate in Spain and prepare to discuss the five questions.

Discussing the printed questions should take about half of the five minutes allotted. A further two and a half minutes should be spent on follow-up questions relating to the sub-topic of friendship. Suggestions are given below, but it is important to react to what students say and pursue the conversation naturally, rather than simply ask pre-prepared questions one after another.

Possible follow-up questions :
– *Preferirías casarte por lo civil o por la iglesia? ¿Por qué?*
– *¿Crees que es imprescindible vivir con tu pareja antes de casarse?*
– *¿Hay que casarse para formar una familia?*
– *¿Qué piensas del matrimonio homosexual?*
– *¿Piensas que la madre se debería quedar en casa y cuidar de los hijos?*
– *¿Te plantearías ser madre soltera en el futuro si no encuentras la pareja ideal?*

9 Students choose a topic, either A Relationships within the family or B Friendships and prepare answers to the questions, which they will discuss in conversation.

Note that a list of discussion questions on "El matrimonio y las parejas" can be found on a Unit 12 Assessment copymaster.

Unit Assessments 10–12 offer additional assessment on the topic of family/relationships.